NETS OF AWARENESS

NETS OF AWARENESS
Urdu Poetry and Its Critics

FRANCES W. PRITCHETT

University of California Press

BERKELEY LOS ANGELES LONDON

University of California Press
Berkeley and Los Angeles, California

University of California Press, Ltd.
London, England

The Urdu calligraphic designs based on the words *āgahī* ("awareness") and *dām* ("net") were done by Adil Mansuri, an artist/calligrapher and poet from Ahmedabad, Gujarat, who now lives in New Jersey.

The calligraphy on p. v is from the edition of Ġhālib's *Dīvān-e Ġhālib* edited by Ḥāmid ʿAlī Ḳhān (Lahore: Punjab University, 1969).

Library of Congress Cataloging-in-Publication Data

Pritchett, Frances W., 1947–
Nets of awareness : Urdu poetry and its critics / by Frances W. Pritchett.
p. cm.
Includes bibliographical references and index.
ISBN 0-520-08194-3 (alk. paper).—ISBN 0-520-08386-5 (pbk. : alk. paper)
1. Urdu literature—History and criticism. 2. Azād, Muḥammad Ḥusain, ca. 1834–1910—Criticism and interpretation. 3. Ḥālī, Khvājah Alṭāf Ḥusain, 1837–1914—Criticism and interpretation. I. Title.
PK2151.P75 1994 92-43826
CIP

Printed in the United States of America
9 8 7 6 5 4 3 2 1

The paper used in this publication meets the minimum requirements of American National Standard for Information Sciences—Permanence of Paper for Printed Library Materials, ANSI Z39.48-1984.♾

آگہی دامِ شنیدن جس قدر چاہے بچھائے
مُدّعا عنقا ہے اپنے عالَمِ تقریر کا

No matter how awareness spreads its net,
My realm of words shelters the imaginary bird.

ĠHĀLIB

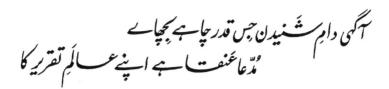

CONTENTS

Acknowledgments ix

A Note on Transliteration xi

Preface xiii

PART ONE A GARDEN NOW DESTROYED

1. The Lost World 3
2. Beyond a Sea of Blood 16
3. Reconstruction 31
4. The Water of Life 46

PART TWO FLOWERS ON THE BRANCH OF INVENTION

5. Tazkirahs 63
6. Poems Two Lines Long 77
7. The Art and Craft of Poetry 91
8. The Mind and Heart in Poetry 106

PART THREE LIGHT FROM ENGLISH LANTERNS

9. The Cycles of Time 127
10. From Persian to English 140
11. "Natural Poetry" 155
12. Poetry and Morality 169

Epilogue 185

Appendix: A Ghazal Observed 191
Glossary 195
Notes 201
Bibliography 225
Index 231

ACKNOWLEDGMENTS

Everything I've ever done with Urdu has helped to guide me toward this book. So first of all I thank my teachers: Moazzam Siddiqi and Bruce Pray at Berkeley, C. M. Naim at Chicago, and Khaliq Ahmad Khaliq in Lahore. Their knowledge, dedication, and encouragement have been most precious gifts. And I pay tribute also to my literary mentor Ralph Russell, lifelong foe of academic pretentiousness and unnecessary jargon, who insists that scholarly writing should be kept as open as possible to all interested and intelligent readers. Since he has always practiced what he preaches, his lucid, straightforward books have influenced me from the beginning.

As ever, I owe thanks to my own family, and to the whole community of Urdu-lovers, many of whom have been generous with their time and help on this project. In Karachi, Dr. Aslam Farrukhi presented me with a copy of his own indispensable two-volume biography of Azad; he and Janab Jamiluddin Aali, Dr. Farman Fatahpuri, Dr. Asif Aslam, and the whole group at the Anjuman Taraqqi-e Urdu provided me with an excellent forum for trying out some of the ideas argued in this book. In Lahore, I had the good offices of old friends like Begam Altaf Fatima, and Janab Ahmad Nadeem Qasimi very kindly found me a copy of Dr. Farman Fatahpuri's out-of-print tazkirah book. In Delhi, Maulvi Niyazuddin and his son Nizamuddin of the Kutubkhanah Anjuman Taraqqi-e Urdu were an invaluable source for rare books, new friends, and other *ġhanīmat*s. Dr. Gopi Chand Narang in Delhi, and especially Dr. Naiyar Masud in Lucknow, have helped with advice and counsel. I am also grateful for the useful suggestions and general moral support provided by interested friends and colleagues in America, especially Susham Bedi, Aditya Behl, Nadine Berardi, Michael Fisher, Laura Freseman, William L. Hanaway, David Lelyveld, Philip Lutgendorf, David Magier, C. M. Naim, Carla Petievich, Bruce Pray, Ibrahim Quraishi, David Rubin, Vijay Seshadri, and the late Barbara Stoler Miller, whose recent death has been a sad loss to us at Columbia. Any book is a node in a network of such practical and intellectual exchange, and I have received more kindnesses over the years than I can even record.

The National Endowment for the Humanities provided a research fellowship that gave me a year (1987–88) of leave from teaching so that I could lay the groundwork for this book. Special thanks are also due to my friends and colleagues at the Middle East Center and the South Asia Regional Studies Center at the University of Pennsylvania, who during the last few years have played the largest role in bringing Shamsur Rahman Faruqi to this country several times for talks and seminars. The South Asian Area Center at the University of Wisconsin at Madison also invited him for a month-long lecture series in 1990.

Lynne Withey of the University of California Press did much to make this book possible; I'm grateful for her encouragement and support. One of her best deeds was to suggest that I work with Pamela MacFarland Holway, whose thoughtful advice and insight helped to shape not only the intellectual contours of the book, but its visual design as well. My friend Adil Mansuri was kind enough to provide some of his elegant calligraphic creations.

In the making of this book my best colleague and friend, Shamsur Rahman Faruqi, has played so substantial a role from start to finish that it seems almost inappropriate merely to thank him. He not only suggested many refinements and saved me from many errors at every stage of my work, but did much of the original research on which the middle third of the book rests. As always in our long-standing collaboration, it is both an honor and a pleasure to work with him closely enough to be so deeply indebted. Any remaining errors are, needless to say, mine alone.

A NOTE ON TRANSLITERATION

The letters of the Urdu alphabet have been transliterated as follows:

alif as: a, i, u, ā

b	p	t	ṭ	ṡ
j	ch	ḥ	ḳh	
d	ḍ	ż		
r	ṛ	z	zh	
s	sh			
ṣ	ẓ			
t̤	z̤			
ʿ	ġh			
f	q			
k	g			
l	m			
n				

vāʾo as: v, ū, o, au
h
ī
baṛī ye as: y, e, ai
nūn-e ġhunnah: ñ
hamzah: ʾ
iẓāfat: -e

For the sake of consistency, Persian words have been transliterated as they are pronounced in Urdu. Indic words have been treated as though they were written phonetically in Urdu script.

PREFACE

Long ago at Berkeley, when I was just learning to read the Urdu script, my teacher introduced the class to the poetry of Ġhālib. It was much too hard for us. We spent a whole hour grappling with a single two-line verse. But then, as a reward, we heard it sung by Begam Aḳhtar—and I was hooked. These little verses were dense, tight, intricate structures, made of beauty and energy held in perfect balance. They resonated so well with my own inner life and my own sense of poetry that I loved them even before I understood them. I knew I wanted more.

In the library I found just the sort of book I had been looking for: Muhammad Sadiq's magisterial *A History of Urdu Literature* (1964), published by the Oxford University Press in India. East meets West, I thought, and here is the best of both worlds: a book in English, equipped with references, notes, index, diacritics in the Western scholarly style—by an author who comes from within the Urdu tradition, who in fact is a senior professor at a college in Lahore. Here is a much more knowledgeable ghazal lover who will interpret the tradition for me, and will share with me an insider's appreciation of the poetry.

Alas for my innocence. Professor Sadiq made it clear that I was wrong to value the ghazal so highly. For the ghazal has had a rotten streak from the beginning: it was "tainted with narrowness and artificiality at the very outset of its career." As a result, it has innumerable flaws. The ghazal "lacks freshness"; it "has no local colour"; its deficiency in "truthfulness," "sincerity," and a "personal note" has made much of it into a "museum piece." Its imagery is "fixed and stereotyped"; it is "incapable of showing any feeling for nature"; it displays "fragmentariness" and is "a patchwork of disconnected and often contradictory thoughts and feelings." In fact it is generally held to be "the least poetic of all forms, because it least admits of inspiration," and there is "a large element of truth in the argument." It envisions love as "a torture, a disease," a "morbid and perverse passion"—a view that is a "legacy from Persia" and is "ultimately traceable to homosexual love which had taken deep root among the Persians and Persianized Arabs." Furthermore, over time the ghazal has gone from bad to worse. It has developed "wholly in the direction of fantasy and unreality": "facts give way to fancies," and the imagination explores "curious byways" as the ghazal evolves "in its downward career."[1]

Although Professor Sadiq recognizes that the ghazal has "strong assets," he sees them as outweighed by even heavier liabilities. He sums it all up in a phrase that has lived in my mind ever since—and has goaded me into writing this book. The ghazal, Sadiq says, "stands very low in the hierarchy of literary forms."[2] This is so obviously an erroneous and wrongheaded statement that refuting it is not my main goal; the poetry itself is a more than sufficient refutation. Rather, I want to inquire how this judgment has come to be made. Even if there could be such a thing as "the" hierarchy of all genres (which there cannot be), and if anyone had the authority to define it (which no one does), why would anyone rank such a sophisticated, powerful genre as the ghazal, popular for over a millennium in many languages, near the bottom? And even more to the point, why would someone like Sadiq make such a harsh and hostile judgment? This poetry had, after all, been handed down for generations as one of the chief glories of his own cultural heritage, and he obviously valued his heritage enough to spend many years studying it and writing books about it. Why did he devote years of his life to this heritage—and then produce a sweeping denunciation of the genre that lay at the heart of it? Instead of providing a subtle, nuanced analysis of the ghazal, why did he attack it with a blunt instrument?

To my further surprise, I found that Sadiq was far from alone in his views. Classical Urdu literature has very commonly been presented in English either disdainfully or apologetically—or both. Of course, such modes of presentation not only irritate the serious student, but also discourage the newcomer from pursuing the subject further. The distinguished Urdu scholar Ralph Russell has recently expressed his own exasperation at this state of affairs in an article called "How Not to Write the History of Urdu Literature"—an article replete with horrible (and humorous) examples and offering among its conclusions the polite advice, "If you don't think much of Urdu literature, please don't go to the trouble of writing a history of it."[3]

In Urdu too, as I gradually realized, Sadiq's views were only a relatively complete inventory of attitudes many critics held in part. Disdain has sometimes been expressed not only openly but even extravagantly: according to one well-known critic, the ghazal is "a half-barbarous form of poetry."[4] By contrast, defense of the ghazal has usually been halfhearted at best. Most apologists have freely conceded such fundamental defects as artificiality, lack of unity, and so on, and have then sought merely to reduce the charges by pointing out some mitigating circumstances and redeeming features.[5] Or else they have sought to justify the ghazal not as poetry, but as a vehicle for conveying an alleged political or religious message.[6] "Even today," as one perceptive critic recently put it, "we are ashamed of the greater part of our literary property—or we do not consider it worthy of esteem." The result is that "our tongues never tire of finding fault with our cultural possessions."[7]

Why could I, knowing so much less Urdu, admire and appreciate Ġhālib more than many of his cultural heirs? How far back did this critical intolerance toward the ghazal—and other traditional genres—go? I eventually traced the attitude straight back to the earliest (and still much the most important) history of Urdu poetry, Āzād's *Water of Life* (1880), and found it reaffirmed and elaborated in the earliest (and still much the most important) work of modern Urdu literary criticism, Ḥālī's *Introduction to Poetry and Poetics* (1893). As I investigated the lives of Azad and Hali,[8] I discovered that these two uniquely influential literary pioneers had shared certain formative experiences both in their youth and afterward. Gradually I came to understand why and how their views had developed. They who had inherited the mansion of classical poetry made a desperate resolve: to condemn large portions of the structure, in order to shore up and renovate the rest. Against the background of their lives, such a resolve made sense. But over the past century it has also done immense cultural harm—and this harm continues into the present. When I discovered that Muhammad Sadiq, my original bête noire, had in fact written his doctoral dissertation on Azad, I knew that the wheel had come full circle.

Nets of Awareness is a study of an episode in the cultural and literary history of late-nineteenth-century North India: a look at how the classical ghazal, which for centuries had been the pride and joy of Indo-Muslim culture, was abruptly dethroned and devalued within its own milieu, and by its own theorists. The break with tradition was so sharp that nowadays some aspects of the ghazal are obscure, and others even markedly distasteful, to most modern readers. I argue that the cause of this abrupt "paradigm shift" was not ultimately literary so much as political. The violent "Mutiny" of 1857, and the vengeful British reaction to it, destroyed the old world of the Indo-Muslim elite. After 1857, the victorious British had the only game in town: they were obviously, "naturally," superior, and they made sure everyone realized it. Azad himself, in another context, described the result: "The important thing is that the glory of the winners' ascendant fortune gives everything of theirs—even their dress, their gait, their conversation—a radiance that makes them desirable. And people do not merely adopt them, but are proud to adopt them. Then they bring forth, by means of intellectual arguments, many benefits of this."[9]

Such adoption of a new culture may be a fine thing; certainly both Azad and Hali were officially and strongly committed to the benefits of Westernization. But however good a face they managed to put on it, the result was clear: after 1857 they found themselves having to perform radical surgery on their own culture, to enable it to survive in a world defined by the victors. Azad and Hali set out to replace their inherited Indo-Persian concept of poetry with what they understood to be the contemporary English one: a Wordsworth-like vision of "natural" poetry.

If Wordsworthian poetry was the touchstone of naturalness, however, the whole Indo-Muslim poetic tradition was bound to appear "unnatural" in comparison—not just literarily decadent, artificial, and false, but morally suspect as well. And if, as many English writers argued, poetry was inevitably a mirror of society, then the cultural rot must go much deeper. The result was a sweeping, internally generated indictment with which Urdu speakers have been struggling ever since. *A History of Urdu Literature* was reprinted in 1984, shortly before its author's death, in an expanded second edition. Professor Sadiq added much new material; but he did not change a word of his harsh attack on the ghazal.

The present study has three parts. In the first part I locate the lives of my two central characters, Azad and Hali, within their cultural and literary setting; in the second part I seek to reconstruct the orally transmitted poetic concepts that Azad and Hali inherited—concepts that are now little known and even less understood; in the third part I analyze the new anticlassical poetics that Azad and Hali defined with such urgency and power.

I hope, of course, that this book will be useful to lovers of Urdu literature both here and in South Asia, and to scholars of North Indian culture and history. But I have also tried my best to make the subject as vivid and interesting to others as it is to me. I will be delighted if people who know little or nothing about Urdu literature can find in this book a starting point. For this reason, I have included not only a glossary of key literary terms, but also an appendix containing an example of a ghazal, literally translated and with its parts explained. Also for this reason, I have used English sources wherever possible, so that the reader can consult them independently; usually, however, there aren't any, and in such cases all translations are my own.

This story takes place in North India only a little over a century ago, the blink of an eye in historical time. Worlds were in collision. The powerful momentum of the advancing British Raj encountered the political inertia of the declining Mughal Empire. The irresistible force met the heretofore immovable object—and rolled over it. Azad and Hali, survivors of this great historical collision, were absolutely determined that their literature—and with it their culture—would not die from the shock. Their urgent attempts at triage, surgery, and sometimes euthanasia were not always successful. But their larger purpose was achieved. The Indo-Muslim community survived its darkest hours, learned to play the new game by the new rules, and was able once again to face the future with purpose and hope. Now, a century later, it can consider reclaiming some of the best achievements of the old game.

Our own generation can take pride in a widening range of cultural encounters that has opened over time to more and more people. We expect cultures to clash, and we try to appreciate the dissonances. But we also know that (as Azad put it) "if you examine the temperaments of individual men who live thousands of miles apart and in countries with different characters, you will see, since human nature is one, to what extent their thoughts resemble each other's" (46). Across the continents and the decades I salute Azad and Hali: with their backs to the wall, they had the courage to fight for survival and renewal. They tried desperately to reorganize their culture into lines of defense that could resist the Victorian onslaught. Even when they attacked their own poetry most bitterly, their love for it was never in doubt. And even when I disagree with them most strongly, I know that they would understand my own larger purpose. For we can now see that the poetry itself has stood firm over time. The Victorians are dead, and the ghazal lives.

Or at least, the British Victorians are dead; but many South Asian Victorians remain. They view the ghazal through the special distorting lenses provided by Azad and Hali—yet in many cases, such is the power of the poetry, they guiltily find themselves loving it anyway. This book is dedicated to the memory of Azad and Hali, and to everyone who loves classical Urdu poetry. For nowadays cultures belong to those who choose them. And I am proud to consider myself an heir to the rich and inexhaustible tradition of the ghazal.

Part One

A GARDEN NOW DESTROYED

So there is now no hope at all of another such
master of poetry being born in India.
For he was the nightingale of a garden
that has been destroyed.

AZAD, *Water of Life*

1 THE LOST WORLD

By the late eighteenth century, the once-mighty Mughal Empire was in rapid political decline. The magnificent Red Fort itself had been sacked over and over by a series of plunderers: first by Nādir Shāh and his Persians (1739), who carried off the famous Peacock Throne; then by Aḥmad Shāh Abdālī and his Afghans (1757); and finally by Ġhulām Qādir and his Rohillas (1788), who not only despoiled the library but even dug up the palace floors looking for concealed valuables. Toward the end of this period the unfortunate emperor Shāh ʿĀlam II (r. 1759–1806), Aurangzeb's great-great-grandson, had much to endure. He was crowned while a fugitive in Bihar, and did not even manage to return to Delhi until 1772. His political impotence became proverbial; as the saying went, "The realm of Shāh ʿĀlam—from Delhi to Palam."[1] The emperor knew humiliation, helplessness, and actual poverty. He was "only a chessboard king" (253).

At length he accepted the Marathas as his protectors, and from 1785 to 1803 they were the real power behind his throne. Even then, though, his tribulations were not over. For when the brutal Ġhulām Qādir seized the city in 1788, he was outraged at finding so small an amount of loot—and had Shāh ʿĀlam blinded. The Marathas later came to the rescue, retook the city, and restored the blind emperor to his nominal throne. But gradually, amidst the military and political turbulence of the period, the British gained the upper hand over the Marathas; finally, in 1803, Lord Lake took Delhi. For the first time in decades, stability returned to the city. The new conquerors, like the old, valued the Mughal dynasty for its time-honored legitimating power, its continuing hold on the Indian imagination. The British kept Shāh ʿĀlam II on the throne until his death three years later, at the age of seventy-nine.[2]

Despite Shāh ʿĀlam's legal sovereignty, his throne rested uncertainly on layers of nostalgia and remembered glory. He himself as an "emperor" was hopelessly vulnerable. But he had another calling as well: he was a serious poet, as well as a notable connoisseur and patron of poetry. Toward the end of his life, poetry became his chief pursuit. And as a poet, he could feel an unchallengeable pride and confidence. He came from a tradition that knew itself as the center of its cultural world—and knew that its cultural world was the only one that counted. For he wrote in the beautiful court language, Persian, and took full advantage of its rich classical literature and its sophisticated, highly developed array of genres. As Persian poets had done for centuries, he often composed in the brief, intense lyric genre of ghazal (*ġhazal*), with its endless romantic and mystical possibilities. And as Persian poets had also done for centuries, he chose a personal pen name (*taḳhalluṣ*), which he incorporated into the last verse of each ghazal: he called himself "Āftāb" (Sun).

Moreover, as North Indian poets had been doing since at least the beginning of the eighteenth century, he composed ghazals not only in Persian, but also in Urdu. Urdu, while still resting firmly on its Indic grammatical and lexical base, was steadily enlarging its repertoire of Persian genres and imagery. As a literary language, Urdu was absorbing almost everything that Indians loved in Persian—so that it was in fact gradually supplanting Persian. Thus it is not surprising that when Shāh ʿĀlam II wrote in Urdu, he, like most poets, used the same pen name as he did for his Persian verse. When he composed poetry in the Indic literary language of Braj Bhasha, however, he used a different pen name: his own title "Shāh ʿĀlam" (Ruler of the World). He was also fluent in Panjabi, and is said to have known Arabic, Sanskrit, and Turkish. During his reign "the Red Fort once again became a center of literary enthusiasm."[3] It was the scene of frequent mushairahs (*mushāʿirah*), or poetry recitation sessions.

Shāh ʿĀlam's eldest son, Javān Baḳht, shared his love for poetry. "This exalted prince was so inclined toward poetry that he arranged for mushairahs to be held twice a month in his apartments; he used to send his own mace-bearer to escort the distinguished poets on the day of the mushairah, and encouraged everyone by showing the greatest kindness and favor."[4] Javān Baḳht, however, died young. When Shāh ʿĀlam himself died, the British installed his second son on the throne as Akbar Shāh II (r. 1806–1837). Akbar Shāh composed poetry only casually, because it was the thing to do; playing on his father's pen name, he called himself "Shuʿā" (Ray). But the new heir apparent, Akbar Shāh's son Bahādur Shāh (1775–1862), vigorously sustained the family poetic tradition: he brought poets into the Red Fort, held mushairahs, and pursued his own strong literary interests.[5]

Bahādur Shāh was a very serious poet. The famous pen name he chose for himself, "Ẓafar" (Victory), was actually part of his given name, Abū Ẓafar Sirāj ud-Dīn Muḥammad Bahādur Shāh. His mother, Lāl Bā'ī, was a Hindu. Bahādur Shāh had been educated entirely within the Red Fort, under his grandfather's supervision, and had mastered not only Urdu and Persian but Braj Bhasha and Panjabi as well; he composed a volume (*dīvān*) of poetry in each of these four languages. Like his grandfather, he used two separate pen names: "Ẓafar" for poetry in Urdu and Persian, "Shauq Rang" (Passionate) for the rest of his verse.[6]

When Akbar Shāh II died, Bahādur Shāh, who was sixty-two years old at the time, duly replaced him on the throne—a throne behind which the British were definitely the real power. The new emperor Bahādur Shāh II (r. 1837–1857) was a man of parts: he studied not only poetry but mystical philosophy as well, and practiced calligraphy, pigeon flying, swordsmanship, horse breeding, riding, and other aristocratic arts. While his dress and most of his tastes were simple and dignified, he enjoyed the company of women: he was much influenced by his favorite wives, and continued to marry an occasional new one even into his sixties and seventies. Living on a fixed British pension, he nevertheless had royal traditions of largesse to uphold, as well as many relatives and dependents to support, so that he was hard-pressed for funds; he used every possible means to increase his income, and his financial affairs were always in disarray.[7] He certainly felt the difficulty of his position—and sometimes wittily used it as a source of poetic imagery. As he wrote in one of his poems, "Whoever enters this gloomy palace / Is a prisoner for life in European captivity."[8]

Bahādur Shāh was a man of "cultured and upright character," who as a "philosophic prince" could have "adorned any court," and whose "interests and tastes were primarily literary and aesthetic." The British certainly viewed him with less and less respect over time; yet, as Percival Spear argues, a large part of their disdain was a function of their own increasingly limited, utilitarian outlook on life. The emperor was "a poet, and so could expect no more consideration than the same men gave to Shelley or Byron or Keats." But since the emperor was so much loved and esteemed in India, motives of prudence kept British disdain in check.[9] Even when the physical power of the Mughal emperor was close to nonexistent, his symbolic power as a cultural icon was a force to be reckoned with. As the governor general put it in 1819, the British should seek to avoid any behavior that "might be misinterpreted into a wanton oppression of a dignified tho' unfortunate Family."[10]

Even as the emperor's royal prerogatives slowly eroded, the decline was managed for the most part with decorum: the hostile British Resident

Hawkins, who made a point of violating court etiquette, was soon sent home. "After this, in the deft hands of William Fraser and then Thomas Metcalfe, even the gradual withdrawal of British recognition of the imperial status was smoothed by dignified deference."[11] C. F. Andrews makes a similar point: although "real power passed more and more, every year, into the hands of the English," nevertheless since "the English were, throughout this whole period, very few in numbers," and since they "did not interfere more than they could possibly help," the result was a kind of "dual control" that was "not altogether disturbing."[12] Peter Hardy notes that in studying the period "one is impressed by how little in feeling and in style of life the educated classes of upper India were touched by the British presence before 1857."[13] As Azad later put it, "Those were the days when if a European was seen in Delhi, people considered him an extraordinary sample of God's handiwork, and pointed him out to each other: 'Look, there goes a European!'"[14]

Narayani Gupta describes a lively Hindu-Muslim cultural life—conducted entirely in Urdu, by people who had consciously chosen not to learn English. The father of the great Urdu novelist Nażīr Aḥmad (1836–1912) went so far as to tell the boy he would rather see him dead than learning English. As the recently founded (1825) Delhi College developed, not its English section but its Urdu-medium "Oriental" one flourished—and showed itself especially zealous in pursuing the new Western sciences.[15]

Spear characterizes this period, especially the second quarter of the nineteenth century when the "English Peace" was well established, as a time of prosperity, confidence, urban growth, and religious and cultural harmony. "The Court was the cultural centre, the Hindus dominated the commercial life and the British conducted the administration"; daily life was a matter of mutual accommodation and shared festivals, with "much interchange of civilities and much give and take." Spear paints an almost (though not quite) idyllic picture: "Old and new for a time met together in the short-lived Delhi Renaissance."[16] C. F. Andrews agrees: the "impact from the West" in fact "led to a cultural renaissance which proceeded remarkably from within."[17] This Delhi Renaissance was rich in the arts, and extraordinarily influential. Lucknow, untouched by the kind of repeated plundering that Delhi had endured, was a great magnet and center of patronage; but Delhi, as the last Mughal capital, had a special nostalgic appeal. The court was "the school of manners for India" and "a cultural influence of great value"; its prestige and patronage made it "the natural centre of all the arts and crafts."[18] Urdu poetry was widely and seriously cultivated: there were not only frequent mushairahs at the Red Fort, but also weekly ones held on the Delhi College premises,[19] as well as numerous privately sponsored ones. When it came to poets, Bahādur Shāh's circle included, besides himself, one great poet, several major ones, and literally dozens of highly competent minor poets.

· · ·

The great poet, Mirzā Asadullāh Ḳhān (1797–1869), who used the pen name "Ġhālib" (Victorious), is now universally recognized as either the first or second greatest classical ghazal poet of Urdu; his reputation is rivaled only by that of Mīr Taqī "Mīr" (c. 1722–1810). Ġhālib came of Turkish stock, and was always proud of his family's military tradition: his father had died fighting in the raja of Alwar's army, while his uncle Naṣrullāh Beg had been in the service of the Marathas and then in 1803, when the British took Delhi, had become a commander under Lord Lake. The British pension inherited on this uncle's death was the mainstay of Ġhālib's finances throughout most of his life. He was raised in Agra by his mother's well-off and aristocratic family. At the age of eleven he began writing Persian poetry; he had already, according to his own account, been writing in Urdu for some time. When he was thirteen he was married—by family arrangement, as was customary—to a girl from a wealthy and socially elite background; a year or two later he settled in Delhi, which became his home for the rest of his life.[20]

Ġhālib's life in Delhi was firmly grounded in the aristocratic Persianized culture surrounding the court. He always knew who he was, and knew his own worth as a poet; despite his lifelong financial and personal vicissitudes, neither his confidence nor his sense of humor ever really failed him. His complex, metaphysical, "difficult" poetry, however disturbing to conventional tastes, was arresting and undeniably powerful; even during his lifetime he began, so to speak, to be Ġhālib.

But he also had many friends in the British administration, including the Resident John Fraser. He made a two-year journey to Calcutta and took a strong interest in the English influence on view there—including newspapers, as yet unknown in Delhi. (Although he knew neither English nor Bengali, Persian served as an effective link language.) And he certainly thought the Emperor Akbar's administrative style inferior to that of the English, as he made clear on one occasion to the great reformer Sir Sayyid Aḥmad Ḳhān (1817–1898).[21]

Ġhālib met the new culture on his own terms and tried throughout his life to make it behave like the old. In some respects, of course, it obliged him. The elaborate etiquette of English ceremonial gatherings was directly borrowed from that of the Mughal court, and Ġhālib set considerable store by it: "In the Government durbars I occupy the tenth place to the right, and the marks of honour prescribed for me comprise a ceremonial robe, seven gifts of cloth, a turban with an embroidered velvet band and jewelled gold ornament to wear in it, a string of pearls and a cloak."[22] Such feudal honors were as consciously manipulated by the English as they had always been by the Mughals.[23]

Ġhālib tried to extend his aristocratic status into more modern realms as well. In 1842 he was invited to be interviewed for the newly created post of Persian professor at Delhi College. A famous anecdote gives a vivid picture of Ġhālib's arrival, in his palanquin, for the interview. He alighted, but refused to enter the building until Mr. Thomason, the secretary, appeared and gave him the formal welcome to which his aristocratic rank entitled him. Time passed. Finally, Mr. Thomason came out to try to resolve the situation:

> [Mr. Thomason] came out personally and explained that a formal welcome was appropriate when he attended the Governor's durbar, but not in the present case, when he came as a candidate for employment. Ghalib replied, "I contemplated taking a government appointment in the expectation that this would bring me greater honours than I now receive, not a reduction in those already accorded me." The Secretary replied, "I am bound by regulations." "Then I hope that you will excuse me," Ghalib said, and came away.[24]

Despite his poverty and indebtedness, Ġhālib made the grand gesture with a flourish. Honor was honor, it was clear where it lay, and that was the end of the matter.

Ġhālib tried again and again to teach the new regime manners, especially when it came to the vital question of patronage. He reminded the English that poetry was a uniquely potent art, conferring immortal fame not only on its creators, but also on the patrons whose generosity it celebrated. In 1856 he composed a Persian ode (*qaṣīdah*) to Queen Victoria, and forwarded it to London through Lord Ellenborough. But he then received a bureaucratic letter suggesting "that the petitioner, in respect to the norms of administrative procedure, should channel his petition through the administrator in India." He therefore sent his ode again, through the proper channels, along with a letter in which he politely reminded the queen of the well-known and long-established duty that sovereigns owed to poets. (It was indeed a long-established one: more than five centuries earlier, the Indo-Persian poet Amīr "Ḳhusrau" (1253–1325) had used exactly the same line of argument on one of his own patrons.)[25] Ġhālib pointed out to Queen

Victoria that since great kings had customarily "rewarded their poets and well-wishers by filling their mouths with pearls, weighing them in gold and granting them villages and recompense, the exalted queen should bestow upon Ghalib, the petitioner, the title of *Mihr-Khwan*, and present him with the robe of honour and a few crumbs from her bounteous table—that is, in English, a 'pension.'" He was eagerly awaiting a response—but by then it was 1857.[26]

The natural source of patronage for Ġhālib would have been the Red Fort. Poets were so much a part of Persianized court life that they often became intimate "boon companions" to the king; in some cases they became "part of the royal paraphernalia" and changed hands along with the throne.[27] Ġhālib indeed found some support from the court, though never what he needed and felt he deserved. In 1850 he wrote to Bahādur Shāh:

> I swear that you too must feel pride in the great kindness of fortune, that you possess a slave like Ghalib, whose song has all the power of fire. Turn your attention to me as my skill demands, and you will treasure me as the apple of your eye and open your heart for me to enter in. . . . And why talk of the poets of the Emperor Akbar's day? My presence bears witness that your age excels his.[28]

The absolute, passionate confidence of Ġhālib's claim has no bombast in it. He speaks with the impatient certainty of one who knows beyond doubt both what his craft is worth, and what he is worth as a master craftsman.

But although Ġhālib had many admirers and shagirds (*shāgird*), pupils who studied poetry under his guidance, Bahādur Shāh Ẓafar was not inclined to be one of them. Like any other serious poet, Ẓafar made his own choice of a master or ustad (*ustād*), who would criticize and correct his verses; apprenticeship was, in poetry as in other arts and crafts, the accepted way to acquire a skill. Ẓafar's first ustad was Shāh Naṣīr ud-Din "Naṣīr" (Helper) (d. 1838), who was more or less Ẓafar's contemporary and an important poet in his own right. At the middle and end of every month Shāh Naṣīr sponsored mushairahs, some of which were notorious for the complicated meter and rhyme patterns (*ṭaraḥ*) assigned to be used in the poems recited. Around 1803, however, Shāh Naṣīr left Delhi for the Deccan. Ẓafar then briefly named as his ustad 'Izzatullāh "'Ishq" (Love); and after him Mīr Kāẓim Ḥusain "Beqarār" (Restless), a shagird of Shāh Naṣīr; Beqarār eventually resigned to become Lord Elphinstone's chief secretary. Ẓafar's true ustad was Beqarār's replacement, the major poet Shaiḳh Ibrāhīm "Żauq" (Taste) (c. 1788–1854), who had also been a shagird of Shāh Naṣīr. Żauq and Ẓafar developed such a satisfactory relationship that it remained firm for four decades.[29] Ġhālib, by contrast, received only a minor token of royal favor: he was commissioned to compose, in Persian, a Mughal dynastic history—a task he found tedious and uninspiring.[30]

Only when Żauq died in 1854 did Ẓafar finally appoint Ġhālib, the obvious choice, to fill the prestigious post of royal ustad. Ẓafar seems to have done this somewhat grudgingly, and Ġhālib accepted only because he needed the pension that went with the job.[31] Though he was proud of his position at court—"The Emperor loved me like one of his sons"—Ġhālib complained that the pension was "tiny."[32]

While we know a great deal from many sources about the lives of major figures like Żauq and Ġhālib, we know relatively little about their hundreds of less famous contemporaries. Most of our information about minor poets comes from the tazkirahs (*tażkirah*), traditional anthologies of poetry. One especially interesting and comprehensive tazkirah, *The Garden of Poetry* (1855) by Mirzā Qādir Bak̲h̲sh "Ṣābir" (Patient),[33] lists among its 540 contemporary poets no fewer than fifty princes related to Ẓafar. Such royal relatives were usually dilettantes rather than serious poets; their sheer numbers show how socially correct it was in their world to affect literary tastes. An interest in Urdu language and literature had even come to be considered a hallmark of the city itself: "Anyone who had not lived in Delhi could never be considered a real knower of Urdu, as if the steps of the Jāmaʿ Masjid were a school of language," as Maulvī ʿAbd ul-Ḥaq put it. In Delhi poetry "was discussed in every house," for "the emperor himself was a poet and a connoisseur of poetry" and "the language of the Exalted Fort was the essence of refinement."[34]

The Garden of Poetry includes fifty-three Delhi poets who seem from their names to be Hindus (mostly Kayasths and Kashmiri Brahmans) and describes a scattering of poets from unexpected walks of life: "Pairā" (Adorner), a poor water-seller in Chandni Chauk; "Sharīr" (Naughty), a merchant in Panjabi Katra; "Zirġhām" (Lion), a young wrestler; "Ẓarāfat" (Wit), a lady with a colorful past who had now settled into respectability; "Banno" (Girl), a courtesan, who had caught the taste for poetry from her lover, one Gulāb Singh; "Faṣṣād" (Cupper), a barber who was inspired by the company of Shāh Naṣīr; "Farāso," a Western protégé of Begam Samrū; and others.[35]

Ṣābir treated the poet Ẓafar, however, as a special case, for he was also the Emperor Bahādur Shāh, "refuge of both worlds, for whom angels do battle, ruler of time and space, lord of crown and seal . . . at whose command which is the twin of Fate, the revolution of the sky is established." His literary powers were equally exalted: "*Maẓmūn*s [themes][36] of submission in his poetry are equal in rank to pride and coquetry," and "the radiance of meaning [*maʿnī*] is manifest through his words." For when it comes to poetry, not only words but even the very letters that embody them on paper are magically potent:

> The sequences of lines, through the reflection of *maẓmūns*, are lamp-wicks for the bedchamber of the page. The circular letters, through the effect of meaning (*maʿnī*), are the wine-mark on the flagon in the festive gathering of pages. The colorfulness of festive meaning is the glistening of wine; in martial verses, the wetness of the ink is blood and perspiration. In mystical verses, the circular letters are seeing eyes; and in romantic verses, tear-shedding eyes. And in spring-related verses, [the decorations] between the lines are flowerbeds; and in sky-related verses, the Milky Way. The breath, through the floweringness of the words, is the garden breeze; and vision, through the freshness of the writing, is the vein of the jasmine. The line (*miṣraʿ*) has the stature of a cypress; the verse is the eyebrow of the beautiful ones of Khallukh and Naushad.

In short, the emperor's poetry deserves praise so endless that if "the messenger of Thought" ran for a thousand years, it would still only cover as much distance as "the footprint of a weak ant" by comparison. For, as Ṣābir puns, "from the East/opening verse (*maṭlaʿ*) to the West/closing verse (*maqṭaʿ*) is the excursion ground of that Sun whose domes are the skies."[37] In principle, the emperor was still the center of the universe, just as his ancestors, with their vast domains and absolute powers, had always been.

· · ·

Not surprisingly, literary people flocked to the court of such an impressive poet-emperor, seeking both learning and patronage. During the period of the Delhi Renaissance two remarkable young men studied in Delhi: Muḥammad Ḥusain, who chose for himself the pen name "Āzād" (Free), and Alṭāf Ḥusain, who first called himself "Ḳhastah" (Worn Out) but later changed his pen name, very possibly at Ġhālib's suggestion, to "Ḥālī" (Contemporary). The power that these two came to exercise over Urdu literature and criticism has been unequaled ever since.

Muḥammad Ḥusain Azad was the older of the two. He was born in Delhi, in 1830; his mother Amānī Begam, who came from a Persian émigré family, died when he was only three or four years old. His father, Maulvī Muḥammad Bāqir (c. 1810–1857), who also came from a family of learned Persian émigrés, was a man of versatile talents and played a significant role in the cultural life of his day. Educated at the newly founded Delhi College, Maulvī Muḥammad Bāqir stayed on for a time as a teacher; but he found the salary too low. He then for many years held a series of administrative positions on the collector's staff, while also erecting a market for foreign merchants, a mosque, and a Shīʿa religious hall (*imāmbāṛah*) in which he himself sometimes preached. In addition, he involved himself in prolonged and acrimonious Shīʿite religious controversies.

And as if all this were not enough, he also bought a lithograph press, and in early 1837 launched the *Dihlī Urdū Akḥbār* (Delhi Urdu Newspaper), probably the first Urdu newspaper in North India.[38] The *Dihlī Urdū Akḥbār* had, like almost all newspapers of the period, an extremely limited circulation (69 subscribers in 1844, 79 in 1848). It followed a dexterously balanced political line. In a general way it was solidly pro-British, but particular instances of official injustice, corruption, or other wrongdoing came in for criticism. And although it reported—and deplored—many cases of flagrant misgovernment by Indian rulers, including Bahādur Shāh, these were almost always ascribed to the machinations of (evil) courtiers who pulled the wool over a (good) king's eyes.[39]

Around 1845 Maulvī Muḥammad Bāqir enrolled his only son in Delhi College. Muḥammad Ḥusain did well there. He was enrolled in the Urdu-medium "Oriental" section, which offered Arabic and Persian rather than English. In both 1848 and 1849 his Urdu essays won prizes; these essays, as his teachers noted, showed the good effects of his family background in newspaper work.[40] At some point during these years his family arranged his marriage to Āġhā'ī Begam, the daughter of another Persian émigré family. After completing Delhi College's eight-year curriculum, Muḥammad Ḥusain graduated, probably in 1854. He had started to assist his father in his newspaper work, and in the 1850s his name appears as "printer and publisher" of books produced by the Dihlī Urdū Akḥbār Press. He continued with this work until 1857.[41]

Muḥammad Ḥusain Azad later claimed that throughout his childhood and youth he had spent a great deal of time with the poet Żauq, the royal ustad, who was a close friend of his father's. He claimed Żauq as his own ustad—although at this early stage in his life Azad went to few mushairahs and wrote almost no poetry. He claimed to have been especially intimate with Żauq, and to have received many confidences from him. It seems probable that he had a considerable amount of contact with Żauq, but we have only his word for the nature and intensity of their relationship. His most painstaking and fair-minded biographer, Aslam Farruḳhī, speaks of his "Żauq worship."[42] Azad certainly exaggerated at times: he claimed, for example, to have sat constantly at Żauq's feet, absorbing both "outer" and "inner" (that is, mystical) wisdom, for "twenty years."[43] Azad made even more extravagant assertions as well. He claimed that under Żauq's direction he had read, and made abridgements from, no fewer than 350 volumes of the work of classical poets; later the figure somehow became 750! These claims are quite impossible to accept, though they certainly show the kind of classical literary study Azad most admired.[44]

Żauq's death in 1854 must have been a heavy blow. But Azad eventually undertook a project that offered consolation: the editing of Żauq's ghazals for publication. He planned to do this task slowly, carefully, and lovingly. Moreover, he pursued his own literary work. He took Ḥakīm Āġhā Jān "ʿAish" (Luxury) as his new ustad, in a working relationship that continued until 1857. Azad's first known poem, a nineteen-verse "continuous ghazal" (*ġhazal-e musalsal*), was published in the *Dihlī Urdū Akḥbār.* The poem was a meditation on the fleetingness and untrustworthiness of life, and it was called "A History of Instructive Reversals." It was published, with excellent timing, on May 24, 1857.[45]

· · ·

Alṭāf Ḥusain Hali, born in 1837, was seven years younger than Azad; he came from an old family in the famous town of Panipat, north of Delhi.[46] Although he was orphaned at the age of nine, he had an affectionate older brother (an inspector of police, who also wrote Persian poetry) and two older sisters who looked after him. He was a bright and promising child, tremendously eager to learn, and was given a traditional basic education. His first teacher was a *ḥāfiẓ*, someone who had memorized the whole Quran; Panipat was "famous for the number of its Hafizes,"[47] and Hali too achieved this formidable feat. Then he began to learn Persian; along with the language, he studied the history, literature, and especially poetry of Iran—but he always described these studies as "elementary." As he grew older, he himself took the initiative in arranging for an Arabic teacher, but his lessons ended before he had a chance to make as much progress as he wished. He was left unsatisfied: "Although the spontaneous passion for learning in my heart was unbounded, I never had the chance for a regular and continuing education."[48] What he longed for was the classical Persian and Arabic training of a traditional Indo-Muslim scholar.

His brother and sisters, however, had other plans for him. When he was seventeen years old, they arranged his marriage to a cousin, Islām un-Nisā, and thus inducted him into the ranks of adulthood. They then pressured him to find work and augment the family income, which was none too large. The young Alṭāf Ḥusain was a dutiful boy, and everyone in the family made sure he saw his duty clearly. Alṭāf Ḥusain's scholarly aspirations were obviously destined to wither on the vine. Given the circumstances, the time and place and culture in which he lived, this was a foregone conclusion.

Alṭāf Ḥusain, however, then did the only truly astonishing, defiant, flagrant deed in his long, sober, impeccable life. He waited for a night when his new bride was at her parents' house—and he slipped away. He was not yet eighteen, and had never been anywhere. Yet without hesitation he simply ran away from home. Hali himself, years later, gave his own account of this event: his relatives had "forced" him to marry, and unfortunately this "yoke that was placed upon my shoulders" meant that "apparently now the doors of education were closed on every side." He took flight, and never apologized for it: "Everyone wanted me to look for a job, but my passion for learning prevailed." Besides, he added in extenuation, "my wife's family was comfortably off."[49]

Penniless, traveling alone for greater anonymity, he set out to walk the fifty-three miles to Delhi. Even after he arrived, he was sometimes homeless, and so often hungry that his health was affected. But he was able to slake his thirst for knowledge. In later years, far from having regrets, he looked back nostalgically on this time: "I saw with my own eyes this last brilliant glow of Delhi, the thought of which makes my heart crack with regret."[50]

In Delhi, he studied Arabic language and literature, including poetry and meter, at a flourishing, "very spacious and beautiful" traditional school (*madrasah*), the Madrasah of Ḥusain Bak̤hsh.[51] Many years later he described his cultural background at the time.

> Although the old Delhi College was then in all its glory, I'd been brought up in a society that believed that learning was based only on knowledge of Arabic and Persian. Especially in the Panipat area, first of all nobody even thought about English education, and if people had any opinion about it at all it was as a means of getting a government job, not of acquiring any kind of knowledge. On the contrary, in fact: our religious teachers called the English schools barbarous. When I arrived in Delhi, at the school in which I had to live night and day, all the teachers and students considered graduates of the college nothing but barbarians.

Hali regretted that during his year and a half in Delhi he hadn't even gone to look at Delhi College, and had never chanced to meet his distinguished contemporaries who were being educated there. He named three in particular: the great teacher and translator Maulvī Żakā'ullāh (1836–1907?), the famous novelist Nażīr Aḥmad, and Muḥammad Ḥusain Azad.[52]

If he failed to meet his peers, he lost no time in seeking out the greatest of his elders: he often went to visit Ġhālib, and persuaded him to explain difficult passages in his Urdu and Persian poetry. Treating Ġhālib as an ustad, he showed him his own earliest ghazals. Ġhālib is said to have duly given him *iṣlāḥ*, "correction," as an ustad should, and to have encouraged him to persist with his writing. Unfortunately, none of this early poetry—written under the pen name of "Ḳhastah"—has survived.

Hali lay low so successfully that for a year and a half his family had no idea at all where he was, or even whether he was alive or dead. There is no evidence that he would ever have voluntarily returned to them. But in 1855 they learned of his whereabouts, recaptured him, "compelled" him "forcibly, willy-nilly" (as he put it) to leave Delhi, and took him back to Panipat. He had the nerve to run away, but not the nerve to look his elders in the eye and defy them. So ended the great period of his education.

By 1856 Hali had an infant son, and he himself had recognized—or had been forced by family pressure to recognize—the need to find a job. He went alone to Hissar, without connections or references, and managed to get a position in the deputy collector's office. The salary was small, but at least it would be steady. Hali did his work most conscientiously, and rapidly mastered the office routines. But by then it was 1857.[53]

· · ·

1857—the end of this particular world. An upheaval like an earthquake, opening a chasm so deep that no one could see to the bottom. It was the end of the court, and thus a profound "break in cultural as well as political tradition."[54] As Andrews puts it, "The renaissance at Delhi gave a sudden illumination to the age. . . . Light flickered and leapt up for a brief moment before it died away." But the light did not die of its own accord—Andrews is very clear about that. The light was killed. "More than any other single cause, the Mutiny killed it."[55]

2 BEYOND A SEA OF BLOOD

The story of 1857 has been told and retold, from numerous points of view. It indeed began as a mutiny, and the "Mutiny" it has remained in the British historical imagination. It soon spread beyond the army, however, and thus became much more than a mutiny; South Asian historians often describe it as the "First War of National Independence." For our present purposes we can call it the Rebellion.[1] By whatever name, it had profound effects on the lives of virtually all urban North Indians.

Bahādur Shāh "Ẓafar," poet-emperor and English pensioner, was utterly undone by the events of 1857. On the one hand, it has been argued that he was an ardent participant in the Rebellion—that he had been secretly informed about it in advance, that he tried energetically to take charge of it and give it an inclusive, nationalistic character.[2] It has also been argued that although the Rebellion took him by surprise, at the crucial moment the "Imperial yearnings in his heart" suddenly awoke, and he "entered into the full spirit" of the rebels, for "rather than continue in slavery, it would be preferable even to die."[3] On the other hand, he has also been blamed for the collapse of the Rebellion: he failed to rise to this "great occasion" and uphold the kingship, so that although the common people participated in the Rebellion, "the elite remained prey to vacillation," and "the English had the chance to destroy Delhi."[4]

No doubt the prospect of wielding in practice the power he had always claimed in theory was alluring. But Bahādur Shāh was eighty-two years old, and was never able to control the rebels—or even to restrain his own headstrong sons from atrocities like the killing of captured English women and children. He was almost certainly taken by surprise on May 11, when the first rebel soldiers arrived from Meerut and appeared beneath his balcony; he clearly disapproved of their ill-bred, unmannerly behavior. Once they seized the city and claimed him as their emperor, however, he displayed considerable activity on behalf of their cause. He became, in Spear's words, "a contingently willing accessory after the fact."[5]

For he tried to restore order in the city, maintain communal harmony, raise and allocate revenues, and inspire the troops to fight the English instead of despoiling the citizens.[6] His power was far from absolute, but it was also far from nonexistent. May 17: "The King summoned many of the Sepoys to his presence and spoke to them very severely." June 17: "The King sent for the chief of the mutineers, and threatened to take poison unless greater discipline were enforced and the oppressions discontinued. The chief promised immediate compliance." July 2: "The King said it was no use his giving orders, as they were never obeyed, and he had no one to enforce them, but his decree was that the English should be caused not to exist." August 4: "'We have here 60,000 men in the city, but they have not been able to win a clod of dirt from the English.'" August 22: "'If the Sepoys would only leave the city, and employ themselves in collecting the revenue, I should be in a position to pay them, and to protect the lives and property of the citizens.'"[7] His exasperated tone is not that of an absolute ruler, but neither is it that of a helpless, fearful victim.

The emperor's leverage lay in the fact that the rebels could not afford to lose his services as their symbolic source of authority. Thus his frequent threats to withdraw his cooperation: to hold no more public audiences, to renounce the throne, to retire to some holy place, to "swallow a diamond" and die.[8] Such threats were noted with pathos and hope in the *Dihlī Urdū Aḳhbār:*

> His Majesty has issued a proclamation wherein he has drawn attention to the fact that the majority of the powerful and influential people cause misery to the loyal subjects of the Emperor. . . . If the prevailing state of affairs continues, His Majesty wrote, then he would be obliged, since he had little love for worldly goods, to retire to Ajmer, to the shrine of the Khwaja. . . . It is heard that the abovementioned had a great effect on the audience when it was read out.[9]

At other times, however, Bahādur Shāh made strongly anti-British remarks, and even composed martial verses that he sent to his commanding general: "May all the enemies of the Faith be killed today; / The Firinghis be destroyed, root and branch!"[10] When the British recaptured Delhi on September 18, Bahādur Shāh hesitated, then ultimately refused to accompany the rebels in their flight from the city.

The unfortunate emperor had been placed from the start in an almost impossible position. The British, however, perceived (or chose to perceive) his court as the heart and soul of the Rebellion—and avenged themselves accordingly. They summarily executed a number of Bahādur Shāh's sons and grandsons and other princes of the blood; still others were sentenced to life imprisonment. The Red Fort, which housed the Mughal court, had always been called the Auspicious Fort; so many of its inhabitants met dire fates that Ġhālib later renamed it the Inauspicious Fort.[11] As for the emperor himself, he was held for a time in a humiliating kind of captivity, available to be stared at by chance British visitors. Finally he was placed on trial, on ill-conceived charges of sedition. Later historians would recognize that in fact he had never formally renounced his sovereignty: while he might be a defeated enemy king, therefore, he could not properly be considered a rebel.[12] He was also charged with the death of the British women and children who had been murdered in the Red Fort.

At the trial, the prosecutor argued that "to Mussulman intrigue and Mahommedan conspiracy we may mainly attribute the dreadful calamities of the year 1857"; he sought to show "how intimately the prisoner, as the head of the Mahommedan faith in India, has been connected with the organisation of that conspiracy either as its leader or its unscrupulous accomplice." Bahādur Shāh's defense rested on the plea of helplessness: "All that has been done, was done by that rebellious army. I was in their power, what could I do? . . . I was helpless, and constrained by my fears, I did whatever they required, otherwise they would immediately have killed me. . . . I found myself in such a predicament that I was weary of my life."[13] The emperor was judged guilty on all counts, exiled to Rangoon, and kept under discreet house arrest; he was by this time in a condition of vagueness and partial senility. When he died a few years later, the British buried him secretly in an unmarked grave in a wide field, which was then sown all over with grass.[14] The last surviving members of the Mughal dynasty were left in conspicuous and humiliating poverty; as Ġhālib later wrote to a friend, "The male descendants of the deposed King—such as survived the sword—draw allowances of five rupees a month. The female descendants, if old, are bawds, and if young, prostitutes."[15]

· · ·

In 1857 Ġhālib was fifty-nine years old, partially deaf, and in uncertain health. He took no significant part in the Rebellion, though it appears that he prudently "continued to maintain relations" with Bahādur Shāh by composing celebratory verse and perhaps appearing once or twice at court.[16] But he suffered much anxiety and grief, and endured financial hardship when his British pension ceased to arrive. For the most part he shut himself up in his house and began to write an elaborate history of what was happening—in ancient Persian, avoiding all Arabic words. In his history Ġhālib wrote of the disastrous effects of the revolt: one must, he said, "shed tears for the destruction of Hindustan," which was a ruined land. "City after city lies open, without protectors. . . . House after house lies desolate, and the abodes of grieving men invite despoliation."[17] Delhi College, where Azad had studied, suffered the total loss of its library. The rebels looted the Persian and Urdu books, and tore the English books into fragments that "carpeted all the college gardens to a depth of two inches."[18] The prisons had been emptied, and the streets were in a state of anarchy; the city was full of the kind of lower-class ruffians with whom the aristocratic Ġhālib could never feel empathy. Perhaps most painful of all, the postal service had entirely broken down, so that Ġhālib—an indefatigable correspondent, writer of the most irresistible letters in Urdu literature—could no longer get news of his friends in other cities.

When the British recaptured the city in the autumn, however, things suddenly grew much worse. For several days after the assault, British troops ran wild, not only looting and plundering but also killing every able-bodied man they found. Then there followed "a more systematic reign of terror"—indiscriminate shootings, drum-head court-martials and summary hangings—that lasted for several weeks.[19] During this period Ġhālib and his family led "a prisoner's life," barricaded inside their house, so deprived of all news that "our ears were deaf and our eyes were blind." When Ġhālib's brother died after many years of insanity, the curfew was so strict that it was difficult even to bury him. "And in this trouble and perplexity, a dearth of bread and water!"[20]

Even so, Ġhālib was one of the luckier ones: his street contained some houses owned by courtiers of the loyalist maharaja of Patiala, who had arranged for special guards. He and some neighbors were eventually interrogated by a British officer. Ġhālib, ever the aristocrat, reported that the officer had "asked me my name and the others their occupation." Ġhālib later claimed that he had established his credentials by producing the letter that acknowledged his ode to Queen Victoria. When asked why he hadn't come over to the British camp, he replied, according to Hali's account, "My rank required that I should have four palanquin-bearers, but all four of them ran away." According to his own account, he described himself as "old and crippled and deaf," unable to do anything but pray for English success. In any case, he was sent home again without harassment.[21]

Apart from a few such privileged, barricaded, and guarded neighborhoods, however, almost all the people of Delhi, and especially the Muslims, were driven out of the city. Ġhālib said there were hardly a thousand Muslims left in the whole city, while many were living "in ditches and mud huts" outside its boundaries.[22] They were still outside in December, shelterless in the cold and the winter rains. Not until early 1858 did the Hindus begin to return; the city regained something like a quarter of its former population. Mosques were occupied by troops; many beautiful old buildings had been damaged or destroyed in the fighting or were systematically razed by the British. It was not until July 1858 that the civil courts reopened, and only late in 1858 did Muslims gradually begin to reenter the city.[23] It was in 1858 that Ġhālib wrote, in a private letter to a friend, an unusual verse-sequence (*qiṭ'ah*) full of bitterly direct description:

> Every armed English soldier
> can do whatever he wants.
> Just going from home to market
> makes one's heart turn to water.
> The Chauk is a slaughter ground
> and homes are prisons.
> Every grain of dust in Delhi
> thirsts for Muslims' blood.
> Even if we were together
> we could only weep over our lives.[24]

Even by the end of 1858 a general permission to return had still not been granted, as Ġhālib noted; it was not given until November 1859, more than two years after the Muslims of Delhi had been expelled from their city—and the city to which they returned was irrevocably transformed.[25]

A number of the changes made in the city were pointedly symbolic. After 1857 the densely built-up urban areas within three hundred yards of the Red Fort were razed to the ground. The fort itself was "almost entirely cleared of buildings, only a few relics of the old Mughal Palaces being allowed to stand," with the resulting space occupied by "barracks for European troops." The majestic Lahore Gate became a bazaar "for the benefit of the European soldiers of the Fort"; the famous Dīvān-e 'Ām (Hall of Public Audience) was "used as a canteen." The general effect of the many kinds of punitive measures taken after the Rebellion was that people "had been taught to know their masters"; the Delhi area "received a lesson which will never be forgotten."[26] Sikh troops were quartered in the Jāma' Masjid until 1862; several other mosques were not restored until the 1870s, and the Sunahrī Masjid, outside the Red Fort's Delhi Gate, not until 1913.[27] The well-known Madrasah of Ḥusain Baḳhsh, where Hali had studied, stayed closed for eighteen years.[28] And Delhi College, its library destroyed by the rebels, was kept closed by the British until 1864, when it reopened; but despite its steadily increasing emphasis on English at the expense of Urdu, it was closed again in 1877.[29]

In the immediate aftermath of the Rebellion, moreover, the invasions, occupations, looting, slaughter, and expulsion of population were followed by further disasters. As Hali put it, after the British reconquest the city became a "howling wilderness."[30] In 1860, Ġhālib summed up the sufferings of Delhi:

> Five invading armies have fallen upon this city one after another: the first was that of the rebel soldiers, which robbed the city of its good name. The second was that of the British, when life and property and honour and dwellings and those who dwelt in them and heaven and earth and all the visible signs of existence were stripped from it. The third was that of famine, when thousands of people died of hunger. The fourth was that of cholera, in which many whose bellies were full lost their lives. The fifth was the fever, which took general plunder of men's strength and powers of resistance.[31]

Normalcy was very slow in returning. Ġhālib continued to mourn the death of a great number of his friends—on both sides. Among the British dead, "some were the focus of my hopes, some my well-wishers, some my friends, some my bosom companions, and some my pupils in poetry." And among the Indians, "some were my kinsmen, some my friends, some my pupils and some men whom I loved." Now "all of them are laid low in the dust."[32]

The destruction of the neighborhoods, landmarks, and customs of the city was such that, to Ġhālib, Delhi itself had died: Delhi was "a city of the dead." Did someone ask about Delhi? "Yes, there was once a city of that name in the realm of India." Whenever his friends inquired about some notable Delhi person or occasion, he replied that Delhi was finished: "All these things lasted only so long as the king reigned."[33] In a pessimistic letter to a friend, Ġhālib quoted one of his own *shiʿr*s (two-line verses): "A sea of blood rolls its waves—if only this were all! / Wait and see what else now lies before me."[34] The image obviously rang true for him: two years later he described his life since the Rebellion as that of "a swimmer in a sea of blood in this city."[35]

But life had to continue somehow. From 1858 onward, Ġhālib sought to get his pension restored; this proved to be difficult, for he was suspected of collaboration with the rebels, a charge he vehemently denied. He needed the support of the chief commissioner, Sir John Lawrence: "I therefore wrote in the praise of this man of high splendour a ghazal on the theme of spring, congratulating him on his victories and singing of the freshness of the breezes of the unfolding season, and sent it off by post." He received instructions to resubmit his petition through the commissioner; but when he did so, he was told that "there was no call whatever for a letter comprising nothing but praise and congratulation."[36]

Ġhālib had literary sufferings to endure as well. He himself had never kept copies of his own verse, and the two great private libraries in which his friends had carefully collected his works had been sacked and wantonly destroyed by British troops—as had the library at the Red Fort, too. He feared the loss of the poetry that was his life's great achievement. "A few days ago a faqir who has a good voice and sings well discovered a ghazal of mine somewhere and got it written down. When he showed me it, I tell you truly, the tears came to my eyes."[37]

Finally, in May 1860, after so much uncertainty and so many rebuffs that Ġhālib had almost given up hope, the pension was restored and the arrears paid in full. Ġhālib received from Sir John Lawrence a formal letter in Persian, duly written on paper sprinkled with gold dust, thanking him for his laudatory ghazal. This, together with a regular pension he had been receiving for some time from the nawab of Rampur, eased his financial situation somewhat. In February of 1863, his courtly rights—to attend at government durbars and to have the traditional robe of honor bestowed on him—were finally restored. He attended his last durbar in December 1866, where for the first time since the Rebellion these ceremonial robes and gifts were actually presented to him.[38] Although Ġhālib's health was failing, and his finances were never what he wished, the flow of letters to and from his many friends and shagirds continued to sustain him. He died in 1869.

· · ·

In 1857 Azad, twenty-seven years old, had been working with his father at the Dihlī Urdū Aḳhbār Press. The rebels arrived so suddenly, and seized the city so rapidly, that people were left stupefied. This abrupt downfall of the British was, as the *Dihlī Urdū Aḳhbār* editorialized, a reminder of the Day of Judgment, and was thus "meant to scourge us into obedience to the Divine Will." It was an event so amazing as to be scarcely credible: "Did what we saw really take place in fact, or did it pertain to the realm of dreams?"[39]

After the initial shock, Maulvī Muḥammad Bāqir successfully readjusted his loyalties. He apparently tried to save the life of his friend and former colleague, Francis Taylor, the principal of Delhi College, by hiding him from the mob that sacked the college and destroyed its library. The next day the presence of the fugitive was discovered; Francis Taylor, forced to flee in disguise, was caught and beaten to death in the street.[40] But when Maulvī Muḥammad Bāqir published an article about the killings of various Englishmen, he went out of his way to blacken Francis Taylor's character. With his years of experience in the collector's office, Maulvī Muḥammad Bāqir then did what many others were doing: he reported to the new center of authority, the court. The emperor presented him with a robe of honor, and he became a regular advisor, performing a variety of administrative duties.[41] It seems that on one occasion he even took to the field in command of "two companies of infantry and one of cavalry," to rescue a revenue train that was being attacked by bandits on its way to Delhi.[42]

The *Dihlī Urdū Akḥbār* took note of the widespread looting, violence, oppression, and economic hardship, expressing the hope "that the Divine Dispenser might so will things that the present anarchy comes to an end and the cause of His Majesty's worry is totally removed."[43] As the weeks wore on, Maulvī Muḥammad Bāqir's editorials grew more hortatory and anti-British. He changed the name of the paper to *Akḥbār-e Ẓafar*—doubly appropriate since *ẓafar* means "victory"—and pointedly issued it on Sundays, "in defiance of the Christian sabbath."[44] He wrote at least one pamphlet arguing that the fight against the English was a religious struggle (*jihād*), which it was the sacred duty of Muslims to support.[45]

Azad himself reacted to the shock of the Rebellion by publishing, as we have seen, his first known poem, "A History of Instructive Reversals." This nineteen-verse "continuous ghazal" appeared on May 24, 1857, about two weeks after the arrival of the rebels. The poem begins with a series of rhetorical evocations of famous dead kings ("Where is the realm of Solomon, and where the sovereignty of Alexander?") but soon becomes altogether direct and immediate:

> Right now it is said that the Christian community of yesterday
> was the possessor of ascendant fortune (*iqbāl*), world-bestowing,
> world-upholding,
> was the possessor of learning and skill and wisdom and
> cleverness,
> was the possessor of splendor and glory and a powerful army.
> There was no help! When there emerged
> in the world the sword of wrath of the Lord of Fury,
> all their jewels of wisdom could not be employed,
> all the fingernails[46] of devising and wisdom became useless,
> wisdom and craft and knowledge and cleverness availed
> nothing—

> the Telingas from the East [*sic*] killed them all right here.
> This is an event that no one has ever seen or heard of—
> the revolving of the heavens is a strange revolving!
> Indeed, just open the eye of instruction a little, oh heedless one—
> here, the lips of speech of the people of language are closed.
> If you have eyes, the whole reality of the world has been revealed:
> beware, oh heart—never place any trust in it!
> For instruction, this event is enough for the people,
> if God should give a steady wisdom and an alert heart.
> What can I say—there's not enough scope for a breath!
> All are gaping like mirrors, with their backs to the wall,
> that despite the Christian rulers' wisdom and vision
> they should be erased like this, all at once, without a trace in the world!
> When Azad wanted a chronogram (*tārīḳh*) of this event,
> his heart said, "Say, 'Oh you of sight, you should derive a lesson from it.'"[47]

Literarily speaking, this poem can only be called uninspired; but it has a unique historical interest. It is Azad's only known reflection on the Rebellion, and it emerges from the very midst of the turmoil, from those few months in Delhi when the revolving—the "revolution"—of the wheel of fortune had indeed turned the world upside down.

In the poem the British are referred to only in religious terms, as "Christians," and the Rebellion too is depicted entirely as a religious lesson arranged by God: it is a stern rebuke to the vanity of kings, and indeed to all human illusions of power. The fate of the Christians reveals "the whole reality of the world," and "the people" are to take warning: "Beware, oh heart—never place any trust in it!" God may give you sovereignty one day, and the next day He may, without warning, utterly cast you down. The pages of history are full of famous cautionary examples, and now a new one has been added to the series. Azad's view is typical of contemporary newspaper commentary on the Rebellion.[48] Although nationalist, anticolonial, politically modernizing responses to the Rebellion no doubt existed, they do not seem to have been widespread within the Muslim elite of Delhi. Azad's poem shows us how Maulvī Muḥammad Bāqir could change allegiances almost literally overnight: since God had chosen to overthrow one set of rulers and raise up another, what else should one do but accept His manifest verdict? Similarly, when a few months later God chose to restore the British to power, that too had to be accepted—and indeed, by then people must have been somewhat inured to such shocking but "instructive" reversals.

Azad himself apparently seconded his father's journalistic efforts on behalf of the Rebellion; and after the British retook Delhi, Azad too became, as Farrukhī writes, "a swimmer in this ocean of blood." Maulvī Muḥammad Bāqir was arrested, and Azad was summarily expelled from his house at bayonet point, together with his whole joint family including old women and young children.[49] As Azad later described the scene:

> The soldiers of the victorious army suddenly entered the house. They flourished their rifles: "Leave here at once!" The world turned black before my eyes. A whole houseful of goods was before me, and I stood petrified: "What shall I take with me?" My eye fell on the packet of his [Żauq's] ghazals. I thought, "Muḥammad Ḥusain, if God is gracious, and you live, then all this can be restored. But where will another ustad come from, who can compose these ghazals again? . . . While these exist, he lives even after his death; if these are lost, his name cannot survive either." I picked up the packet and tucked it under my arm. Abandoning a well-furnished home, with twenty-two half-dead souls I left the house—or rather, the city. And the words fell from my lips, "Hazrat Ādam left Heaven; Delhi is a heaven too. I'm his descendant—why shouldn't I leave Delhi?" (450)

As they made their halting way out of the city, a stray bullet struck Azad's year-old baby daughter; after some days in a coma, she died. Having wandered on foot for several days, half-starving, under conditions of the greatest hardship and danger, the travelers made contact with reliable friends. Azad sent the rest his family off to safety, but despite their tears and entreaties, he refused to go with them. Instead he went back to Delhi, to learn his father's fate.[50]

There he sought out a Sikh general who was an old friend of his father's, and who now took pity on his plight. Disguised as the general's groom, Azad followed him as he rode his horse past the field where Maulvī Muḥammad Bāqir and other prisoners were awaiting execution. Under these painful conditions, father and son exchanged a last long look. Two weeks afterward, Maulvī Muḥammad Bāqir was shot. Azad was hidden by his friend the general and then smuggled out of the city. Although details of this account may be uncertain—Azad's father was probably not shot but hanged, and probably rather sooner than later—the main outline is at least plausible, and this is the account Azad passed down in his own family.[51]

Then began a lost time in Azad's life. There was rumored to be a British arrest warrant out for him; in fact, it was a remarkable piece of luck that he hadn't been arrested along with his father. While his family stayed with relatives in a town near Delhi, he himself kept moving from city to city, fearing arrest, unable to find a secure niche. For two years or so he wandered, spending time in Lucknow, in Madras, in the Nilgiri hills, in Bombay, in Malwa, and elsewhere; then he spent longer periods in the Punjab, first in Jind, then in Jagraon, where he worked as a calligrapher in a newspaper office.[52]

Finally, in early 1861 he reached Lahore, where a relative helped him get a low-level job in the postmaster general's office. Azad was now working directly for the "Christian rulers" who had, only four years earlier, killed his father and destroyed his world. He held the postal job until the end of 1862. It is not clear what he did in 1863—except that during this whole period he was actively seeking a job in the Department of Public Instruction. In pursuit of this goal he composed his first book, a small textbook (now lost) for schoolgirls, and showed it to the appropriate officers. In February 1864, Azad was finally appointed to a clerical position in the Department of Public Instruction.[53]

During this year he wrote another textbook, *The Earring of Good Advice,* also for schoolgirls. In this textbook he found occasion to speak elegiacally of "the renowned city, the ancient royal capital of India," Delhi. "Although it's been entirely devastated and destroyed, and the inhabitants have been slain and exiled and laid low in the dust, even in their ruined, poverty-stricken condition its people showed an elegance and sophistication that I haven't seen anywhere else."[54] Azad struggled to get on with his life, but it was clear that he bore deep scars. Within a single month he had lost his father, his baby daughter, his work, his friends—and his city. The "terrible sufferings" of the Rebellion "had a crushing effect on his mind," quenching his youthful high spirits, making him seem older than his age. Even years later, when he used to reminisce with an old friend about 1857, "all these talks ended in tears."[55]

· · ·

Hali suffered less bitterly during the Rebellion. He was in Hissar, it will be remembered, working in the deputy collector's office. Suddenly Hissar, like many other North Indian cities, was in turmoil. As Hali put it, the "mischief caused by rebellious soldiers broke out in India, and even in Hissar dire events manifested themselves, and government authority disappeared."[56] As was so often the case, the rebels in Hissar acted independently: word was brought to the emperor after the fact that five companies of soldiers, who had been joined by three hundred bandits (Mevatī), had murdered the collector and plundered the treasury, and were on their way from Hissar to Delhi.[57]

Hali, "taking his life in his hands," set out for Panipat. The roads were now very dangerous; during his journey he was set upon by bandits, and the horse on which he was riding was seized. By the time he at length reached Panipat, traveling on foot, enduring much hardship and danger, the fatigue and bad food had given him a case of dysentery so acute that he was sick for more than a year. Even after a famous physician (*ḥakīm*) finally cured him, his stomach, chest, and lungs stayed weak all his life, so that he had to live with much more caution and restraint.[58]

Although Panipat itself remained quiet during 1857, it rapidly filled with refugees who had been expelled from Delhi without money or possessions. Though only twenty years old, Hali worked so devotedly, compassionately, and soberly among the refugees that he seemed, it is said, like a much older man. Some of the refugees who had taken shelter in his own household stayed on and on. One of these was a ten-year-old girl whose whole family had been killed, and who lived for the rest of her long life with Hali's family. Writing forty years later, Hali referred to the events of 1857 as "extremely tragic," such that "even to describe them again as they happened is like rubbing salt into a wound."[59]

After the Rebellion itself was over, for a long time "the condition of the country was such that people were afraid to leave their houses. Factories, offices, schools, colleges were all closed. . . . They say that there was not a neighborhood in Delhi without its gallows," writes Ṣāliḥah ʿĀbid Ḥusain, Hali's granddaughter and biographer. Hali stayed in Panipat for four years; as his health improved and most of the refugees left, he began studying in an impromptu but persistent way with the most eminent local scholars. But more children were born to him. With extra mouths to feed, the family's finances grew even more straitened. It was time once more for Hali to look for work.[60]

In 1861 Hali once again went to Delhi. There he led a hand-to-mouth existence of uncertainty and unemployment. In 1863, however, he fortunately encountered Nawab Muṣṭafā Ḳhān "Sheftah" (1806–1869), who invited Hali to his city of Jahangirabad, near Meerut, to tutor his children. Sheftah was an important poet and biographer in his own right; his ustad had been the major Delhi poet Momin Ḳhān "Momin" (1800–1852). Since then, Sheftah had been a shagird of Ġhālib's. Hali and Sheftah formed a warm friendship, and Hali stayed at Jahangirabad for the remaining years of Sheftah's life. Hali treated Sheftah as an ustad, and later claimed that Sheftah's correction (*iṣlāḥ*) of his poetry was even more useful than

Ġhālib's. Both Sheftah and Hali, however, shared a great respect and love for Ġhālib, and occasionally visited him in Delhi. Hali's life in Jahangirabad was a quiet, retired, congenial one.[61] It came to an abrupt end in 1869. In February, Ġhālib died; Hali wrote an elegy (*marśiyah*) full of grief at the loss of such an ustad: "With his death, Delhi has died"; "There was one light in the city, and it is gone."[62] Late in the same year Sheftah too died, so that Hali lost both his ustads almost at once. During this same crucial period, Hali met Sir Sayyid Aḥmad Ḵhān, who was to play a large role in his future. And having no choice, Hali began to look for another job.[63]

· · ·

The Rebellion of 1857, together with its brutal, destructive, and long-lasting aftermath, marked the real end of aristocratic Muslim culture in North India. The effects of this deep slash through the fabric of nineteenth-century Indian history have been so profound that it is impossible to enumerate, or even envision, all of them. Metcalf concludes that the "most pervasive legacy" of the Rebellion was perhaps to be found in the "intangible sphere of human relations," for "a year of bitter racial warfare left an abiding mark on all concerned."[64]

There was enormous physical destruction, especially in Delhi. The ruin wrought on lives and property in Delhi was in fact much greater than in any other rebellious city. People were haphazardly killed, systematically executed, imprisoned, expelled from the city, subjected to terrible hardships, arbitrarily stripped of all their property. Many of Delhi's old Muslim families were almost entirely rooted out. Survivors were scattered and reduced to grief, helplessness, and silence. Libraries were looted, precious manuscripts lost, buildings razed, the city's old culture devastated.[65] After the initial "reign of terror" when British troops first retook the city, most of the continuing reprisals were selective and were directed against upper-class Muslims who were thought, with or without reason, to have had ties to the court.

Above all, after more than three hundred years the Mughal court itself was now gone—hopelessly gone, gone forever. Bahādur Shāh had left an equivocal legacy. He certainly joined with the rebels to at least some extent, as indeed his own imperial claims would have almost required him to do. But then he surrendered to the English, and during his "trial" he emphatically repudiated the Rebellion. Nostalgic sympathy for him was widespread: he was a romantic symbol of imperial grandeur and tragic loss. But his legacy could not provide a cultural rallying point for his demoralized people. Not until 1903 was any real effort made to locate his grave and build him a tomb. Even then it was a small effort, and the British created obstacles; only in 1934 was a modest tomb actually built.[66] It was not for nothing that the Auspicious Fort had been renamed by Ġhālib the Inauspicious Fort.

The Mughal idea of the king as divinely ordained focus and center of the society, axis of the culture in time and space, was still very much alive in eighteenth- and nineteenth-century India. Even new would-be dynastic founders often aspired to such a vision of kingship. When Ṭīpū Sulṭān assumed royal power (with Mughal approval) in Mysore in 1786, he felt empowered to "reconstitute the universe around himself." By his command, "measures of distances and weights, names of towns, administrative departments and official titles, units of coinage, and the entire calendar including the days of the week, months, and years, were all transformed."[67]

Even as late as 1819, when Ġhāẓī ud-Dīn Ḥaidar, nawab of Avadh, assumed (theoretically) independent kingship—thus setting himself up with British encouragement as a rival to the Mughal dynasty—most of his implicitly universal claims, including a throne and royal canopy apparently based on the Peacock Throne, were drawn directly from Mughal precedent. He created new coins and a new dating system for them, a new royal coat of arms, a new and much more elaborate code of court etiquette based on the sacredness of his person, and a set of newly exalted titles for all and sundry including "Lord of the Age" for himself and "Lord of the World" and "Lord of the Era" for certain of his nobles.[68] As we have seen, the British, too, had been drawn into this system, holding durbars and bestowing robes of honor, writing formal Persian letters on paper sprinkled with gold dust. These tendencies reached their height in Lucknow: the resident was attended wherever he went by no fewer than forty ceremonial macebearers, and "the Residency buildings themselves became ever more like a palace complex."[69]

Whatever the actual political facts, the medieval Mughal vision of kingship as absolute universal sovereignty was still widespread and powerful. When such a symbolically awesome king, the center and embodiment of a whole cultural world, falls in some irrevocable way, a great deal may fall with him. His people may well fear for their culture. Thus could Ġhālib write of the lost glories of Delhi, "All these things lasted only so long as the king reigned." Since the king Bahādur Shāh was also the poet Ẓafar, and preeminently the patron of Urdu and Persian poets, it is not surprising that his fall tended to drag the classical poetry down with him. Azad later expressed surprise that even the Urdu language itself had survived the debacle: "Urdu emerged from Delhi—and its lamp ought to have been extinguished with the kingship of Delhi" (61). But survival meant living through a time of devastation and disaster. So many poems in various genres lamented the ruin of the city that a number of them were ultimately gathered into a melancholy anthology, *The Sigh of Delhi* (1863).[70]

The loss, and the mourning, were painful enough. But the vengeful English often went out of their way, in those first months and years, to rub in the humiliation, to show their contempt for the whole culture that had presumed to give them such a horrible moral and practical shock as the "Mutiny" had been. In the immediate aftermath of 1857 many Englishmen wished "to raze Delhi to the ground, or at least to destroy the Jama Masjid," and the "most bitter and widespread hostility was reserved for the Muslim community."[71] Many Muslims grieved for the rest of their lives: their ancient, much-cherished culture seemed to have been hopelessly discredited, even in their own eyes, by its ignominious collapse.

The British, "at the climax of their power," confronted a Muslim community that was "at its lowest ebb"; even a Westernizer like Sir Sayyid Aḥmad Ḳhān feared that the Muslims could never again prosper or "receive esteem," and considered emigrating to Egypt.[72] "I could not even bear to contemplate the miserable state of my people," he wrote. "For some time I wrestled with my grief and, believe me, it made an old man of me." In any case, he planned to leave Delhi after his retirement from government service, for "everyone knew," as Hali put it, that "he did not want to be constantly reminded of the awful conditions in which the Muslims of Delhi were living after the Mutiny."[73] Another survivor of this period, Maulvī Żakā'ullāh, showed a more typical reaction: he refused, even years later, to talk about his memories of what he had seen and experienced. To him "the shock of those last Mutiny days" had been "beyond all bearing," so that he succumbed for a time to "a melancholy that bordered on blank despair."[74]

Decades later, Nażīr Aḥmad's markedly pro-British son Bashīr ud-Dīn Aḥmad wrote of the period, "Delhi was very much suppressed, and so beaten down that—God forbid! There are still some people alive who saw the Rebellion; when I hear from them about its devastation and sufferings, my blood runs cold." The Rebellion had "shaken the foundation of Delhi, and so destroyed it that even today it hasn't been able to flourish."[75] As Sadiq put it very simply, "the whole system went down with a crash after the Mutiny."[76]

3 RECONSTRUCTION

The process of reconstruction had to start with basic, pragmatic concerns: finding a job, finding a way to live in the new world. In the years immediately following the Rebellion, Azad and Hali had to cut their coats according to their cloth. And since India was now to belong directly to the queen-empress, it was more and more clear that the only cloth available would be imported fabric. Quixotically aristocratic attitudes like that of Ġhālib, who rejected a job because he was not formally escorted to the interview, were no longer sustainable. It was less and less possible even to please the British in classic courtly ways, with odes to Queen Victoria and ghazals in praise of the commissioner; the British had started to de-Mughalize themselves.[1]

Nor was there any real guidance from the older generation. Hali had grown up fatherless; Azad's father had been executed by the British. Moreover, Azad and Hali had both lost their much-admired ustads, the mentors who were empowered to shape and guide their literary lives. This was an irretrievable loss, for it was clear that such ustads would never be seen again. "The molds in which they were shaped have been altered, and the breezes that nourished them have changed direction," Hali later wrote of Ġhālib and his circle.[2] "So there is now no hope at all of another such master of poetry being born in India," Azad later wrote of Żauq, "for he was the nightingale of a garden that has been destroyed" (420).

Still, Azad and Hali had their lives to live. We have seen that Azad, after wandering for several years, ended up in Lahore in 1864, at the age of thirty-four, with a minor clerical job in the Department of Public Instruction—a job he had worked hard to get. As it happened, Lahore's new Government College was also founded in 1864, with the remarkable Dr. G. W.

Leitner as principal. Azad had been supplementing his office salary by tutoring Englishmen in Urdu; in 1864–65 he tutored Dr. Leitner, who formed an excellent opinion of him. Dr. Leitner, a scholar of Arabic, Persian, and Urdu, worked all his life to promote the development of Western learning in Indian languages. He was somewhat autocratic by temperament, but a most effective popularizer and shaper of opinion.[3]

In 1865 Dr. Leitner founded what is commonly known as the Anjuman-e Panjāb, the "Punjab Society"—an organization "of which he became Secretary and, indeed, dictator."[4] Its objects were "the revival of ancient oriental learning, the advancement of popular knowledge through vernaculars, the discussion of social, literary, scientific, and political questions of interest, and the association of the learned and influential classes with the officers of the government." Over time, the Anjuman succeeded in such projects as arranging public lectures, setting up a free library and reading room, compiling educational texts and translations in Indian languages, and establishing Lahore's famous Oriental College. The Anjuman was actively supported by leading British officials, including the commissioner, the deputy commissioner, officers of the Department of Public Instruction, and even the lieutenant governor himself; it inspired the formation of similar societies in Delhi, Rawalpindi, Amritsar, Hissar, and elsewhere. The Anjuman was considered a great success: soon people in many cities began to manifest "a growing interest in vernacular literature impregnated with the spirit of the West."[5]

The Anjuman made Azad's career. He threw himself energetically into its activities from the first. Most of its thirty-five original members were directly employed by the government; in fact, as Farruḳhī makes clear, "the whole Anjuman was called into being by Government fiat." Azad himself, as a pillar of the Anjuman, was almost more royalist than the queen. In the first essay he ever read before the group, in February 1865, he thanked God for the government's educational program and fully endorsed its paternalism: "If the parents don't take care of their children, who else will?" In his second essay he argued that people ought to help themselves by their own efforts, and in his third essay he discussed measures for increasing trade.[6] Azad's Anjuman activities so solidly established him that he was sent by the government on a special information-gathering tour of Central Asia in 1865, and on a mission to Calcutta in 1866. His part in the Rebellion had left him under a cloud; but now that cloud had been entirely dispelled.[7]

In 1866 Azad became a regularly paid lecturer on behalf of the Anjuman; in 1867 he became its secretary. He continued to work hard for the society. The minutes he kept show that among the subjects discussed at meetings were programs for the relief of the poor, the limitation of polygamy (to cases of the wife's illness or barrenness), the suppression of foul language among women, the reduction of marriage expenses, and the improvement of the postal service. The papers Azad read before Anjuman meetings were well received; out of a total of 142 papers the Anjuman eventually published, twenty-two were Azad's.[8] Azad was so much in favor now that in early 1867 he was invited to a party given by the lieutenant governor and presented with a "trinket" in token of his services.[9] From March through December 1867 Azad produced no fewer than thirty-six lectures and essays, on all manner of cultural and social topics; he also edited the Anjuman's journal. Gradually his lecture and essay topics came to be drawn more and more from the realm of literature.[10] He also wrote another school textbook, the extremely successful *Stories of India* (*Qiṣaṣ ul-hind*).[11]

In 1869 Azad was appointed assistant professor of Arabic at Government College, on Dr. Leitner's recommendation; with this the best period of his life began. But it was never a bed of roses. In 1870 he started to edit a newspaper for the Anjuman, but the paper was soon accused of being English-influenced to an unacceptable degree, and in 1871 Dr. Leitner ordered it handed over to someone else. The files of the Anjuman were also taken from Azad, and it was clear that Dr. Leitner no longer looked upon him with complete favor. Still, Azad was able to enjoy his teaching and get on with his literary work.[12] His students remembered him fondly: his lectures about Persian and Urdu poetry were fascinating, and he often treated the boys to iced lemonade after class. He became a well-known school character: he wore a long loose robe (*chuġhah*), with one sleeve "kept out of use and slung at his back," and is said to have been followed around the campus by a riding pony that he never rode. Azad not only won loud applause in the school's mushairahs but sometimes held small Urdu mushairahs in his own classes as well.[13] His life in Lahore was now settled and productive.

Then in 1870 Hali too arrived in Lahore. He had been looking for a job, and had just found one with the Punjab Government Book Depot. His new job involved going over books that had been translated from English into Urdu, editing them and checking them for mistakes. "I stayed in Lahore and did this work for almost four years," Hali later wrote. "From it I acquired a general feeling for English literature, and somehow or other my admiration for Eastern—and above all Persian—literature began gradually to diminish."[14]

Azad and Hali met for the first time in Lahore. It might have been social contacts that brought them together, or perhaps it was the Anjuman and its activities. Sharing as they did a deep, nostalgic love for the old lost Delhi, and seeing eye-to-eye on many literary questions, they became friends; and their friendship endured through the years.

· · ·

On May 9, 1874, Azad delivered to the Anjuman his famous lecture on the reform of Urdu poetry. The audience included a number of Englishmen of high official rank (director of public instruction, high court judge, secretary of the Punjab government, colonel, commissioner, deputy commissioner). The text of Azad's speech was printed the next day in a local newspaper, and there is no doubt about the boldness of his message: he called for a new Urdu poetry and a new poetics, both based on English models. The traditional adornments of poetry have now fallen into desuetude, he argued. "New kinds of jewelry and robes of honor, suited to the conditions of the present day, are shut up in the storage-trunks of English—which are lying right here beside us, but we don't realize it."[15]

In the course of his speech he accused classical Urdu poetry of ignoring the Indic side of its heritage, the colloquial language of Braj Bhasha with its simplicity and expressive vigor, in favor of the charms of Persian: Urdu poets had "reproduced in Urdu a photograph (*foṭogrāf*) of all the meters, and interesting and colorful ideas, and types of literary composition, found in Persian." This had indeed given Urdu not only sophistication and polish but also "the power of expressing, through metaphors and similes, extremely subtle and refined thoughts." However, it had also led to the growth of dark, obscure tangles of poetic verbiage, in which meaning had been reduced to a kind of firefly: "now it lights up, now it vanishes."[16] Moreover, the verses in this rich language were devoted to an extremely narrow, limited circle of traditional *maẓmūns* (themes), mostly those of love: "some to the joy of union, many to longings, even more to bewailing separation; to wine, to the cupbearer, the spring, the autumn, complaints against the heavens, and flattery of the powerful"—all "absolutely imaginary" topics. Urdu poetry languished in captivity within this "limited circle" of related themes, and must be helped to break free.[17]

At the heart of Azad's talk was an emotional plea for a radically new vision of the nature and goals of poetry:

> Oh gardeners of the Garden of Eloquence! Eloquence is not something that flies along on the wings of exaggeration and high-flying fancy, or races off on the wings of rhyme, or climbs to the heavens by the force of verbal ingenuity, or sinks beneath a dense layer of

> metaphors. The meaning of eloquence is that happiness or sorrow, attraction or repulsion, fear or anger toward something—in short, whatever feeling is in our heart—should as we express it arouse in the listeners' hearts the same effect, the same emotion, the same fervor, as would be created by seeing the thing itself.[18]

The touchstone of poetry was thus to be its power to express and communicate natural feelings—feelings, reactions to the world, which are first present in the poet's heart, and are then passed on to the listeners as well. Verbal adornments in poetry were to be treated like salt in food: they should be used in small, judiciously planned quantities.

Azad made it clear that he did not underestimate the difficulty of this task, or the seductive power of the old poetry. But he warned that if the effort was not made, the old poetry would decay into hopeless obsolescence, and Urdu would end up with no poetry at all. He then explained candidly, "Although some of my countrymen and myself have long been aware of these matters, the reason I speak about them now is that I see that lately our government, and its officers whose hearts have taken responsibility for our education, have turned their attention in this direction."[19]

Azad's speech was followed by the remarks of Colonel W. R. M. Holroyd, the director of public instruction. Speaking in English, Colonel Holroyd began, "This meeting has been called to discover means for the development of Urdu poetry which is in a state of decadence today." Quoting the lieutenant governor, Colonel Holroyd emphasized the usefulness of poetry as a teaching tool and deplored the dearth of poetry suitable for the classroom. To fill this need, he suggested that verses from Mīr, Żauq, Ġhālib, and others should be compiled, "aiming at moral instruction, and presenting a natural picture of our feelings and thoughts."[20]

At the end of his speech Colonel Holroyd proposed that the Anjuman should start a new mushairah series, but that instead of setting the traditional formal pattern line (*miṣraʿ-e t̤araḥ*) to which all the poetry should conform, the Anjuman should "propose a certain subject on which the poets should write." He had high ambitions for this scheme: "Should this proposal succeed, the year 1874 would be a landmark in the history of India, and people would remember the poets through whose efforts poetry rose out of decadence and reached the height of perfection." He concluded, "I propose that we should hold monthly meetings, and that for the next month the poets should write in praise of the rainy season."[21] This meeting turned out to be the most memorable and controversial in the Anjuman's whole history.

Azad was immediately attacked by a number of his contemporaries for his proposed new poetics. He was accused of writing a language that was "outwardly Urdu and inwardly English, such as the present rulers want to create." His rejection of the traditional repertoire of poetic adornments and figures of speech was "as if some beautiful woman were stripped of her jewelry and clothing, and made to stand absolutely naked." After all, "without metaphors and similes, there's no pleasure in poetry!" And far from being restricted to themes of love, "Urdu poetry has incorporated every kind and every sort of *maẓmūn*, so excellently and subtly that if a hundred societies are formed, and make such futile efforts for a hundred years, and give out a hundred thousand rupees as a reward, they still won't be able to improve on it!" In short, Azad was exhorted to honor Żauq and Ġhālib and to stop trying to "ruin Urdu poetry by remaking it in the English style."[22] He also, however, received a certain amount of support.[23]

As for Hali, he seems to have welcomed the new mushairah series.[24] A quarter of a century later, he diplomatically divided the credit for the initiative: "Under the auspices of Colonel Holroyd, director of public instruction, Punjab, Maulvī Muḥammad Ḥusain Azad fulfilled his longstanding desire—that is to say, in 1874 the foundation was laid for a mushairah absolutely new of its kind in India." Hali noted that he himself had shared in the mushairah series by writing four *maṡnavīs* (narrative or reflective poems)—on "The Rainy Season," "Hope," "Patriotism," and "Justice."[25] He spelled out the goal of the project: "that Asian poetry, which has become entirely the domain of love and exaggeration, might be broadened as much as possible, and that its foundation might be laid on realities and events."[26] And he specifically urged the organization of more such "new-style mushairahs."[27]

The Anjuman's new mushairahs proceeded exactly along the lines laid down by Colonel Holroyd. After the first one praised "The Rainy Season," the second addressed itself to "Winter." This second mushairah went so well that the official journal of the Anjuman predicted full success in "removing from Urdu poetry licentious subjects and obscene images, and replacing them by scenes descriptive of things in this world." After the third mushairah, on "Hope," a sarcastic newspaper article sneered that "the poets of the Punjab and of Delhi have well understood the intention of the director of public instruction"—which was that they should "abandon the mention of wine and song" in order to "describe the phenomena of nature."[28]

Then followed "Patriotism," "Peace," "Justice," "Compassion," "Contentment," and "Civilization." By this time, a great many poets were attending, some from far away; still others who were unable to attend sent their poems to be read. But many of the poems were full of the "worn-out *maẓmūns*" that Azad wished to drive out of circulation. At the fourth mushairah, people were said to have listened "all ears" to Hali's poem on "Patriotism," while when Azad's turn came his delivery was praised but his poem found to be in need of *iṣlāḥ*, "correction." At the fifth mushairah a modernist newspaper correspondent complained that Hali was still using the old *maẓmūns*: he "again mentioned wine and drunkenness, the nightingale and the rose, and destroyed the hopes one had conceived for his talent." By the sixth mushairah it was reported that "Hali's poem was, as usual, the high point," and he was praised as "the only glory of these gatherings." Strict generic standards were maintained: some poets who had inappropriately brought odes or satires (*ḥajv*) were forbidden to recite them. Colonel Holroyd was very pleased with the mushairahs.[29] And he was not the only one: at some point Hali wrote a brief but extravagant Persian poem, "Verse-sequence in Praise of the Kindness and Generosity of the Honorable Colonel Holroyd."[30]

But the mushairahs became the center of much controversy. It was announced that poets who distinguished themselves would be awarded not merely prizes but monthly stipends as well, and this raised the stakes considerably. A newspaper called *Panjābī Aḳhbār* began a kind of vendetta against Azad, making a series of charges: that he was an incompetent poet and no real shagird of Żauq's, but only a kind of young "nephew"; that he was arrogant and put on superior airs; that he presided over the mushairahs in a biased way; that he quarreled with senior poets, who he feared would eclipse him; that he used his influence unfairly, to manipulate the prize giving in favor of junior poets; that he made the mushairahs "the resort of youngsters, green-grocers, and confectioners," among whom he could easily shine.[31] Azad's own poems were repeatedly subjected to the most exacting kind of *iṣlāḥ* and were invariably found by hostile critics to be wanting. One criticism was especially ironic: Azad, who reproached Urdu poetry for excessive borrowing of imagery from Persian, was accused of depicting, in his own long *maśnavī* on "Winter," entirely foreign and fantastic scenes. "Has there ever been such cold in our country, that the rivers froze into ice, and people began crossing them without boats?" Azad's reindeer, sleighs, and perpetual snows came in for marked disapproval.[32]

Azad felt the attacks keenly, especially since it happened that no shagird or admirer came forward at the time to respond on his behalf. However, he behaved with dignity in this difficult situation. He has been accused by ʿAbd ul-Ḥaq of being jealous of Hali's greater popularity as a poet. Whether or not this was the case, he apparently did think that the venomous newspaper articles, although they appeared anonymously, were composed by a shagird of Hali's. Azad seems to have felt that if Hali didn't encourage the newspaper attacks, neither did he do anything to discourage them. For a time there was a coolness between the two. But, as Farruḳhī points out, it could not have been of major importance, for ten years later they were still exchanging warm and friendly letters.[33]

One person who did encourage and support Azad was Sir Sayyid Aḥmad Ḳhān. He advised Azad to ignore the critics and recommended a strong and simple literary creed: "Bring your work even closer to nature (*nechar*). The extent to which a work comes close to nature is the extent to which it gives pleasure." Sir Sayyid took the same line in an article in his own journal *Tahẕīb ul-Aḳhlāq* (The cultivation of morality) in 1875: he praised Hali, invoked Milton and Shakespeare, and called for a "natural poetry" (*necharal po'iṭrī*).[34] Another journal under his influence lamented the dearth in Urdu of poetry "with a feeling for nature" and maintained that the date of the first "mushairah for natural poetry" marked "the beginning of the improvement of Urdu." It urged Urdu poets to "turn at last toward natural subjects and seek inspiration from the ideas of Milton and Shakespeare"—to write not just about "love and imagination," but about "real events" and "visible objects."[35]

It seems that there were nine mushairahs altogether, ending in March 1875. Why did they end? Certainly the mushairah series generated a damaging competition for money and prestige; personal conflicts and rivalries were responsible for many of the attacks on Azad's leadership. Sadiq argues that the mushairah series ended because it could not please its audience: "The academic verse it produced failed to touch the heart of the generation to which it was addressed."[36] According to Dr. Leitner, the "collapse" came because the series aggravated its participants: the "poets did not want to be told by any one that they had, hitherto, debased their genius by celebrating love"; they refused to accept "dictation in poetic inspiration."[37] Taking a longer view, Farruḳhī maintains that the mushairah series ended not because it failed, but because it succeeded. The officers of the Department of Public Instruction "came to feel that it had fulfilled its purpose": the new literary movement had now been well launched and was gradually spreading by itself.[38] The Anjuman's own journal indeed proclaimed success: the mushairahs "will leave permanent traces" on the young; thus "the moral purpose which the founders of the mushairah had in view above all else will be attained."[39]

And what of the real, inner relationship of Azad and Hali to all this? Sadiq takes a cynical view: far from being "a spontaneous growth" based on real cultural needs, the new poetry was "an exotic tended and watered by official patronage." Government patronage was the crucial factor, and government employees could not afford to disregard it. "The fact is that both Azad and Hali wrote to order at this stage."[40] Farrukhī takes a more generous view: though all the government really wanted was some new textbooks for use in the schools, Azad himself saw his chance and "took advantage of this movement" for his own purposes, seeking to "turn the face of Urdu poetry in a new direction," widen its range, and free it from its narrow circle of concerns. Azad had in fact expressed some such wish as early as 1867.[41] As we have seen, Ṣāliḥah 'Ābid Ḥusain makes similar claims for Hali.

The psychological truth of the situation is surely impossible to disentangle. People tend to adjust their behavior to suit the strong concerns of powerful patrons: it would not be surprising, under the circumstances, if Azad or Hali had indeed in some fashion "written to order." But people also tend to identify with the institutions that shape their lives: Azad and Hali would have been unusual if they had been entirely unaffected by the milieu of the Department of Public Instruction, especially when Colonel Holroyd's views were couched in a rhetoric of solicitous concern for Urdu and its "decadent" condition.

In fact, both Azad and Hali were deeply ambivalent about the loss of the old poetry and its projected replacement with the new. Hali, even as he participated in the new mushairah series, also recited at another Lahore mushairah during the same year an elegy that mourned the irretrievable loss of the old world of Delhi: "Oh friend, don't speak of Delhi as it used to be, / I cannot possibly bear to hear this story." Hali identified the loss of the poets of the pre-1857 generation in Delhi with the loss of poetry itself: "Poetry is already dead, now it will never live again, friends, / Don't torment your heart by remembering and remembering it."[42] Azad's own inner turmoil was even more poignant. As Farrukhī puts it all too accurately, "He struggled his whole life long to adopt a Western way of thinking; he advocated the development of new concepts and new principles; but mentally he lived in the past."[43]

· · ·

The new mushairahs ended after less than a year, but the conflicts they precipitated lived on—and gathered strength. Both Azad and Hali spent much of the rest of their lives with literary storms swirling around them. They never entirely stopped trying to reconstruct the endangered mansion of Urdu poetry. Which of the old timbers should be reinforced and refinished, and which ones were hopelessly rotten and had to be removed? After the restoration, what new kind of structural integrity could be achieved? If it was not quite necessary to destroy the mansion in order to save it, it was certainly necessary to pull down parts of it in order to shore up the rest. The cause was urgent, and it absorbed the fullest energies of these two powerful minds.

Azad stayed on in Lahore for the rest of his life. For years he taught at Government College, and wrote books. Most conspicuously, he wrote school textbooks; they gained him a great popular reputation, and *Stories of India* was a perennial favorite. By the early 1880s he had written twenty-three textbooks in all, of which eighteen were published in his lifetime. Most were in Urdu, with a few devoted to Persian or Arabic language and literature. Azad's prose style, in his textbooks as elsewhere, won him lasting fame. "In addition to being the greatest prose stylist of Urdu, Azad is our most important educational writer as well."[44]

From about 1875 to 1877 Azad worked on *The Wonder-World of Thought* (*Nairang-e ḳhiyāl,* 1880), a set of thirteen allegorical essays, mostly by Samuel Johnson (seven) and Joseph Addison (four), that he translated—or rather transcreated—into Urdu.[45] These selections were introduced by two prefatory essays, in which Azad further developed the basic themes of his "new poetry" lecture of 1874. He continued to urge radically Westernizing approaches to poetic problems: "Just as English arts and sciences are improving our clothing, houses, conditions, thoughts, and knowledge, in the same way English literature too goes on giving *iṣlāḥ* to our literature." He concluded with an exhortation to writers of Urdu: they must create such a powerful and living language that the Indians will think the age of Mīr has come again, and "the English will say, 'Shakespeare's soul has emerged in India.'"[46] Hali wrote a review in which he strongly praised *The Wonder-World of Thought*; he spoke of Azad as writing a new and useful kind of book, seeking to "express the poetic thought of a broad, learned, refined, and regulated language like English, by means of a limited and unregulated and imperfect and unlearned language like Urdu."[47]

Also in 1880 Azad published his masterpiece, *Water of Life* (*Āb-e ḥayāt*). It was a magnificent achievement, recognized widely and immediately as the definitive history of Urdu poetry. Hali wrote a long and glowingly favorable review.[48] *Water of Life* at once became, and has remained, the single most influential sourcebook for both anecdotes and historical theories about Urdu poetry. The first edition sold out quickly. Azad published a much revised and expanded second edition in 1883; Hali was one of the friends and correspondents who helped him gather new material for it. Both *The Wonder-World of Thought* and *Water of Life* were incorporated into the official Punjab University examination curriculum. Sadiq calls *Water of Life* "one of the most brilliant reconstructions of the past that we possess."[49] If Azad had done nothing else except write this book, he would still be one of the most important figures in Urdu literature.

Azad's life had always had rocky patches, and it became even rockier toward the end. In 1875 one of his sons died, and 1876 another son died as well. Azad's relationship with Dr. Leitner deteriorated further: Dr. Leitner, with whom he had had an unsatisfactory collaboration on a book, now found him "as inaccurate as he is occasionally brilliant," given to "intrigue," and definitely "unworthy of trust."[50] In 1877 a beloved aunt who ran his household died. In 1883 Government College was placed under the jurisdiction of Punjab University; with his exuberant gift for metaphor, Azad envisioned the university as a frightful witch eating the college alive. He was anxious about his job, but then in 1884 he was finally confirmed as a professor of Urdu in the university. At about this period his house caught fire. And—the worst blow of all—his beloved and talented daughter Amat us-Sakīnah suddenly died. As the grieving father wrote, "She was in truth more precious than seven sons, when I was writing she was my right hand; her death has shattered my heart." Azad was so affected by this blow that for a time he lost his mental balance.[51]

Obtaining leave from his teaching position, he planned a trip to Iran, his family's ancestral home, to gather books for his library. His nine-month tour in 1885–86 included visits to a number of cities in Iran, then a return through Afghanistan. The trip was generally successful, and Azad lectured and wrote about his travel experiences. In 1887 he began working to create the "Azad Library." He obtained a small grant of government land for it and managed to pay for the library building himself. The library, and the rare books with which he endowed it, were much praised; Azad was soon awarded the honorific title "Sun among the Learned" (Shams ul-ʿulamā).[52] Azad also finished work on two books about the Persian language, literature, and culture, for which he had been collecting material for many years. Of these, *On Iranian Poets* (*Sukḥandān-e fārs*) was much the more important. It was completed in 1887, but was not published until 1907—fully twenty years later.[53]

The reason for this hiatus was the tragedy of Azad's later life: the attacks of insanity that began increasingly to afflict him. His madness came on gradually, but he was legally certified in 1890 and was retired on a pension. For the last two decades of his life, intervals of complete lucidity alternated with abrupt descents into madness. Farruḳhī suggests several causes: his too-intense work on editing the ghazals of Żauq; his grief over his daughter's death; and his sufferings during 1857. Moreover, he had had "fifteen or sixteen" children, but except for one surviving son, Āġhā Ibrāhīm, he saw them all die "before his eyes" at early ages. His madness took pathetic forms. Sometimes he used a planchet to summon the spirits of Mīr and other Urdu poets. Sometimes, suffering terribly from insomnia, he paced the floor all night, reciting verses, calling on the great ustads, hearing their voices, replying to their words. In one fit of madness he even set out on foot for Delhi.[54]

At another time, he managed somehow to reach Aligarh, where he appeared without warning at the house of the amazed Sir Sayyid Aḥmad Ḳhān. He told his host that Abu'l-Fazl and other spirits had been speaking to him—dictating a book, which he was taking down in their own words. This book, *The Court of Akbar* (*Darbār-e akbarī*), grew into a massively long and extravagant paean to Akbar for his religious tolerance and other qualities. It was colorful, vivid, anecdotal, idealizing, repetitive, full of long authorial asides—and so seductively written that it won immediate popularity and remains a favorite today. Azad worked on it at intervals for twelve years, and it was finally published in 1898. All accounts agree that Azad's madness was fitful: for five minutes, ten minutes, half an hour, he would be entirely his normal self, then suddenly an attack would overcome him. But remarkably enough, he not only continued to write, creating a series of bizarre and fascinating books, but produced some works that were actually published. Over the years, though, the lucid intervals grew fewer, and the madness worse.[55] Azad died in Lahore in 1910, at the age of eighty. Hali enshrined the date of his death in a chronogram: "Urdu literature has ended."[56]

· · ·

While Azad lived and died in Lahore, Hali never did feel at home there; he missed Delhi, and seized the first possible chance to go back. This chance came in 1875, when he was offered the post of head Arabic teacher in the Delhi Anglo-Arabic College. Hali taught in this school for the next twelve years. His growing admiration for Sir Sayyid, combined with the influence of the Lahore mushairah series, made him dissatisfied with the state of Indo-Muslim poetry and culture in general. This discontent gave rise to his most famous poem, usually known as the *Musaddas-e Ḥālī* (1879). In 456 six-line stanzas (*musaddas*) the poem, which Hali called "Madd o jazr-e Islām" (The high tide and low tide of Islam), deplored the "present decline and lowness of the Muslims' condition."[57] The *Musaddas* was published first in Sir Sayyid's reformist journal *Tahżīb ul-Aḳhlāq*, and then—since it became a tremendous popular success—over and over again in pamphlet form. Azad is said to have snidely compared the didactic verse of the *Musaddas* to the bland, boring flavor of roasted chick-peas: it was, he reportedly said, neither sweet nor spicy.[58]

Hali next wrote a book that looked backwards: it was *The Life of Sa'dī* (*Ḥayāt-e Sa'dī*, 1884–86), an admiring biographical and literary study of the great thirteenth-century Persian poet. At about the same time, he endured a heavy personal grief: his beloved older brother fell sick, came to Delhi for treatment, and died after a protracted illness. In 1887 Hali received a notable reward for his literary achievements: he was granted a pension for life by Sir Āsmān Jāh, chief minister of the state of Hyderabad. The arrangement was mediated by Sir Sayyid, who asked Hali how much the pension should be; with characteristic simplicity, Hali named exactly the amount of his salary as a teacher. Hali then retired from the Anglo-Arabic College and returned to Panipat, where he lived for the rest of his life.[59] But he did travel a bit, especially to Aligarh, where he served as a kind of poet laureate for Sir Sayyid's controversial Muhammedan Anglo-Oriental (M. A. O.) College: he composed and recited suitable poems to mark important events in the life of the college.[60]

Hali's poems gradually grew so numerous that it was time for them to be collected and published in a volume. This volume reflected the duality of his poetic history and sensibility. It contained unabashedly traditional poems: many ghazals (including the one containing his elegiac lament for Delhi), some quatrains (*rubā'ī*), odes, and chronograms. But it also included a number of poems that, while they observed the rules of traditional forms like the verse-sequence and the *tarkīb band*, were nevertheless very much in a new style: passionately hortatory and didactic, seeking to inspire action in the real world. While some of these poems were moralistic in a general way—urging, for example, courtesy, dignified behavior, kindness to servants, cleanliness, financial prudence, better treatment of women—others were more partisan and contentious. Hali defended Sir Sayyid by name against charges of irreligious behavior; he went on the attack against Sir Sayyid's enemies; he paid tribute to the M. A. O. College; he composed long versified addresses for meetings of the Muhammadan Educational Conference. He also called for poetic renewal ("The Decline of the Poetry of Delhi") and took a surprisingly strong nationalist line ("The Freedom of England and the Slavery of India").[61]

By way of a preface to this volume, Hali wrote a long essay known as the *Introduction* (*Muqaddamah*) (1893), setting forth his own views on poetry. This essay became a small book in itself, and is by far the most influential work of Urdu literary criticism ever written. It will be discussed at length in the final part of the present study.

During his later life, Hali lived more and more in retirement. By 1896 he had prepared a small separate house, where he could live and work apart from his family and visitors. There he completed his other greatest literary achievement, *A Memoir of Ġhālib* (*Yādgār-e Ġhālib*, 1897); it contained anecdotes, selected verses, and a lucid, unpretentious, deeply affectionate portrait of Ġhālib as a person. Today, this elegant and nostalgic memoir is perhaps even more popular than the *Introduction*.[62]

Hali had long had a close, mutually admiring friendship with Sir Sayyid Aḥmad Ḳhān. When Sir Sayyid died in 1898, Hali lost the man who was the ustad of his mature years, the most vigorous and unfailing supporter of his all-too-controversial literary work. In his last major work, *An Immortal Life* (*Ḥayāt-e jāved*, 1901), Hali paid tribute to his close friend and mentor. To his disappointment, this biography never found much favor with the public; its thousand-page length and hero-worshiping tone were perhaps largely responsible.

In 1904 Hali was officially awarded the title of "Shams ul-ʿulamā"—the same title that had been bestowed on Azad. He continued to write much occasional verse and many essays along reformist lines. One of his favorite causes was the education of women. His didactic novel *Conversations among Women* (*Majālis un-nisā*, 1904–5), originally written during his days in Lahore, earned a government prize of four hundred rupees arranged by Colonel Holroyd and was widely used in girls' schools; his poem "In Praise of the Silent" ("Chup kī dād," 1906) paid homage to women's unsung virtues.[63] Like Azad, he always managed to make time to write school textbooks; the range and extent of his literary output is remarkable.[64] And he too, like Azad, founded a library—using money he collected from the citizens of Panipat in memory of Queen Victoria when she died in 1901.[65] For the occasion, he composed two elegies in her honor.[66] Hali died in 1914.

· · ·

Azad and Hali were denied by history the chance to feel about Urdu poetry the way the great classical ustads had felt. They were unable to feel the supreme confidence shown by Ġhālib when writing to Bahādur Shāh—a confidence that impatiently assumed both his individual mastery, and the self-evident, unchallengeable excellence of the literary tradition within which he worked. Azad and Hali were of the generation hardest hit by the deep slash of 1857. Their lives were almost cut in half by its force. They had grown up in the old world, which they had deeply loved. They were forced to witness its terrible death throes; and then they had to live most of their lives in the new world.

They not only saw their culture being torn apart in the outer world, but felt it collapsing within their hearts. Both of them devoted their best energies to shoring up a framework within which the past could survive—and on which the future could build. This sense of mission gave a compelling sincerity and urgency to their arguments. Moreover, both were immensely talented: they managed to give their words an impetus that remains powerful even a century later. To a surprising extent, Urdu poetry is still imagined and described in the very terms they used; the house still stands as they reconstructed it.

4 THE WATER OF LIFE

We have had a glimpse of Azad, forced to flee in confusion from Delhi in 1857, snatching up the packet of Żauq's ghazals and tucking it under his arm. This vivid image, like so many others, was created for us by Azad himself in his masterpiece, *Water of Life*. Azad made his feelings at the time vivid as well: "Hazrat Ādam left Heaven; Delhi is a heaven too. I'm his descendant—why shouldn't I leave Delhi?" (450). The bitterness and poignancy of his words linger in the memory. Azad's magic with words has proved so potent that even the hostile critic ʿĀbid Peshāvarī has called *Water of Life* "the most often reprinted, and most widely read, Urdu book of the past century."[1]

Water of Life reconstructed the "lost heaven" of the old Delhi culture, to keep its memory alive into the future. In the introduction, Azad explained his reasons for writing. The passage is so important that it deserves to be quoted at length.

> Moreover, those with new-style educations, whose minds are illumined by light from English lanterns, complain that our tazkirahs describe neither a poet's biography, nor his temperament and character; nor do they reveal the merits of his work, its strong and weak points, or its relationship to that of his contemporaries; in fact, they even go so far as to omit the dates of his birth and death. Although this complaint is not without foundation, the truth is that information of this kind is generally available in families, through accomplished family members and their circles. It's partly that such people have been disheartened at the change in the times and have given up on literature, and partly that knowledge and its forms of communication take new directions with every day's experience. In

> Arabic and Persian, this progress and *iṣlāḥ* have been blocked for many years. The English language is a magic world of progress and *iṣlāḥ*. But in the beginning, people of [good] family thought it undesirable for their children to study it. And the style of our old literature was such that it never occurred to people to write about such things in books. They felt all these minor points to be the small change of conversation, suitable tidbits to be told when groups of friends were gathered together, so they weren't aware of the new ways and their advantages. And how could they know that the page of history would be turned—the old families destroyed, their offspring so ignorant that they would no longer know even their own family traditions. And if anyone would tell them something of these matters, they'd demand proof! In short, these thoughts made it incumbent upon me to collect all that I knew about the elders or had found mentioned in various tazkirahs, and write it down in one place. (3–4)

The complexity of Azad's own situation is manifest: he stands apart from the tazkirah tradition, for he perceives its flaws; he stands apart from the older generation, for he knows they are wrong to reject printed books and English, both full of promise for the future; yet he also stands apart from the "ignorant" younger generation, who are so Westernized that they demand written "proof" of what they should have learned in childhood from their elders.

But it is not really anyone's fault; the root of the problem is the unexpected, unimaginable cataclysm of 1857. Thus the note of melancholy, of resignation. The page of history has been turned, "the old families destroyed"; the elders are "disheartened" and have "given up," the traditional channels of oral transmission lie in ruins. (When Hali reviewed *Water of Life*—in the *Aligarh Institute Gazette* in 1881—he too devoted more than a page of his comments to the sufferings of the old elite: "reading about them, the heart grows full.")[2] Since Azad belonged to the only generation that could look both backwards and forwards, he sought to pour the old wine of anecdote and oral tradition into the new bottle of printed form, before the chance was lost forever. This was not just a public service, but a personal imperative. Despite—or because of?—his commitment to innovation and Westernization for the future, Azad himself held on with a death grip to the world of the past.

Water of Life has been incomparably influential; but amidst a great outpouring of praise there has been, right from the start, a steady undercurrent of criticism. Hali consoled Azad for such attacks, reminding him that anyone who writes a book exposes himself to criticism, and urging him to stand firm and ignore it completely: "Useful works cannot be abandoned through fear of nitpickers; if there are two nitpickers, there are a thousand appreciators." As the two friends corresponded, Hali helped Azad gather and check new material for the second edition.[3] In his review, Hali strongly defended his friend: Azad wrote "in the greatest detail" about the poets' lives, provided illuminating anecdotes, and "did not use a poetic exaggeration that cannot be proved."[4] Hali's words of support emphasize a conspicuous fact about the reception of *Water of Life*: while people indeed picked—often accurately—at dozens of small nits, not a single contemporary came forward to challenge the whole achievement, to deny the plausibility of the work as a cultural vision. The early readers of *Water of Life* included hundreds of authoritative eyewitnesses who had lived much of their lives in the world that Azad was depicting; it should be noted that not one of these opinionated, articulate critics questioned Azad's basic vision of that world.

Most of the criticism centered on Azad's prejudiced use (or abuse) of sources for facts, dates, and particular anecdotes. Was Mīr really as much of a curmudgeon as Azad represents him to be? From which tazkirahs did Azad derive his information? How trustworthy were his oral sources? What kind of liberties did he take with them? Why did he omit Momin from the first edition, and why did he insert him with such lame excuses into the second? Why was he so cool toward Ġhālib? Although Azad has been strongly defended by his biographer Muhammad Sadiq,[5] and by scholars as distinguished as Masʿūd Ḥasan Rizvī Adīb,[6] critics have successfully poked innumerable small—and sometimes quite large—holes in the factual fabric of his narrative.[7]

Above all, however, it is Azad's "Żauq worship" that makes him vulnerable. Certainly Azad had complex uses for an ustad like Żauq. Azad could "save" Żauq from the wreck of the old world by rescuing and promoting his poetry; he could save this "uncle," his father's close friend, as he could not save his father. Żauq thus could be of the most obvious psychological value to Azad. Moreover, Żauq could be an excellent primary source: anecdotes could be directly attributed to him, and Azad could bolster his own authority by claiming privileged access to such a well-placed and revered ustad. ʿĀbid Peshāvarī says that Azad invokes Żauq's name 115 times in *Water of Life*.[8] And when the time finally comes to write about Żauq himself, the hyperbole, the "unbounded Żauq worship," is such that the whole rest of the book seems "merely a preface" to it.[9]

Azad did not merely praise Żauq in the most extravagant terms, but also distorted the facts to add to his glory.[10] One unhappy result of this distortion was a notable injustice done to Bahādur Shāh Ẓafar, for Azad asserted that much of Z̤afar's poetry had in fact been written by Żauq. According to Azad, Z̤afar would write the first line of a verse and give it to the royal ustad to complete, or he would compose a few verses and leave it to Żauq to finish the rest. "Thousands" of Żauq's poems, Azad said, are in circulation under the name of Z̤afar (454); a large part of Z̤afar's first volume, and all of his later ones, are Żauq's creations (472). These allegations have been examined at length, and disproved.[11] (In an interesting counterpoint, Hali suggested—though he did not actually claim—that a number of Z̤afar's later ghazals had in fact been written by Ġhālib.)[12]

Another unhappy result of Azad's Żauq worship was, paradoxically, its damage to Żauq's own reputation. For it led Azad to commit a kind of bizarre forgery unique in the annals of Urdu literature, when he finally published his much-edited *Dīvān-e Żauq* (1888). While it is a permissible part of the teaching process for ustads to radically alter, or even entirely compose, ghazals that are then recited under the names of their shagirds, it would be an almost unheard-of piece of insolence for a shagird to compose ghazals and attribute them to his ustad. Yet this is what Azad did. While editing the bundle of Żauq's ghazal manuscripts that he had rescued from Delhi, he not only tampered with the texts, seeking to "improve" them and modernize their language,[13] but even composed whole new ghazals himself, which he added to the volume. Along with much circumstantial evidence, conclusive proof has been found: marked-up first drafts of some of "Żauq's" ghazals—on the backs of letters and papers dated thirty years after his death.[14] But since Żauq was a much better poet than Azad, the effect of Azad's tampering was ironic: "It's a strange kind of ustad worship, that the shagird performs *iṣlāḥ* on the ustad's fine poetry and weakens it before he presents it to the world!"[15]

Why did Azad do it? Surely because he needed more from Żauq than the real Żauq could ever supply. It has been argued that Żauq was never his ustad at all, and that Azad had to co-opt him into the role after the fact.[16] But even if Żauq was an ustad to him as well as an "uncle," obviously Żauq's actual poetry was not enough for Azad, either in quantity (so that Z̤afar's poetry and Azad's own forgeries had to be pressed into service) or in quality (so that Azad had to perform a modernizing *iṣlāḥ* on Żauq's work); nor was Żauq's actual biography enough (so that hyperbole had to be added, and facts constantly distorted, to augment his glory). Azad needed a lifeline back to the lost "heaven" of old Delhi—a lifeline magically strong, a lifeline tough and elastic enough to bear all the weight he needed to put on it. Żauq had to be more than a mere human being: he had to be this lifeline.

In *Water of Life* Azad's nostalgic need for such a lifeline shows itself again and again. People of earlier times were lucky, he says, not to live to see this age (207). Doorkeepers were more cultured in those days than nobles are today (225). Friendships were deeper in those days than anyone in the present "enlightened age" can understand (327). People really cherished their few books in those days, unlike people today who merely browse on books ignorantly "like goats who have entered a garden" (296). Although he himself wants "a thousand times over" to be attracted to the new culture, it can't make any impression on his heart (297). The world of the "New Light people" is darkness to him; he wanders in it as a stranger in a foreign country: it is a world in which mushairahs have been replaced by "committees" (328). Again and again Azad mourns for his lost Delhi: "Oh my Delhi, everything about you was unique in the world!" (133). He ends his great work with a long, moving tribute to the old world, and finally addresses his elders collectively as a kind of venerable ustad: "As time goes on, we keep lighting our lamps from yours. And however far we go forward, we move in your light alone. Only offer me your blessed foot, so I may touch my eyes to it. Place your hand on my head in blessing, and accept my gift" (528).

It was said of Azad that in his hands prose turned to poetry—and poetry turned to prose. There is not a lot to say about Azad the poet, except that his real gifts lie elsewhere. When it comes to Azad the prose writer, however, it is impossible to overstate the case: almost every important Urdu literary figure of the past century is on record as deeply admiring Azad's prose. But Azad himself preferred to use his prose in the service of poetry. In his view, poets are the supreme language-makers: whatever "power of expression," whatever "verbal inventiveness," whatever richness of imagery Urdu possesses, all "came from its poets" (27). Poetry is "such an addiction that its relish makes all other pleasures pleasureless" (118). Poetry is, in short, "water of life to the spirit."[17]

In *Water of Life* Azad tells an archetypal anecdote about Mīr, whom he calls the "crest jewel of poets" (243). A local nawab of Lucknow provided the penniless Mīr with a fine house; it had a sitting room overlooking a garden. But the shutters chanced to be closed when Mīr moved in, and he never opened them. "Some years" passed.

> One day a friend came and said, "There's a garden out here, why don't you sit with the shutters open?" Mīr Sahib replied, "Oh, is there a garden here?" His friend said, "That's why the nawab brought you here, to divert and refresh you." Mīr Sahib's old crumpled drafts of his ghazals were lying nearby. Gesturing toward them, he said, "I'm so absorbed in thinking about this garden, I'm not even aware of that one." (210)

The anecdote exemplifies one of Azad's favorite themes: that poets lived in a special, compelling world of their own. Kings had power over the outer world—but poets had power over the world of imagination.

In anecdote after anecdote, in the life of poet after poet, *Water of Life* explores the relationships between these two kinds of power. If Azad's masterpiece is full of encounters between poets and kings, it is even fuller of encounters between poets and poets, for these are the means by which ustads develop, test, and display their special powers. Azad takes no interest in family relationships, in women or children, and makes only the briefest and most cautious references to religious experience and to inner life generally. Poets have only the kinds of personal traits that make them suitably picturesque and ustad-like: we are told of people's appearance and attire, of their hobbies and eccentricities, of the eating habits of Shaiḳh Imām Baḳhsh "Nāsiḳh" (1776–1838) in some detail (333–34), and even of Żauq's calling out to Azad while in "the necessary place" (471). Azad's anecdotes depict lives in which the great central value is poetry—poetry as a consuming art that demands not only talent and training but also a lifetime of skilled practice.

Water of Life is a mine of these anecdotes. As a point of entry, one example from the early days of the tradition commends itself: the anecdote about Mirzā Muḥammad Rafīʿ "Saudā" (1713–1780) and Mirzā Fāḳhir "Makīn." One of Azad's longest anecdotes, it is a kind of melodrama in several acts, complete with poets and kings, ustads and shagirds, *iṣlāḥ* and professional rivalry.

> In those days, there was a man of good family named Ashraf ʿAlī Ḳhān. Using Persian tazkirahs and the volumes of the ustads, he had worked for fifteen years to create an *intiḳhāb* (selection). And for editing, he took it to Mirzā Fāḳhir Makīn, who in those days was the best known of the Persian poets. Mirzā Fāḳhir, after many refusals and protestations and insistences, took the *intiḳhāb* and began to examine it. But here and there he thought the ustads' verses meaningless and struck them out; here and there he wounded them with the sword of *iṣlāḥ*. When Ashraf ʿAlī Ḳhān Sahib learned of this state of affairs, he went and, after much to-ing and fro-ing, took the *intiḳhāb* away. The manuscript had been disfigured by the *iṣlāḥ*s, which caused him much grief. He took it in this state to Mirzā [Saudā], told him the whole story, and asked for justice. And he also said, "Please edit it yourself."

A classic beginning: poetry is a pursuit for "men of good family"; it is to be found most abundantly (during this early period especially) in Persian sources; it is a lifetime pursuit, and one may well spend "fifteen years" gathering individual verses from here and there into an *intikhāb*, a selection of carefully chosen verses that displays one's own taste and critical judgment. It would be sensible to show the manuscript then to a noted Persian poet, in case minor errors had crept in. It is traditional good breeding for Makīn to make a show of modesty and reluctance. But how arrogant of him to perform major *iṣlāḥ* on the verses of the great masters!

The appeal against one ustad can only be to another. The manuscript is shown to Saudā; he too, mindful of the proprieties, is at first coy about accepting it.

> Mirzā Saudā said, "I'm not a practicing Persian poet. I simply string together a few words of Urdu, and God knows how they've managed to receive the robe of honor of acceptance in people's hearts. Mirzā Fākhir Makīn knows Persian and is masterfully accomplished in Persian. Whatever he did, he must have done for a reason. If you want *iṣlāḥ*, then there's Shaikh Āyat Allāh 'Ṡanā,' the shagird of the late Shaikh 'Alī 'Ḥazīn'; and there's Mirzā Bhachchū, with the pen name of 'Zarrah,' the shagird of Mīr Shams ud-Dīn 'Faqīr.' There's Ḥakīm Bū 'Alī Khān 'Hātif' in Bengal. There's Niẓām ud-Dīn 'Ṣāni'' Bilgrāmī in Farrukhabad. There's Shāh Nūr ul-'Ain 'Vāqif' in Shahjahanabad. This is a task fit for those people."
>
> When Mirzā mentioned the names of these renowned Persian scholars, Ashraf 'Alī Khān said, "Mirzā Fākhir wouldn't give them the time of day." In short, because of his insistence Mirzā accepted the *intikhāb*. When he looked at it, he found that the verses of accomplished poets, poets who have been taken as established masters from ancient times to today—those very verses all lay wounded and writhing. Seeing this state of affairs, Mirzā too was grieved. Appropriately to the circumstances, he wrote the essay *Reproof of the Heedless*, and he exposed Mirzā Fākhir Makīn's foolishness and misunderstandings with regard to the principles of literature. Along with this, he cast an eye over Mirzā Fākhir's own volume as well, and mentioned its errors; and where it was possible, he gave suitable *iṣlāḥ*.

Saudā duly mentions a number of well-known contemporary Persian poets and scholars, establishing their credentials in some cases by naming their ustads as well. But he is finally prevailed upon to look at the manuscript. Irritated by Makīn's presumption, Saudā then attacks him in an essay—one no doubt designed, in this pre-print culture, to be circulated among a small but influential group of connoisseurs.

In response, Makīn sends one of his senior shagirds to assess the situation and try to conciliate Saudā.

> Mirzā Fāḳhir learned of this. He was very much alarmed. And he wanted to wash out these stains with oral messages. Thus he sent Baqā Allāh Ḳhān "Baqā" to speak with Mirzā [Saudā]. He was Mirzā Fāḳhir's shagird, and a very practiced (*mashshāq*) and knowledgeable poet. Mirzā [Saudā] and he had various full discussions, and certain of Mirzā Fāḳhir's verses, the objections to which had reached him in the form of rumors, also came under disputation. Thus one of his [Persian] verses was:
>
> > In this company my heart was constricted like a wineglass
> > The bloom on the wine's face made me blossom out.
>
> Mirzā [Saudā]'s objection was that it was inappropriate to speak of a wineglass as having a constricted heart. Master poets had always used for the wineglass the simile of a blooming flower, or that of laughter, because a wineglass must necessarily be open. Baqā, in response, grew wet with the "sweat of *shāgirdī*." And at length he brought in a [Persian] verse by "Bāżil" as a warrant (*sanad*):
>
> > What pleasure would wine give to me, desolate without you?
> > Because the wineglass is like a constricted heart without you.
>
> When Mirzā Rafīʿ heard this, he laughed heartily and said, "Tell your ustad that if he's going to keep examining the verses of ustads, he should also try to understand them! For this verse supports my objection: although the wineglass is proverbial for laughter and bloomingness, and the wineglass is part of the equipment of pleasure, even *it* has the attributes of a sad heart."

Saudā's objection is based on traditionally accepted networks of imagery: the wineglass may be compared, by virtue of its wide, rounded bowl, to a blooming flower or to an open, laughing mouth. In Persian and Urdu, it is sad hearts that become constricted, not happy hearts or wineglasses. Baqā tries to reply with a "warrant," an authoritative precedent from the work of an accepted ustad. Saudā points out that Bāżil's verse is deliberately taking advantage of the normal imagery by reversing it for poetic emphasis: I am so desolate without you that *even* the wineglass itself—which is (by definition) always open and happy—seems to me to be constricted and sad. Makīn's verse, by contrast, violates the tradition while failing to create any special effect.

But now the action moves into an entirely new realm. Makīn, having been bested in the literary arena, tries to shift the battle into different territory, through a macabre blend of violence and intimidation.

> In short, when this scheme didn't succeed, Mirzā Fāḳhir took another tack. He had many shagirds in Lucknow, especially the Shaiḳhzādahs, who at one time [before Akbar's conquest] had been the

> rulers of that very land of Avadh; the vapors of impertinent aggressiveness and arrogance had not left their minds. One day Saudā, all unaware, was sitting at home, and they forcibly invaded his house and surrounded him. They placed a knife against his stomach and said, "Take along everything you've written and come before our ustad, so things can be resolved." Mirzā was very skilled at inventing the roses and flowers of poetic *maẓmūns*, and creating the parrots and mynahs of speech, but this was quite a new *maẓmūn!* He was completely at a loss. The poor man gave his folder of poems to a servant, and himself climbed into the palanquin and went with them. That Satanic crew were all around him, he was in the middle. When they reached the Chauk, they wanted to dishonor him there. After some argument, they again began to harangue him. But who can dishonor him to whom God has given honor? By chance Sa'ādat 'Alī Ḳhān and his entourage came by that way. Seeing the crowd, he halted; and inquiring about the circumstances, he seated Saudā with him on his elephant and took him away. Āṣif ud-Daulah was in the ladies' apartments, having a meal. Sa'ādat 'Alī Ḳhān went and said, "My dear brother, it's an awful thing—while you rule, such a calamity in the city!" Āṣif ud-Daulah said, "What is it, brother, is everything all right?" He replied, "Mirzā Rafī'—whom Father used to call 'Brother' and 'Kind and generous friend' when he wrote letters to him, whom Father used to beg to come, but who never came—is here today, and in such a state that if I hadn't arrived, the ruffians of the city would have dishonored the poor man." Then he told him the whole matter.

Poor Saudā is abducted at knifepoint; Azad, even while sympathizing with him, has a little gentle fun at his expense: this was quite a new *maẓmūn!* But after all, God is watching over him, and he is rescued by the nawab's brother.

The nawab himself, Āṣif ud-Daulah, prepares to avenge his "uncle" by throwing the culprits out of the city, but Saudā dissuades him: "Your Excellency, our wars by their very nature settle themselves in the domain of the pen." The final act of the drama, a return to the literary arena, then takes place before the whole court. Āṣif ud-Daulah challenges Makīn: "If you're a champion in the field of poetry, compose a satire right now in Saudā's presence." Makīn of course fails to do so. But when Saudā's turn comes, "without the least delay" he recites an extemporaneous Persian quatrain—in which by clever wordplay he conveys the idea that Makīn is an ass with his mouth full of excrement and expresses the hope that God will strike him dead. After that the dispute cools down, and the two poets merely continue to "abuse each other from a distance in satires." But it is very clear who has won: "The entertaining part is that no one even knows the satires of Mirzā Fāḳhir; while whatever Saudā composed against him is on the lips of thousands" (157–60).

How did Azad know all this in such detail? According to his own account, he used to stroll through the streets of old Delhi with Żauq, as Żauq told stories about Saudā and his times (141). The original source for this particular anecdote is apparently a verse account by Saudā, but Azad takes a number of liberties with it, to improve its dramatic effect; the result is riddled with historical inconsistencies and attributes to Saudā a quatrain that certainly antedates him.[18] But the anecdote evokes, in its assumptions, a whole cultural world.

The anecdote records a clash not merely between two poets but between two ustads. By no means every poet was considered to be an ustad. No detailed discussion, no concise definition, of the concept of *ustādī* is provided in *Water of Life*—or anywhere else, as far as I know. It seems to be a South Asian tradition, with no counterpart among poets in Arabia or Iran; it may well have originated in the latter part of the seventeenth century.[19] Azad himself noted, as we have seen, that "the style of our old literature was such that it never occurred to people to write about such things in books." What was the need? Everybody already knew, by a kind of cultural osmosis: basic poetic knowledge was "available in families, through accomplished family members and their circles" (4). Although Azad, foreseeing "ignorant" future generations, aimed to put the old oral culture on paper, he was so much a product of this culture himself that it never occurred to him to define its most basic terms. Still, he has given us rich enough anecdotal data so that we can perform a kind of triangulation.

An ustad was known above all by his pen name, which he either chose for himself or received from his own ustad, and by the name of his city.[20] He was also identified by his literary ancestry: he was often described as a shagird of so-and-so. Although he was not usually identified through his literary progeny (ustad of so-and-so), an ustad without shagirds was almost a contradiction in terms. Secondarily, an ustad was identified through the names of his immediate male forebears, usually on the father's side of the family. Names were very important: Azad said only half jokingly that a man's name was a fine indicator of the worth of his elders who had chosen it (225).

Age, too, played a part in an ustad's reputation; in general, senior ustads of many years' standing outranked junior ones who had just begun their careers. A senior ustad had a larger body of poetry in circulation and had built up over time a larger group of devoted shagirds. Above all, a senior ustad had had time to become more "practiced" in poetry than a junior one; the term *kuhnah mashq*, "long-practiced," was also used. As Azad always recognized, "practice (*mashq*) is very powerful" (344). Żauq taught Azad that ustads can make even unpromising rhymes and meters work (475); Azad records an anecdote in which, at Ẓafar's command, Żauq instantly turned a casually spoken phrase, metrical only by chance, into the second line of a *shiʿr* (463–64)—a feat we will consider at more length later on. Veteran ustads become so practiced that they can compose extemporaneous verse perfectly suited to any occasion—as Saudā did, according to the anecdote, when insulting Makīn.[21] *Water of Life* offers numerous examples of such fluent improvisation. Ustads come up with verses for every situation: to tease a delinquent shagird (117); to humiliate a court jester (119); to deflate even Mīr's self-praise with laughter (207–8); to deplore a delayed pension payment (226); to hasten the bestowal of winter clothing (234); to ridicule a mis-tied turban (273); to lament a pension cut when a rival ustad appears at court (302); to appreciate the beauty of a sleeping boy (352); and so on.

An ustad is necessary to a young poet, says Azad, the way a rider with a whip is necessary to a spirited horse: only such a rider can guide the horse, cause him to perform at his best, and keep him from running wild and ultimately being "spoiled" (248). The ustad must "pull in the promising colt, and guide him with the reins of theory" (342). Hali too, when discussing Ġhālib, is in agreement on this point: he attributes to Mīr the prophecy, "If this boy [Ġhālib] finds a worthy ustad to put him on the right road, he'll become a peerless poet; otherwise, he'll babble nonsense." Hali depicts Ġhālib as running wild in his youth with obscure, convoluted poetry "just as very bright boys often [do] in the beginning"—and then as gradually brought to heel by the influence of senior friends, so that he comes to write more disciplined and intelligible verses.[22]

When an ustad is approached by an aspiring young poet, he may either accept or refuse him as a shagird. If the ustad does accept the shagird, he owes him his best care and attention, and generally does not take money for his services. As we have seen, shagirds were expected to show the most zealous, partisan loyalty toward their ustad, whether in mushairahs, in literary disputes—like that in which Baqā defended his ustad against Saudā—or in street brawls. Shagirds might in fact claim an amount of attention the ustad found burdensome. Shāh Naṣīr was asked why he made a habit, although he was well-off, of exacting small gifts from his shagirds. He explained that his shagirds gave him no peace: "Every day they write down their fiddle-faddle and nonsense on pieces of paper, and come and sit on my head." His exactions, he said, meant that at least they brought their ghazals only every fourth day instead—and that they wrote more carefully, and valued his comments more, since they had paid a small price for them (396). However, an ustad might also, on occasion, delightedly reward a shagird's performance with a valuable gift (353).

This intimate ustad-shagird relationship is the basis of everything else; in the case of mystically inclined poets, it could even blur into the relationship of religious teacher to disciple, *pīr* to *murīd*. Mirzā "Maẓhar" Jān-e Jānāñ is said to have recited a verse to a would-be shagird and told him, "Consider it to be *tabarruk* (a tangible sign of spiritual favor) and *iṣlāḥ* both" (137). As in other intimate relationships, however, tensions and rivalries were often apparent. Azad noted that although master-apprentice relationships existed in many fields of learning, "when I've seen shagirds grapple with their ustads, it has usually been in this art alone" (112).

The ustad has a special personal authority that entirely transcends that of the printed word, as one of Azad's most entertaining anecdotes makes clear.

> When [Mirzā Salāmat 'Alī] "Dabīr" was just beginning his practice, his ustad's advice about some word displeased him. Shaiḳh Nāsiḳh was alive, but he was elderly. Dabīr went to him. At that time he was amidst a group of people, sitting on cushioned stools, in formal assembly. Dabīr petitioned, "Your Lordship! About this verse I said such-and-such, and my ustad gave such-and-such an *iṣlāḥ*." He replied, "Your ustad gave the correct *iṣlāḥ*." Dabīr then said, "Your Lordship, it is written in such-and-such a way in books." He said, "No. What your ustad has said is the proper thing." Dabīr again petitioned, "Your Lordship, please just look at this book." The Shaiḳh Sahib grew irritated and said, *"Aré,* what do *you* know about books! In my presence you invoke books! I've looked at so many books, I've become a book myself!" He was so angry that he picked up a cane that lay before him, and rose. Dabīr fled. Shaiḳh Nāsiḳh was so excited that he pursued him as far as the door. (516)

The veteran ustad, the interpreter of the tradition who over time has "become a book" himself, is the pillar on which the world of poetry rests.

The ustad's unique and precious gift to the shagird is his *iṣlāḥ*, his "correction" and improvement of the shagird's work. We have seen one hostile example of the process of *iṣlāḥ*, when Saudā criticized Makīn's use of the image of the wineglass. Baqā's defense of his ustad rested on the establishing of a warrant, a verse from a recognized master containing the disputed usage. (We will consider the process of *iṣlāḥ* in more detail later on.) The prescriptive force of *iṣlāḥ* means that an ustad has almost royal powers: a shagird who visits his ustad can be said to have "presented himself humbly in the service of his king of speech" (353). A poet has a "lordly temperament"; he is happier finding the one right word than the worldly king is with conquering a realm (65–66). The coins of the "realm of poets" were struck in the name of Żauq (420); Ġhālib, though not rich, possessed "the lordship of the realm of speech, and the wealth of *maẓmūns*" (482). Kings may in fact treat poets royally: a whole village can be earned by an ode (442). On one occasion, a raja impulsively presented Momin with an elephant—a particularly royal gift—from his own stables; Momin later sold it (409).[23]

Poets can also show their royal rank by treating kings with varying degrees of disrespect. Momin refused a lavish pension from the raja of Kapurthala when he discovered that the same amount was being paid to a mere "singer" as well (409–10). Mīr snubbed the nawab of Avadh by declining to compose on demand (197) and by proudly refusing to accept money or a robe of honor despite great need (209–10). When Shāh ʿĀlam himself honored the mystically inclined Ḳhvājah Mīr "Dard" (1721–1785) by visiting him, Mīr Dard scolded the emperor for sitting among Ṣūfīs with his legs disrespectfully stretched out; Shāh ʿĀlam replied that his feet hurt, to which Mīr Dard retorted that in that case he needn't have come at all (178). When Shāh ʿĀlam boasted that he could compose ghazals even while using the toilet, Saudā replied, "Your Majesty, that's what they smell like, too" (142). We have seen that Saudā was known to Āṣif ud-Daulah, the nawab of Avadh, as the man "whom Father used to call 'Brother'" and "whom Father used to beg to come, but who never came."

Yet *Water of Life* recognizes that kings are well capable of getting their own back. Żauq was harassed by Ẓafar, who delighted in thinking up fiendishly ingenious, almost impossible "grounds" (*zamīn*), or meter rhyme patterns, and commanding Żauq to compose in them (472). Nāsiḳh, who offended the nawab of Avadh by contemptuously refusing his patronage, was driven out of Lucknow (338). And, above all, there is the terrible cautionary tale of Mīr Inshā'allāh Ḳhān "Inshā" (1753–1817), whose flippant behavior eventually turned Nawab Saʿādat ʿAlī Ḳhān against him; the nawab kept him in isolation, under a kind of house arrest, until he went mad and finally died in humiliation and squalor (280–85).

When patronage proves unreliable, poets are thrown back on the open market: they must make direct use of their "coins of speech" and "capital of *maẓmūns*" in order to survive (365). Shaiḳh Ġhulām Hamadānī "Muṣḥafī" (1750–1824) in old age sold his best verses to others for money (350); Mīr Mustaḥsan "Ḳhalīq" supported his family by selling ghazals (365). Even theft of this verbal capital is possible: Dabīr was furious enough to take drastic action when his ustad, Mīr "Ẓamīr," sought to read an elegy of Dabīr's in public and claim it as his own (516–17).

But ultimately none of these political or financial vicissitudes matters. The only thing that really matters, the only thing that determines the real victor in every contest, is the sheer quality and enduring fame of the poetry: in the last analysis Makīn loses because "no one even knows" his poetry, while Saudā's verses are "on the lips of thousands." Poets are ustads, they are kings, they are court poets, they are temperamental artists, they are unworldly mystics, they are capitalists—but above all they are masters of their craft. Thanks to both a natural aptitude and a lifetime of technical training and practice, they can perform admired verbal feats that no ordinary person can even dream of achieving. They can, however, teach their art to others, so that the chain of transmission through the generations becomes a kind of poetic *silsilah* (lineage). The unbroken *silsilah* is a source of intense pride, permitting the poetic tradition to grow and develop in each generation without losing touch with its roots.

The aftermath of 1857 fatally damaged almost all the lineages. As time passed, wounds turned to scars, and the old world became steadily more opaque to the new. *Water of Life* is built up from fragments of the old lost world, painstakingly reordered and rearranged in Azad's mind and heart. No one could argue that all Azad's anecdotes are historically accurate; we know that many of them are distorted, manipulated, or simply apocryphal. But if the parts are flawed, the whole vision is nevertheless persuasive—and, in its essentials, true to the world it seeks to depict. Perhaps Mīr never made that remark about the outer and inner gardens—but the anecdote beautifully captures the classical ghazal poet's attitude. Perhaps Baqā never argued with Saudā about wineglasses—but the view of poetic imagery that underlies the argument is one they would undoubtedly have held. Azad's anecdotes, taken all together, give us an invaluable glimpse of the old world of poetic theory and practice. Azad shows us the classical ustad in his glory—lord of the world of speech, ruler of the imagination.

Part Two

FLOWERS ON THE BRANCH OF INVENTION

Mīr Inshā'allāh Ḳhān . . . wrote a grammar of Urdu and caused flowers of rhetoric to bloom on the branch of invention.

AZAD, *Water of Life*

5 TAZKIRAHS

As we have seen, Azad sympathized with those who complained about the tazkirah tradition. Tazkirahs provided too little information: they described "neither a poet's biography, nor his temperament and character"; sometimes they even went so far as to "omit the dates of his birth and death." Hali agreed, maintaining that tazkirah writers often "didn't even try" to seek out this "necessary information." Instead, they engaged in "meaningless and petty" critical discussion.[1] Nor, according to Azad, did tazkirahs shed sufficient light on each poet's achievement—on "the merits of his work, its strong and weak points, or its relationship to that of his contemporaries" (4). Moreover, tazkirahs sometimes gave an unrepresentative selection from a poet's work, so that his real qualities did not clearly appear (88–89).

Yet Azad made it plain that he considered *Water of Life* a "tazkirah of poets" (408), and himself a "tazkirah writer" (499). He defined his territory clearly: he decided, for example, that it was "not the task of an Urdu tazkirah writer" to deal with what poets had written in Persian (499). Certainly the greater part of Azad's material came from tazkirahs. He also drew heavily on oral sources—just as tazkirah writers had always done. He was thus confronted by many of the same problems that other tazkirah writers had faced: accounts given by different earlier tazkirahs were contradictory (118); anecdotes were sometimes vague and poorly told and had "with regret" to be omitted (410); his cherished oral sources conflicted with one another (369). Yet even while oral sources posed special problems, they were a unique treasure of information: verses missing from poets' written volumes were often known orally, by heart, to contemporaries (230–31).

Hali praised *Water of Life*—tendentiously, from his stance as a modernizer—as "the first Urdu tazkirah in which the responsibilities of tazkirah writing have been carried out."[2] Scholars nowadays see *Water of Life* as a kind of hinge. It is both the last work on the list of classical tazkirahs—of which about sixty-eight, out of what was certainly a much larger number, are currently known to be extant—and the first modern literary history. Despite Azad's criticism of the tazkirah tradition, it is not surprising that he placed himself within the most important genre of literary record and commentary that existed in Urdu—a genre, moreover, with a long and rich history.

Like so many other Urdu genres, tazkirahs were taken over from Persian. Indeed, until about 1845 most tazkirahs of Urdu poetry were themselves written in Persian. Etymologically, *tażkirah* is derived from an Arabic root meaning "to mention, to remember." Historically, the literary tazkirah grows out of the ubiquitous little "notebook" (*bayāẓ*) that lovers of poetry carried around with them for recording verses that caught their fancy. A typical notebook would include some verses by its owner, and others by poets living and dead, both Persian and Urdu. Azad himself kept just such a private notebook; it was published some years after his death.[3] The concise two-line length of *shiʿr*s, and the speed with which Urdu script can be written, make it possible to record such verses very conveniently and to memorize and recite them with ease. Lovers of Urdu poetry still frequently keep notebooks, and favorite verses still commonly circulate in conversation.

More serious, or more organized, students might compile notebooks devoted only to certain kinds of poetry: to the work of living poets, for example, or the finest poets, or poets from a particular city, or women poets, or poets in a certain genre. In a pre-print culture such compilations were of the greatest interest and value, for they were often the only means of preserving and disseminating poetry over time and space. There were, as we have seen, a great many occasional poets, but only a few of them were "possessors of a volume" (*ṣāḥib-e dīvān*)—poets who had had a substantial body of their own poetry systematically collected and arranged for dissemination in manuscript form.[4] Compilers of notebooks were thus often moved to perform a public service by sharing their work with a wider circle. With the addition of a certain amount—sometimes a very small amount—of introductory or identifying information about the poets, a notebook could become a tazkirah. Tazkirahs circulated in manuscript form, and as printing developed in North India they began to be printed as well.[5]

The tazkirahs' roots in the "notebook" tradition explain one of their most conspicuous traits: their individuality, their insouciance, the insistence of each one on defining its own approach to its own group of poets. As we might expect from their origins, the earlier ones tend to be more like anthologies, with only brief critical commentary and minimal information about the poets; later ones tend to include more extensive biographical data, anecdotal asides, and/or critical comment. But even then, they are by no means consistent: if the compiler didn't have certain information, or wasn't interested in it, he simply didn't provide it, and there was an end of the matter. After all, if a poet had composed one or two good verses, it was a valuable and enjoyable task to preserve them, even if little or nothing was known about the poet. Sometimes, in an oral culture, even the poet's pen name was lost—yet the worth of the verses themselves remained, along with the pleasure of reciting them and sharing them with others.

The tazkirahs' idiosyncrasies can be clearly seen in their various styles of organization. Although the majority had their contents arranged in alphabetical order by the first letter of each poet's pen name, this scheme was by no means universal; no fewer than twenty out of the sixty-eight extant tazkirahs adopt other arrangements. The earliest three surviving tazkirahs (including a famous one by Mīr), which were all completed around 1752, present the poets in a largely random order; as late as the mid-1830s another tazkirah (no. 29) used the same haphazard approach.[6]

Already by 1755, however, "Qā'im" Chāndpūrī had introduced in his tazkirah (no. 5) a division of poets into three chronologically defined periods: early, middle, and late. One early tazkirah (no. 7) put its poets into order according to the traditional *abjad* system used for chronograms. The writer of another tazkirah (no. 8) used "classes" based on chronology but divided the last class into five subgroups that he identified as follows: "leading new poets; poets of royal or noble lineage and their ministers and courtiers; poets who are local Afghan nobles and non-Afghans from nearby areas; poets who are dear friends of mine; dear friends and relatives and brothers of mine, and novices who haven't yet written much poetry but are vain enough to regard themselves as poets."[7] Mīr Ḥasan's tazkirah (no. 9) integrated both main systems, listing the poets alphabetically but then subdividing the poets within each letter into early, middle, and late. The writer of one tazkirah (no. 12) appended to his alphabetical list a separate category for his close friends; the writer of another tazkirah (no. 17) appended to his alphabetical list what was apparently his own "notebook" of three hundred favorite *shi'rs*, with no attributions at all.

Among the nineteenth-century tazkirahs, alphabetical organization by pen name continued to predominate. Chronological division offered the main alternative, and the scheme most commonly adopted was the tripartite early-middle-late one. One tazkirah (no. 31) that used the chronological scheme introduced it with a kind of handbook of basic poetic knowledge, including sections on Persian grammar and usage, Urdu grammar, Urdu usage, meter, the arts of discourse and poetics, and discussion of the development of the Urdu language.[8] Another (no. 37) arranged the poets as much as possible into poetic lineages starting from the three principal ustads, Mīr, Saudā, and Muṣḥafī, but then adding a large group—poets with unknown ustads—who were left over. Another (no. 45) began with a group of verses by known poets, and then included a separate group for which the authors were not known. Another (no. 49) was divided into three parts: first an Arabic one, then a Persian one, then an Urdu one. One huge tazkirah (no. 40) aspired to be all-encompassing, dividing its 999 poets into four chronological groups.

Others prided themselves on their selectiveness: one (no. 35) confined itself to a mere twelve poets. Another (no. 43) included only verses that had as their refrain (*radīf*) the name of some part of the body—and arranged them in order by body part, working from "head," "mind," "hair," downward to "foot," "heels," "soles." Another (no. 54) focused only on the *vāsoḳht* genre. Several tazkirahs confined their attention to women poets. Two of these (nos. 52 and 62) were alphabetical, while the third and largest (no. 58) was divided into two sections: the first section contained 102 *bāzārī* women poets, the second 49 women poets who lived in respectable seclusion (*pardah*). Two other tazkirahs (nos. 59 and 59a) concerned themselves exclusively with poets from Rampur; one small one (no. 55) was divided into four "gardens," of which three were devoted to poets from Bhopal. The tradition even includes a tazkirah of Urdu poets in French (no. 34) by Garcin de Tassy, and one in English (no. 41) by Aloys Sprenger.

Enough has been said to show that tazkirah writers were a remarkably diverse and freewheeling group. This was only to be expected: since the real value of a tazkirah lay in the poetry it preserved and disseminated, the nature of the presentation was a relatively minor point, left to the personal taste of the compiler. The genre began, after all, with Mīr's brief, mostly randomly organized tazkirah *Nikāt ush-shuʿarā* (Fine points about the poets, 1752), which became notorious for the acerbic adjectives Mīr applied to the many poets he disliked.[9] *The Garden of Poetry* (1855), the last tazkirah published before the Rebellion, contained, as we have seen, extravagant praise of the emperor—yet Ṣābir allotted only a little over two pages to Ẓafar, while he devoted over eight pages of floridly humble rhetoric to his own life and career. Ṣābir also saw fit to begin his tazkirah with a record-breaking 111-page introduction: first a description of his own desperate search for an ustad; then various lengthy—but unfortunately not very coherent—accounts of the origin of the world, poetry, social organization, and so forth, drawn from Arabic, Persian, and also Hindu sources; then theoretical discussions about poetry, including his ideas about meter, rhyme, and genre.

Other tazkirah writers approached their task much more lightly. Many enjoyed the chance to display their own literary virtuosity by writing an elaborate prose full of elegantly rhyming phrases. Some, as we have seen, felt free to make special sections for their close friends and relations. Even more disarmingly, Abu'l-Ḥasan Amrullāh Illāhābādī, author of the early *Taẕkirah-e masarrat afzā* (The enjoyment-enhancing tazkirah, 1780), confides his fears and hopes in his introduction:

> May it not happen that this cruel and powerful age should inflict on me a change in fortune, and I should forget those things that are sheltered in my heart, and that are now prepared to manifest themselves! With this thought I took courage, and made the attempt. . . . I beseech the fair-minded and enlightened reader: if you stroll through this garden, please don't wound its flowers with the fingernails of nit-picking. Because arrangement and pruning (*iṣlāḥ*) are difficult, while tearing apart and scattering are not hard. This tazkirah is a gift—one fit for young poets, to give them joy.

The author shows this candidly personal touch throughout. He tells an occasional corny joke; he confesses ruefully how a dancing girl outdid him in repartee; he complains of a fellow tazkirah writer who won't share material; and he devotes fully eight affectionate pages to his brother, the poet "Ḥasrat."[10] His tazkirah lives up to its title: it is both enjoyable and full of joy.

For our present purposes, one tazkirah in particular, *An Elegant Encounter* (*Ḳhush ma'rikah-e zebā*)[11] (no. 37) by Sa'ādat Ḳhān "Nāṣir," deserves a closer look. It is one of the largest tazkirahs, with 809 poets; its pre-Rebellion date (1846), its focus on Lucknow, its unique arrangement according to poetic lineages, all make it a useful cross-check on *Water of Life*. It proves to be a very consistent supporting witness. Whatever may be the historical reliability of any individual anecdote, Nāṣir's underlying assumptions about the literary life, and about the roles and activities that constitute it, are manifestly the same as Azad's.

At the center of this poetic world, for Nāṣir as for Azad, is the ustad; Nāṣir's lineage arrangement in fact makes ustad-shagird relationships the chief organizing principle of his work.[12] (Azad, by contrast, organizes *Water of Life* into a sequence of five historical periods, an approach we will examine in a later chapter.) Nāṣir makes it clear that ustads often chose the pen names of their shagirds: Āġhā Ḥasan "Amānat" gave all his shagirds pen names like his own, ending in *t;* Shaiḳh Qalandar Baḳhsh "Jur'at" (1748–1810) named one shagird "Mihr" (Affection) because of his friendly disposition—only to find the name already occupied. The most popular pen names were constantly recycled: Nāṣir records, for example, six separate forerunners of our "Azad" and one of our "Hali."[13]

In such an authoritarian world, to change ustads was an awkward and delicate business: Jur'at refused to accept a former shagird of Muṣḥafī's without Muṣḥafī's written consent. Sometimes shagirds grew impatient with this lifelong seniority system:

> In the days when I was writing this tazkirah, [the poet] "Ābād" and I met in Ismail Ganj, above a confectioner's shop. He asked, "How have you described me?" I said, "An inventive poet, shagird of Nāsiḳh." He was disgruntled, and said, "You should have described me as my *own* shagird. . . . I'm better than he is now!"

Nāṣir is scandalized by such unseemly behavior. For a shagird to consider himself better than such a capable ustad as Nāsiḳh is outrageous—"It's nothing but barbarous ignorance!"[14]

For Nāṣir, just as for Azad, the ustad's great glory is his capacity to "adorn" his shagirds' verses with "the jewels of *iṣlāḥ*." Nāṣir gives many examples of *iṣlāḥ* by the great poet Nāsiḳh: he changes "of few words" to "tongueless"; he easily rearranges a troublesome line; he firmly corrects, among others, Nāṣir's own verses, overriding all objections.[15] Junior ustads rely on their elders: when Jur'at is criticized at a mushairah for using the form *gulbāzī* instead of *gul-e bāzī,* he seeks out Saudā, who confirms that his usage is not only permissible but actually more commonly accepted. Ustads often consult each other about minor problems like exotic scansions; Nāsiḳh even sends his shagirds with questions to other ustads, so they can discover who knows and who doesn't.[16]

And sometimes ustads quarrel—preferably by proxy, as in one complex anecdote recounted by Nāṣir. At a patterned (*ṭaraḥī*) mushairah sponsored by one Mirzā Ja'far, two minor poets, "Qamar" and "Ẓamīr," incite Mirzā "Qatīl" to humiliate the Kayasth poet Maujī Rām "Maujī," a shagird of Muṣḥafī's. In front of the whole mushairah Qatīl objects to two of Maujī's usages: he has used the word *gulāb* to mean *gul* ("rose") and has misused the word *sarāb* ("mirage") by stretching its associations beyond "desert" to "sand" and "sun." Controversy develops; Maujī goes to his ustad for support. Muṣḥafī, however, maintains that poets "shouldn't fall out with each other over their shagirds." Nāsiḳh himself therefore intervenes, giving Maujī a written reply to Qatīl to read aloud in the next mushairah: "Such pointless remarks from a poet like you, the pride of the age, are strange indeed! Don't you know that . . . "—and there follow a number of warrants, including verses from several respected poets (among them Muṣḥafī) that support the disputed usages. Then, for good measure, Nā-siḳh carries the war into the enemy's camp, making an objection to one of Ẓamīr's verses: Ẓamīr has used the image of a "fish restless under water," while, on the contrary, "where else can a fish feel peaceful except under water?" And so on—and on.[17]

Azad, as we have seen, shows us that passions sometimes run so high in these literary quarrels that they result in physical violence—always by proxy, which means by shagirds. Nāṣir describes the case of Javāhir Singh "Jauhar," who was so "ignorant of the etiquette (*ādāb*) of gatherings" that during a mushairah held by Sirāj ud-Daulah he rudely laughed at one of the ghazals of Ḳhvājah Ḥaidar 'Alī "Ātash" (1777–1847), and used abusive language. Jauhar then recited a ghazal in reply to Ātash's, in the same pattern, and added some further taunts. Everyone present was upset by his behavior. Someone got Jauhar's attention and gestured to him to make his escape, but "the fool didn't understand." After the ghazal was finished and Jauhar finally rose to leave, some of Ātash's shagirds managed to reach him and "his honor was lost."[18]

· · ·

Nāṣir makes it clear, as does Azad, that these dramatic conflicts between ustads occur very often in connection with mushairahs. Azad describes a mushairah to which rival poets came with "swords and muskets and weapons at the ready" for the "dangerous encounter" of verbal warfare (252); in another case, a loaded gun was brandished. Dr. Leitner called mushairahs "Battles of the Bards."[19] As we have seen, Nāṣir frequently names in his anecdotes the sponsor of the particular mushairah at which some notable incident occurred. He mentions well-known regular Lucknow mushairah series, such as that sponsored by "Ibrat," which took place on the fifth of every month, and that of "Saḥāb," which was held at his house at Qandhari Bazaar.[20] Azad himself describes the glories of the mushairah series sponsored by Mirzā Sulaimān Shikoh (254), as well as other regular Lucknow mushairahs (229, 331, 351, 382).

Mushairah series were of course held in Delhi as well—at the Red Fort, at Delhi College (459–60), at Sheftah's house,[21] at Shāh Naṣīr's house (436)—and in every other city where Urdu poetry was cultivated (364). The poet Āġhā Kalb Ḥusain Ḳhān "Nādir," a deputy collector, was undeterred by official transfers: he established his own mushairah series and always "took his mushairah with him" (358) when he traveled. In Lahore,

Munshī Har Sukh Rāy not only arranged a weekly mushairah but also linked it with his newspaper, the *Koh-e Nūr.* The *Koh-e Nūr* published the best ghazals from each mushairah, and also announced the two pattern lines—one Persian, one Urdu—for the next mushairah. By the end of 1854 the *Koh-e Nūr* had a remarkably large circulation: fully 350 subscribers.[22]

At the very start of the tazkirah tradition, Mīr goes into considerable detail about the mushairah held by his own Delhi circle on the fifteenth of every month: for a time it was located at Mīr Dard's house, but then, at Mīr Dard's request (quoted word for word), Mīr himself began to play host. Mīr mentions several other regular contemporary mushairahs as well.[23] Mushairahs could be simple, informal gatherings held even by poets of very limited means. In Delhi in the late 1730s the respected Persian poet Ḥazīn is described as regularly entertaining his fellow poets: "In the evening the courtyard in his house is swept and sprinkled with water and colourful carpets are spread on a raised platform," in preparation for ghazal recitations.[24]

Mushairahs have been both studied[25] and imaginatively depicted.[26] (According to Azad, there were also gatherings called *munāṡirahs* for the reading of prose [398], but these never became well established in the tradition.) The mushairah can be shown to go back to the earliest days of Urdu poetry.[27] In this agonistic "elegant encounter," rival poets, vying for praise, formally presented their work by reciting it aloud to one another and to a select audience of connoisseurs. Anecdotal accounts of famous poetic battles became part of the oral history of the genre: Azad regrets that in the case of Shāh Naṣīr we don't know "in which mushairahs and in competition with whom, which ghazals were composed" (389).

Audience response could involve quite an elaborate repertoire of reactions—but response there must be. A courteous, stylized show of at least minimal approval was almost obligatory: Azad describes Inshā's public complaint (at a mushairah) that a certain senior poet has been treating him outrageously: "Not to speak of doing me justice—he doesn't even nod his head at my verses!" (253). The real audience may even consist of one uniquely qualified person: when Nāsiḳh died, his great rival Ātash too "ceased to compose verses, because the pleasure of composing was in hearing and reciting" (382).

Mushairahs were not always part of a regular series. They could also be arranged in honor of some special or festive occasion, often on short notice, and might continue for a series of nights. Matters of protocol were taken very seriously. The order in which poets were called upon to recite became a matter of delicate maneuvering: Which senior poet would be accorded the supreme honor of being the very last to recite? How would the poets react to one another's verse, in a situation in which audience response and participation were integral to the performance? How would their unruly shagirds behave? A breakdown of decorum was, as we have seen, only too possible; the polished manners and refined elegance so valued in the culture were sometimes at risk. Mushairahs often started fashionably late in the evening and continued far into the night—thus posing the additional risk of putting some participants to sleep.

Almost all mushairahs were of the sort called "patterned," meaning that the convenor(s) had given out a pattern line chosen from a well-known ghazal by some respected poet. If the mushairah was part of a series, the participating ustads might take turns in choosing the next pattern line (390). Every poet had to compose his ghazal in the same "ground" as the pattern line. This meant that it had to have the same pattern—the same meter, the same repeated refrain, and the same rhyme (*qāfiyah*)—as the given line.

The essence of a patterned mushairah was the extraordinary degree of comparability among the "ground-sharing" (*ham zamīn*) ghazals produced for it. Formally, of course, they were completely identical—the technical specifications of the ghazal are so precise that any two verses in the same ground could be part of the same ghazal. Moreover, the formal parameters tend to produce semantic effects. If the prescribed meter is very short, it may be difficult to express elaborate thoughts in it, or to use polysyllabic words. If the refrain is some notable word or phrase—such as "you may remember or not," "door and walls," "finger"—it may give the poet's imagination a definite slant. Above all, the rhyme words are important. There are only so many words in the language that fit into the prescribed metrical pattern, end in the prescribed rhyme, can be made to occur directly before the prescribed refrain—and can still create an effect that seems *shiguftah*, "fresh, flowering." In a patterned mushairah, most of these two dozen or so effective rhyme words occur over and over in everyone's verses.

Since the same formal constraints and semantic suggestions operate on all the poets, the particular character of each verse stands out in high relief. The very process of hearing dozens of similar verses induces the listener to discriminate among them: a superior verse has an immediate and unmistakable impact. Rival poets gnash their teeth behind careless smiles; or if they are truly overwhelmed, they may even refuse to recite when their own turn comes (258–59). Eager shagirds take note of new possibilities; connoisseurs loudly express their admiration—and the verse is instantly recorded in various "notebooks" and memories. It follows that in a single pattern it becomes harder and harder to keep on writing fresh, striking, piquant verses—since poets are working within constraints that are narrow to begin with and are soon on the verge of exhaustion from overuse.

This very difficulty, however, is precisely what ambitious poets welcome: it becomes an irresistible technical challenge. In *The Garden of Poetry*, the last pre-1857 tazkirah, Ṣābir records an extraordinary anecdote of mushairah behavior. It concerns the famous Shāh Naṣīr, former ustad of the emperor.

> It was during these days that Shah Naṣīr returned from Lucknow to Shahjahanabad [Delhi]. On the persuasion of "Pārsā" (Pious) the pious-natured he took part in a mushairah and recited, by way of repetition, two ghazals in new grounds that he had composed at the behest of the poets of Lucknow.

The first of these two patterns had the refrain *tīliyāñ* ("sticks"), the second *patthar ke* ("of stone"). Shāh Naṣīr's ghazals received so much "praise and admiration" that several other ustads grew jealous and "required some of their shagirds to compose ghazals in both the grounds."

One of these shagirds, Ḳhairuddīn "Yās," scored a minor but genuine success: he "composed a good *shiʿr* in the second ground." The reaction was swift:

> Shāh Naṣīr did not like this too much, and he composed almost fifty ghazals in the first ground and had them recited in the following mushairah under the names of his students. This action made the jealousy even hotter, and after that mushairah the poets made it a condition that from then on every mushairah should have this same ground as a pattern. The result was that for some months they composed nothing but ghazals with the refrain of *tīliyāñ*. And these lovers of poetry were so much taken with this craze that for a long time they did nothing but pick up sticks (*tīliyāñ*) from the ground (*zamīn*) of poetry.

This "craze" generated many hundreds of tightly constrained, formally identical two-line verses, all striving to be different in content but all somehow concerning "sticks." The display of verbal ingenuity under the most impossible conditions can seldom have been carried to such heights. Ultimately, Shāh Naṣīr outperformed and outlasted his rivals.[28] According to Azad, he was always on the lookout, everywhere he went, for fresh *maẓmūns* (395). His unparalleled inventiveness earned him Ṣābir's highest acclaim:

> Other people recited no more than eight or nine *shiʿrs* in the mushairah. A thousand praises to the search [for *maẓmūns*] of Shāh Naṣīr—on every occasion he recited a "double ghazal" of sixty or seventy *shiʿrs*, and the ghazal of each one of his shagirds was not less than nineteen or twenty *shiʿrs* long. The wonder is that all their ghazals too were the creations of that master-rider in the field of poetry.[29]

Out of all the verses in all the immensely long ghazals mentioned in this anecdote,[30] Ṣābir describes only one—the single *shiʿr* composed by Yās that originally provoked Shāh Naṣīr to rivalry—as "good." For the rest, it is the sheer ingenuity of the verses, the fact that they exist at all, that makes them impressive. They are tours de force of technical expertise under pressure; Ṣābir finds that a perfectly valid and sufficient reason for praising their creators.

At length the competition—which must have been growing more and more impossible to sustain—was ended in a graceful and appropriate manner. "Ultimately, Shaiḳh Ibrāhīm Żauq wrote an ode in this ground, praising Hazrat the Shadow of God," the emperor himself.[31] Apparently Żauq participated in the earlier "sticks" mushairah series as well, for a ghazal by him in this pattern survives—twenty-seven verses long, and beginning most grandiloquently with six separate opening verses.[32]

Nāṣir as well, in *An Elegant Encounter*, gives many examples of poets' rivalry in composing "ground-sharing" ghazals. In one notable case, that patron of poets Mirzā Sulaimān Shikoh was offended when Muṣḥafī used "language unsuitable for princes" in his presence; he made Inshā promise to humiliate Muṣḥafī publicly. One day Muṣḥafī recited a ghazal with the refrain *kī gardan* ("neck of"). Inshā instantly responded with an impromptu opening verse in the same pattern: "Your head is a mango, your neck is a picked mango slice / You are one whom neither a grasshopper's nor a wasp's neck fits." This verse was a great success: "The common (*bāzārī*) people loved this opening verse—they even went so far as to make a song out of it." Inṣhā then produced another whole ghazal in the same pattern, which ended with a personal attack: "If you look in the mirror, Shaiḳh, you'll see / The head of an ass, the face of a swine, the neck of a baboon."[33]

Next Mirzā Sulaimān Shikoh himself, who was a shagird of Inshā's, wrote a ghazal in the same pattern, describing Muṣḥafī as a fool. Not only Muṣḥafī himself but also one of his shagirds, "Ḳhalīl," mounted an energetic defense: return salvos in the same pattern were fired at Inshā. Then Mirzā Ḥaidar ʿAlī "Garm," another of Muṣḥafī's shagirds, launched his own attack with another "ground-sharing" ghazal against Inshā. Finally,

Muṣḥafī was advised to conciliate Inshā—which he did with yet another ground-sharing ghazal in which he twisted his previous insulting *maẓmūns*, claiming that they could all bear a favorable meaning if they were "wisely understood." The outcome was an uneasy—and temporary—truce, officially formalized in the one appropriate setting: eventually, "on the night of the fifteenth, when there was a mushairah at the Prince's [Sulaiman Shikoh's]," Muṣḥafī and Inshā were reconciled. But the lull in hostilities was brief. At the next opportunity, the whole thing started up again, with the ustads and shagirds conducting a new round of literary quarrels in a set of insulting ground-sharing ghazals that all ended in the word *uñglī* ("finger").[34]

The connection between mushairahs and the tazkirah tradition can be seen at its strongest in a special kind of tazkirah called a bouquet (*guldastah*). A bouquet reproduces all or part of the poetry recited at one particular mushairah. So many bouquets have been published that "even today hundreds of them are available at various bookstores."[35] One notable tazkirah writer, Karīmuddīn, who owned a press, hit upon a novel plan: he sponsored a personal monthly mushairah series held at his own house, so that he could then publish the verses recited on each occasion in a series of brief pamphlets. Since almost all mushairahs were patterned, a bouquet was usually a kind of "patterned" tazkirah—it was, almost literally, a mushairah on paper.

Tazkirahs were thus somewhat like the kind of chess books that are published for serious players—books that record famous games by great masters, with anecdotal or analytical commentary. These books enable the chess afficionado to study the supreme performances of the past and to relish the great masters' remarkable techniques and strategies. Authorial comment is often brief and cryptic, presupposing considerable background in the game. It would be misguided to criticize such books because they don't teach the fundamentals of the game, or narrate its history, or explain its technical terminology. They are addressed to an audience that neither needs nor wants such information.

Similar complaints against tazkirahs are equally misguided. Azad reproached tazkirahs, as we have seen, for not being literary histories; and almost all modern Urdu critics have echoed his complaints. But tazkirahs address an audience of insiders, and give them what they want—which is above all, in a pre-print culture, access to the poetry itself. As Azad noted, people normally learned about poetry from childhood, "through accomplished family members and their circles." People grew up hearing literary anecdotes as "the small change of conversation, suitable tidbits to be told when groups of friends were gathered together" (4). And if you were so unfortunate as to lack such a cultivated background, you learned about poetry from an ustad, not from a book! Your ustad was better than any book, and gave you all the grounding you needed, for as long as you needed it. After that, the poetry itself was your challenge and your joy.

Alas, as Azad laments, how could the tazkirah writers know that "the page of history would be turned—the old families destroyed, their offspring so ignorant that they would no longer know even their own family traditions"? In the case of Urdu poetry, the page of history was turned abruptly and vehemently—turned with (literally) a vengeance. Nowadays the critical attitudes and vocabulary used by the tazkirahs are all but unintelligible to most scholars—and in fact arouse considerable disdain. About the classical tazkirahs' approach two respected modern critics unite in complaining,

> It's apparent that to the tazkirah writers poetry is a game of words. Its principles have been passed on unchanged for ages. Grammar, discourse, poetics, meter—all the principles come within the circle of these three or four topics and the question of going outside them doesn't even arise. Discussion is confined to errors of grammar, discourse, and meter; terms of word choice (*faṣāḥat*) and rhetoric, the names of the figures—all can be found in abundance. Opinions on the poets' works are so obscured by old-fashioned exaggerated language that it's hard even to understand what they mean.[36]

Although this passage is meant to reproach the tazkirahs for the narrowness of their interests, in fact it goes right to the heart of their poetics: "Poetry is a game of words," and its "principles have been passed on unchanged for ages."

The tazkirahs' "old-fashioned exaggerated language" is thus a shorthand that assumes a prior grounding in the rules of the game. Only a few critics have made any attempt to understand and analyze this vocabulary.[37] But the radical opacity of tazkirah terminology is perhaps not surprising—for modern critics are trying to overhear private, intense conversations never meant for their ears. To Mīr, a tazkirah was almost an extension of a mushairah. At the end of his own tazkirah, he warns off outsiders in no uncertain terms:

> Every person who possesses a proper insight into this art understands the meaning of this; I have nothing to say to outsiders. What I have written will be taken as a warrant by my friends; it is not directed to other people. For the field of poetry is wide, and I

> am aware of the colorfulness of the garden of appearance. Thus, "every flower has a different color and scent."[38]

The diversity to which Mīr refers is enhanced by the smallness of the units of comparison. For modern critics do not always keep in mind one important point: that the whole well-established game of words, played so excitingly in the arena of the mushairah, recorded so vividly in the notebooks and tazkirahs, generally involves poems only two lines long.

6 POEMS TWO LINES LONG

The tazkirahs assume that "poetry is a game of words" and that its "principles have been passed on unchanged for ages." A game of this kind, with well-known rules, will inevitably generate its own techniques, its own standards of proficiency, its own exemplary master players. In the game of classical ghazal, the raw materials are words and *mazmūns*, and the results are a series of well-made *shi'rs*. Each poet's handling of his materials is subject to the most intense and public scrutiny, for he must follow the proper rules; the practice of *iṣlāḥ* is by no means confined to ustad-shagird relationships. Mushairahs are like professional workshops. As we have seen, a poet can be challenged by his peers for misusing a word, for slightly altering it, for unduly extending its associations, or for violating the logic of a traditional *mazmūn* (like that of the wineglass as a "laughing" mouth), for these are all matters in which technical proficiency is involved. An ustad should be highly practiced and impeccable in his skills. His work must sustain—and even invite—comparison with that of the great masters of the past.

This general view of poetry has been well expressed by influential Arabic and Persian theorists, who have often envisioned poetry as a craft. Ibn al-Farāj Qudāmah, for example, likened poetry to carpentry: "Style of expression is the real maker of the *shi'r*; vulgar *mazmūns* and thoughts don't in themselves destroy the *shi'r*." On the contrary, since "the poet is a carpenter," he can display his ingenuity all the more markedly on unpromising material. "The virtues or flaws in the wood don't affect his skill."[1] Shams-e Qais, also writing in the thirteenth century, likens the well-practiced poet first to a "skillful painter" who through his artistry "places every flower somewhere" and "uses each color in some place"; then to a "master jeweler" who knows how to make each verse a perfect pearl of elegance; and later to a "master weaver" who, while he starts with "precious stuffs," works into them "images" that are both "graceful" and "precisely detailed."[2] Ibn Ḳhaldūn, in the fourteenth century, compares the poet to "a builder or weaver": proper word combinations are "selected and packed" by the mind into a form, "just as the builder does with the mould or the weaver with the loom." This process is intellectually stimulating: "The desire to press speech into the moulds of poetry sharpens the mind."[3] Even today such views can be heard: Faiẓ Aḥmad "Faiẓ" (1911–1984) has described poetry as "a craft, like that of a carpenter," which "one must learn," and has also compared it to "a musical composition" in which one must see "if and where a note fits."[4]

Like rival craftsmen (and game players), poets may properly be intensely competitive with each other. Poets may actually insist on the chance to show their mastery by working a single pattern to the point of exhaustion—as in the case of the hundreds of verses about "sticks." Poets may compose many of their ghazals in grounds prescribed for patterned mushairahs, and many more in grounds borrowed from other poets.[5] But even when patterns are forced on poets, willy-nilly, by a patron's whim, the result may be superb. Ġhālib composed several of his finest ghazals in patterns imposed on him by the emperor's command, within time limits set by the emperor's fortnightly mushairah schedule; even in private letters to his friends he never expressed resentment at having to work within such arbitrary constraints. On the contrary, in fact: he gloried in these ghazals and expressed a deep pride in his own virtuosity.[6] Even today ghazal poets often find that the ground comes before all else; as Faiẓ has put it, a ghazal "first requires the emergence of a rhyming scheme," after which "one builds on it."[7]

The setting of patterns for shagirds is something for ustads to decide. An earlier ustad's brilliant use of a pattern may almost retire it from service: Ġhālib peremptorily ordered a shagird to abandon work on a ghazal he was writing in one such pattern and to drop it entirely from his volume.[8] Yet Ġhālib also recognized that, contrary to his own practice, poets traditionally borrowed much more than a pattern from their predecessors: they "put an ustad's ghazal or ode before them, wrote down his rhyme words, and began to add words to these rhyme words."[9] The practice of building *shiʿrs* on those of earlier poets in fact goes back to Ḥāfiẓ and beyond;[10] it was encouraged by the memorization of thousands of verses that was—and to some extent still is—part of the training of every aspiring poet. But to model a whole ghazal specifically on that of another poet had connotations of challenge. Thus, when Żauq produced a ghazal modeled on one of Saudā's, his ustad, Shāh Naṣīr, threw it aside and angrily asked, "So you compose a ghazal on an ustad's ghazal? Now you've begun to fly higher even than Mirzā Rafīʿ!" (423–24). Assigning grounds for ghazals was always an act with overtones of authority and power; in some mushairah series the ustads themselves, not the convenor, set the pattern lines (390). Sometimes an intriguing new ghazal recited in one mushairah would be chosen to provide the pattern line for the following session (460).

Azad offers one especially noteworthy example of such pattern setting and its consequences: an elaborate anecdote designed to show Żauq's coming of age as an ustad in his own right, despite the jealousy of his ustad Shāh Naṣīr.

> After some years, the late Shāh Naṣīr returned from the Deccan and began to hold his usual mushairahs. The Shaiḳh [Żauq], peace be upon him, had reached a high level in his practice; he too attended the mushairahs and recited his ghazals. In the Deccan, the Shāh Sahib had, at someone's request, composed a ghazal of nine verses of which the refrain was "fire and water and earth and air." He recited that ghazal in the mushairah and said, "Anyone who writes a ghazal in this pattern I will consider an ustad."

Żauq promptly composed a ghazal in the specified pattern—and Shāh Naṣīr made some objections to it. Żauq then composed an ode in the same pattern and recited it at court.

Żauq's ode was "widely discussed," and some days later he heard that "objections had been written about it." After having his ode checked over by a connoisseur, he took the logical next step.

> The late Shaiḳh [Żauq] took the ode into a mushairah, to recite it there and have it judged in a public encounter. Accordingly, the ode was recited. The late Shāh Naṣīr presented in the gathering a quick-witted student, who was well-read in the standard books of study, and said, "He has written some objections on this." The Shaiḳh, peace be upon him, humbly said, "I am your shagird, and I don't consider myself worthy of having your objections addressed [directly] to me." Shāh Naṣīr said, "It has no connection with me. He's the one who has written something." The late Shaiḳh said, "Well, writing is useful only when people are at a distance. While we are all here in each other's presence, please speak about it orally."

At this point the battle is joined. Despite Shāh Naṣīr's use of his shagird as a proxy, he is clearly launching a personal attack on Żauq's expertise.

> The opening verse of the ode was:
>
> Even if mountain and storm contain fire and water and earth and air,
> They still won't be able to move today, fire and water and earth and air.
>
> The objector made the objection, "A proof is needed for fire moving inside rock." The Shaiḳh said, "Observation." He said, "Give a warrant drawn from a book." The Shaiḳh said, "It is proved from history that in the time of Hoshang fire came out [from stone]."[11] He said, "In poetry, the warrant of a verse is required. History is of no use in poetry."

A clearer credo for the classical poetry could hardly be formulated. To invent a new *maẓmūn* is to alter the world of poetry, to tamper with the lines of force along which the imagination flows. The innovator is subject to public challenge. The best response is a warrant for the usage. The warrant cannot come merely from observation of the natural universe, and it cannot come simply from history. Only the tradition itself can legitimate its own development. Poetry can only be validated by poetry.

Żauq does not challenge the objector's criteria of judgment. Tension runs high—how can he meet the attack?

> Those present at the mushairah were watching the spectacle of the back-and-forth questions and answers. And they were dumbfounded at the objection, when all at once the Shaiḳh, peace be upon him, recited this [Persian] verse of Muḥsin "Tāšīr":
>
> I burned down even before the appearance of the beloved
> It was just as if there was fire in the stone—I was burnt in my house itself.
>
> The moment they heard this, there was a tumultuous clamor in the mushairah. And along with it, Saudā's line was mentioned, "In every stone there is a spark of Your presence"; and in the same way a number of similar verses were argued and debated. (436–38)

Predictably, Żauq emerges as the winner, his ustadship vindicated and no longer subject to question. In terms of historical accuracy, of course, there is every reason to doubt that these events took place as described—if they took place at all.[12] But, as is so often the case with Azad's creations, the anecdote is memorable and illustrative in a way quite independent of its historicity.

The story is set within a general cultural context that is by now familiar to us. It assumes the use of the mushairah as a kind of professional workshop, where technical issues of poetics can be debated before an audience of connoisseurs. It depicts the tensions that can arise between ustad and shagird, especially at the time of generational change, when the shagird becomes an ustad in his own right. It demonstrates once again the way that an ustad's *iṣlāḥ*, his correcting of verses—normally a private and benign process—can be made into a weapon for public combat, and the way that this combat, for the sake of the ustad's dignity, can be conducted by proxy. Like all the anecdotes we have examined so far, it also assumes that the unit of discourse—the unit to which *iṣlāḥ* can be applied—is not the whole poem, but a single two-line *shi'r*.

In this world poetry is immersed in, and justified by, earlier poetry. The context invoked when one is attacking or defending a *shi'r* is not the poem in which it occurs—not even in the case of longer poems like odes, much less in the ghazal. Rather, it is the universe of admired poems by great Persian and Urdu ustads that provides the warrant for present usage. By no means every poet's work attains such a status. "People say that Sayyid Inshā's poetry is not in every instance fit to be a warrant," Azad notes, and he gives his own judgment at some length (270–72).

It is the ustad, the living bearer of the tradition who has himself "become a book," who decides such questions, mediating between the past and the future. Ideally, he exercises a strict dominion over his shagirds, and his *iṣlāḥ* inspires awe:

> He [Shaiḳh Nāsiḳh] was very scrupulous about the proper conduct of his sessions. He used to recline against a bolster. His shagirds (many of whom were from rich and noble families) sat respectfully around the edges of the floor-covering. They didn't even dare to breathe. The Shaiḳh Sahib would think for a while, then write something down. When he put down a paper he would say "Mm-hmm!" Someone would begin to recite a ghazal. When a word in a *shi'r* needed to be changed, or if it was possible after some thought to improve it, he would correct it. If not, he announced, "This is worthless, strike it out," or "Its first (or second) line is not good; change it," or "This rhyme is good but you haven't developed its full potential; cudgel your brain a bit more." When that person was through reading, another would read. No one else was allowed to speak. (336–37)

The conventions of *iṣlāḥ* were so highly developed that ustads could "correct" written verses almost the way teachers correct papers. In addition to making specific emendations, Ġhālib used to write the letter *ṣvād*, for the word *ṣaḥīḥ* (correct), next to verses he considered quite satisfactory, and draw a line through those he rejected.[13] Other ustads would put the letter *ṣvād* one, two, or three times to show their degree of approval.

Since the continuity of the lineages was based almost entirely on oral transmission, once it was broken it was lost forever. As the pre-1857 generation of ustads died off, they were simply irreplaceable; poets no longer had the same access to the rigorous, personalized technical training their predecessors had enjoyed. While ustad-shagird relationships continued to be established in later generations, they achieved only a shadow of their former authority and power. For decades people mourned the loss of the old lineages, of the old poetic world. The power of collective nostalgia finally produced a remarkable monument: a work called *The Adorner of Poetry* (*Mashshāṯah-e suḵhan*), by "Ṣafdar" Mirzāpūrī, of which the first part was published in 1918 and the second part in 1928.

The work is today extremely rare. But at the time, according to ʿAbd ul-Ḥaq, the first part sold so briskly that within a few years not a copy was to be had anywhere. Starting in 1927, therefore, ʿAbd ul-Ḥaq serialized the second part in his journal *Urdū,* since he considered the work so important:

> An extraordinary tradition of *ustād-shāgirdī* has come down to us, but now its glory and its rules of conduct no longer remain. In those days, the only way to be trained in the practice of poetry was to be accepted as the shagird of an expert ustad, who explained the subtleties of poetics, especially the correct use of words, the appropriateness of language, the clarity of colloquial speech, the principles of discourse, and the ways of expressing a *maẓmūn*. This was the greatest school we had.

He emphasized the technical nature of the expertise involved. The verses offered for demonstration need not be superb ones; the point was to see the process at work.

> Although some of the *shiʿrs* are entirely unworthy of attention, the purpose is only to show the *iṣlāḥ*: how changing only one word, or rearranging the words, or taking out an unsuitable word and putting in a suitable one, lifts the level of the *shiʿr* and the *maẓmūn* to a new height.[14]

The reader who has the necessary "taste" (*żauq*) is promised not merely enjoyment but "insight" (*baṣīrat*) as well.

Then follow 261 pages of exemplary *iṣlāḥ*s, first brief ones by two Persian ustads, then more extensive compilations drawn from sixty-one Urdu ustads from Mīr to "Jalīl," Ṣafdar's own ustad. Ṣafdar is scrupulous about sources: he carefully notes his use of materials sent by his friends—and also by many appreciative readers of the first part who were actively helping with the second. His examples are drawn from letters, diaries, tazkirahs, and personal recollections. After each example, Ṣafdar adds a sentence or two of explanation and comment.

A few of Ṣafdar's examples are framed within anecdotes about the great ustads of the past. One such framing anecdote is particularly evocative.

> When the late Ḳhvājah [Ātash] Sahib had entirely given up the practice of poetry, and neither recited verses himself nor gave *iṣlāḥ* to his shagirds, there was an accomplished poet of Lucknow who prided himself on his prowess, and who claimed that no one could improve on his poetry. It happened one day that when he was discussing poetry with a close friend of his, a disagreement arose over one verse. The poet said that no one in Lucknow could lay a finger on his poetry. His friend answered, "My friend, Ḳhvājah Ātash is still alive!" [With great difficulty the two obtained admission to Ātash's house.] Both gentlemen presented themselves in the Ḳhvājah Sahib's service, and sat respectfully down at the edge of the straw mat. First they expressed their thanks for the honor of being permitted into his presence; then they presented an opening verse, for *iṣlāḥ*. The Ḳhvājah Sahib commanded, "Read it." The gentleman, with extreme pride, recited this opening verse:
>
> *bāt meñ farq nah āne dīje*
> *jān jātī hai to jāne dīje.*
>
> The Ḳhvājah Sahib said, "It's very good, there's no need for *iṣlāḥ*." But the other gentleman spoke up, "It's my deep longing that Your Honor should apply some finishing touch to this opening verse." When he insisted and insisted, the Ḳhvājah Sahib said, "All right, read it again." When he recited the opening verse a second time, he commanded, "All right, change it to this:
>
> *ān meñ farq nah āne dīje*
> *jān jātī hai to jāne dīje."*
>
> My God, my God, when the Ḳhvājah Sahib gave this *iṣlāḥ*, how he showed his poetic mastery and the glory of his ustadship![15]

No more than a single word in a single verse is changed—but the effect is overwhelming. The brash young challenger is crushed, the veteran ustad confirmed in his supremacy. The ustad makes no parade of his power, and in fact is even reluctant to reveal it; but when he is goaded into doing so, the contest is over in an instant. Played out between wordslingers rather than gunslingers, this is the archetypal "fastest gun in the West" scene. If it didn't always happen this way in practice, it undoubtedly could in theory—and in imagination.

Both before and after *iṣlāḥ*, the verse has the same simple, hortatory meaning: "Don't let alteration come into (your) word / If (your) life goes, then let it go." Although *bāt* and *ān* both mean "word" or "promise," and both have the same scansion, the change immensely improves the internal structure of the verse. The first line acquires richer interpretive possibilities, since *ān* also means "dignity, pride, self-respect." Moreover, *ān* and *āne* now echo each other both visually and aurally, just as *jān* and *jāne* do in the second line. As an extra touch of elegance, their relative positions within the lines are the same. The first line has been both enhanced in meaning and internally tightened, while the mutual relationship of the lines has also been tightened by their now much greater parallelism. The *rabṭ* of the verse, its quality of internal tautness and "connection," has been markedly improved.

This quality of *rabṭ* was one of the basic excellences of a *shiʿr*. Of all the examples of *iṣlāḥ* given in *The Adorner of Poetry*, by far the greatest number involve an improvement in *rabṭ*, especially between the two lines of the verse. After one such example, Ṣafdar comments, "This is the meaning of *iṣlāḥ*—that the two lines should become involved in close combat with each other."[16] Such intimacy and tension between the lines can bring an invaluable cohesion to the verse. Ideally, every word comes to seem unchangeable, since it is enmeshed with every other word. The verse feels monolithic and inevitable. Mīr, in his commanding position at the very beginning of the tazkirah tradition, emphasized the importance of *rabṭ*.[17] And Azad, at the end of the tazkirah tradition, attributed just this unchangeability first to Saudā [150] and later to Żauq, whose "poetry has the quality that if you forget a word, until you recall the exact original word the *shiʿr* gives no pleasure." Azad then quotes Mīr Anīs as praising Żauq to the same effect: "In his verbal construction is an inborn tightness that makes his poetry powerful" (456).

One final example may help to clarify the point about *rabṭ*. Azad tells an anecdote that explains the origin of one of Żauq's most famous verses.

> One day there was the usual durbar. The ustad [Żauq] too was in attendance. A prince entered; he was perhaps bearing a message from one of the princesses or ladies of the harem. He said something very quietly to the king, and prepared to leave. Ḥakīm Aḥsanullāh Ḳhān too was present. He petitioned, "Prince, so much hurry? What is this coming, and at once going away?" From the prince's lips there emerged, "I neither came at will, nor went at will." The king looked toward his ustad and commanded, "Ustad! Look what a perfect line of verse that was." The ustad without hesitation petitioned, "Your Lordship,
>
> Life brought us, we came; death took us, we went—
> We neither came at will, nor went at will." (463–64)

From the accident of a metrical line of speech, the consummately practiced ustad, when challenged by his patron/shagird, at once makes a verse—and a wonderful one. He indeed shows "the glory of his ustadship."

What Żauq did on this occasion was called "joining lines" (*miṣra' lagānā*), a highly regarded technical exercise. A similar test was said to have been imposed on Firdausī, and an even harder one on the young Amīr Ḳhusrau, who was required to extemporize a quatrain that mentioned "four discordant things, namely hair, egg, arrow, and melon."[18] The perceptive critic Ṭabāṭabā'ī describes joining lines as not only an excellent form of practice but also "a great art" in itself.[19]

In the present case the second line, metrical only by chance, was supplemented by Żauq's instantly invented first line, to make a complete opening verse for a ghazal:

lā'ī ḥayāt ā'e qaẓā le chalī chale
apnī ḳhushī nah ā'e nah apnī ḳhushī chale

Life brought [us], [we] came; death took [us], [we] went—
[We] neither came at will nor went at will

The omission of subjects, quite permissible in Urdu, here makes for universality—the subject can be "I" (as in the prince's statement), "we," or any "they"—and also for tremendous compression: except for "life" (*ḥayāt*) and "death" (*qaẓā*) every word in the first line is a verb. And these verbs echo each other both phonetically and semantically: *lā'ī* ("brought") is separated by only one word from *ā'e* ("came"), *le chalī* ("took") is immediately followed by *chale* ("went").

The first line is thus full of energy, movement, even confusion—which the second line, with its slower pace and its two negators (*nah*), rejects. The first line consists of two affirmative sentences, the second of one negative one. The two lines are thus "involved in close combat" with each other. The first line has a semantic break at the precise metrical midpoint—just as the second does. Moreover, the word right before the midpoint (*ā'e*, "came") is the same in both lines, as is the last word in the line (*chale*, "went"), which ties the verse strongly together both semantically (by the sequence of came-went) and formally, through the rhythmic movement of the repeated words.

There are, of course, several other repetitions in the second line, which add to its closural force. And there are the strongly marked sound effects of the three long vowels *ā*, *ī*, and *e*: in addition to their other occurrences, one of these vowels falls at the end of every word in the verse except *ḥayāt*, in which *ā* is prominent, and the two inconspicuous little negators (*nah*). The result of so much internal *rabṯ* and so many long vowels is an irresistibly sonorous verse, one that has often been recited and sung, and is still very popular today. However Żauq came to compose this verse—and of course Azad is not to be trusted as an accurate historical source—it is a masterpiece of "connection." It has just the monolithic quality, the sense that every single word is inevitable and unchangeable, that marks a truly *marbūṯ* (*rabṯ*-possessing) verse.

Rabṯ is a protean quality and can involve semantic, phonetic, rhythmic, allusive, and even visual self-reflexiveness.[20] The more *rabṯ* the better: no verse is ever reproached for having too much of it. Having *rabṯ*, being *marbūṯ*, is an utterly fundamental value in a *shi'r*. Nevertheless—or rather, for exactly this reason—no theorist ever sat down to explore its ramifications. To people who had taken it for granted from the beginning of their literary lives, it was entirely self-evident. Who would bother to write about something so fundamental? Who would need to read about it?

The importance of *rabṯ* is bound up with the independent identity of the *shi'r* as a self-contained two-line poem. The verse has, in the immediate sense, only its own resources to exploit—and (except in the case of an opening verse) these resources do not even include rhyme between the two lines.[21] Thus the *shi'r* must exploit to the fullest those resources that it does have. In the hands of a poet like Ġhālib the verse can become packed, crammed, so charged that it almost leaps off the page. So much is going on in the same small space at the same time that some of his *shi'rs* are like atomic particles—they seem to be held together by their own intense and perfectly balanced energies.

The corollary of the pursuit of *rabṯ* is a hatred for verbal flabbiness of any kind. Ġhālib has, for example, a *shi'r* in which the word *qismat* ("fortune, destiny") is repeated: "Alas for the *qismat* of those four measures of cloth, Ġhālib / In whose *qismat* it is to be a lover's collar." The verse relies on the well-known *maẓmūn* that love is madness: the passionate lover rips his collar open, tearing the unfortunate cloth. Some commentators have considered it a defect that the word *qismat* occurs in each line, *without* any poetic use being made of the fact. Editors have even gone so far as to substitute, with no textual justification whatsoever, the word *qīmat* ("price") in the first line, simply to save Ġhālib from such an un-Ġhālibian flabbiness. Other commentators have defended Ġhālib, claiming that the repetition is indeed meaningful and enjoyable.[22]

Two basic assumptions underlie this kind of controversy. First, all parties agree that the repetition of even a single word is not a neutral or minor fact; there is no leeway whatsoever for padding. Especially in a much-admired poet like Ġhālib, every word counts—if not positively, then negatively, as a "defect," a failure to extract the last ounce of poetic effect from the available resources. Second, all parties agree that mere repetition in itself is not a contribution to *rabṯ*, and can even be a threat to it, a failure to involve the two lines of the verse in "close combat" with each other. *Rabṯ* cannot be achieved merely by repetition; it demands a much more exciting tension between likeness and difference, one that makes the mind ricochet from point to point within the verse.

· · ·

If *rabṯ* delights the mind, the quality of *ravānī*, "flowingness," delights the ear. It is a kind of euphonious, harmonious sound that makes people want to recite the verse aloud and savor it. The smooth, sensuous effect of *ravānī* is traditionally described as "pearls sliding on a sheet of silk" (260). The pearl-like words are so full of power and "movingness" (*tāsīr*) that they "come rolling along on the tongue, of their own accord" (455). *Ravānī* seems often to involve a cherishing of long vowels and an avoidance of consonant clusters.[23] No individual word should stand out as strange or obtrusive; the rhythm should be so fluent that the meter feels responsive to the verse, not mechanically imposed on it. While the term *ravānī* has been widely used at least since the time of Amīr Ḵhusrau and Ḥāfiẓ, Mīr was especially inclined to cultivate—and to boast of—the *ravānī* in his poetry. His *ravānī* at times creates such music, such rapid movement, such organic smoothness, that even an ordinary *shi'r* can linger in the memory.[24] And of all qualities *ravānī* is the one most certain to evaporate in translation.

Here, for example, is one of Mīr's masterpieces of *ravānī*, a verse that seems to contain the flow and rhythm of the sea:

> *us kā baḥr-e ḥusn sarāsar auj o mauj o talāṯum hai*
> *shauq kī apne nigāh jahāñ tak jāve bos o kinār hai āj*[25]

Yet how uninspired it appears in translation:

> His ocean of beauty is end-to-end crests and waves and buffeting
> As far as my passionate glance travels, there is kissing and embracing today.

Here the basic *maẓmūn* of the beloved's beauty as an ocean is given a piquant twist: just as waves in the ocean, rising and falling, encounter only each other, so the beloved's airs and graces, as they enhance and "embrace" each other, are available only to the lover's eyes. Moreover, *kinār* ("embrace") strongly recalls the more common *kinārā* ("edge, shore")—and thus suggests how delightful but tantalizing it must be for the lover to see so much narcissistic "kissing and embracing" in the midst of that ocean of beauty, when real embraces require an edge or "shore" of physical contact.

Still, the verse's *ravānī* is its real charm—and how to convey that? Euphonious sound combinations like *sarāsar, auj o mauj o,* and *talāṯum* are only part of the story. The component long and short syllables of the lines can be shown, but no such analysis can convey how swingy and seductive their rhythm is. Let us just say that *ravānī* is a quality lost by definition in translation, but very much present in the Urdu, even if it is hard to describe in words. *Ravānī* is only a bit less fundamental than *rabṯ*: a verse can succeed without it, but no verse can ever have too much of it.

And, of course, *rabṯ, ravānī,* and other qualities are to be sought in the verse alone, not in the ghazal as a whole. The *shiʿr* is the fundamental unit of all presentation—whether oral or written, professional or amateur, classical or modern. When poets recite their ghazals, they often rearrange the order of verses, and even more often omit verses they judge unsuitable to the occasion and the audience's mood. When singers sing ghazals, in concert or for recording, they take the same liberties. The "notebook" preserves selected verses rather than whole ghazals; the tazkirah does the same. (Azad presented whole ghazals in *Water of Life* in order to ensure representativeness, not artistic integrity.)[26] Single verses are the units to which *iṣlāḥ* is applied. Single verses are quoted in conversation or recited among friends. Even the greatest connoisseurs, who know thousands of verses by heart, cannot recite whole ghazals—unless they can reconstruct them verse by verse, and even then they usually do not have the verses in order and often cannot tell whether a verse is missing. Even in a formal printed volume, no one considers it strange if a poet chooses to omit most of a ghazal and present one or two selected verses. The individual verse has always been treated as a small, complete, free-standing poem. The very existence of special terms like *ġhazal-e musalsal* ("continuous ghazal") and *qiṯah* ("verse-sequence") shows that such sequential developments are outside the norm.[27]

In a two-line poem, every word is crucial; and the relationship between the two lines is, if possible, even more crucial. When enjambement occurs—when a single thought overruns the first line and completes itself only in the second—the two lines are woven into one semantic unit. But far more often, the two lines are end-stopped: the break between lines is emphasized and exploited, and the two lines placed in some distinct logical relationship to each other. Azad put it very well: "The pleasure comes when half the thing has been said, half is still on the lips—and the listener suddenly catches it" (51). The first line will often make a general statement or claim (*daʿvā*), followed in the second line by a response (*javāb-e daʿvā*), an illustration (*tamṡīl*), or a supporting argument (*dalīl*). Or a well-known effect may be stated in the first line, then attributed in the second line to a new and unexpected cause (*ḥusn-e ta'līl*). If possible, the two lines are joined not only by this logical relationship but also by wordplay, sound effects, and related imagery; only when interlocked in several ways do they become truly *marbūṭ*.

The pursuit of *rabṭ* is thus one of the "age-old" rules of the "game of words" played by ghazal poets. That the demand for *rabṭ* is never applied to a whole ghazal is further proof of the autonomy of the individual verse. *Rabṭ* is an atomistic, word-based poetic concept, one well suited to competitive arenas like that of the mushairah. There can be winners and losers: judgments can be made clearly on the basis of precise criteria within two-line poetic units. *Rabṭ* is either there or it is not: if it is there, its elements can be identified; and if it is not, the verse remains a mere "two-fragment" (*do laḳht*) failure. Similarly, the presence or absence of *ravānī* becomes very apparent under mushairah performance conditions, in which the verse is heard over and over: a verse may be sung lingeringly, with many repetitions of phrases and lines; or it may be chanted, also lingeringly, in a special melodious style called *tarannum*; or its lines may be rhythmically recited aloud again and again, often by both the poet and the listeners.

This small poem, the two-line verse, thus stands alone, independent of the particular ghazal in which it appears. It may well boast of its extreme compression, for when a river "flows through a narrow gorge between two mountains, it flows with a great tumult and commotion," but when the river's flow is "spread out, no force at all remains" (298). Yet the verse's seeming isolation is also a trick of perspective. For the *shi'r* in fact inhabits the whole ghazal universe, and so becomes one node in an elaborate, richly articulated network. The ghazal universe is founded on the figure of the passionate lover, and mirrors his consciousness. The lover, while longing for his inaccessible (human) beloved or (divine) Beloved, reflects on the world as it appears to him in his altered emotional state. To him its highs are infinite heavens, its lows abysmal depths, its every scene and every moment charged with intense and complex meanings—meanings to which nonlovers, the ordinary "people of the world," are blind.

The geography of the ghazal universe includes settings for the lover's every mood: the garden for metaphors of harmony between "nature" and man, the social gathering for human relationships, the wine house for intoxication and mystic revelation, the mosque for ostentatious piety or impiety, the desert for solitary wandering, the madhouse or prison cell for intransigence and frenzy, the grave and its aftermath for ultimate triumph or defeat. The human inhabitants of the ghazal universe include all, and only, the supporting characters proper to a love affair: the lover's confidant, his messenger, his rivals; the beloved's door-guard; the *sāqī* who pours the wine; the fellow drinkers; the smug "advisor"; the ostentatiously pious *shaiḳh*; archetypal earlier lovers like Majnūn; and so on. This whole universe exists in the consciousness of the ghazal knower—who constructs it by reading or hearing verses, and constantly refines it by reading or hearing yet more verses.

It is time to look more closely at the ways in which the ghazal universe is defined and elaborated. For this whole interpretive universe, while it implicitly surrounds each small two-line poem, must be evoked and creatively exploited by the words of the poem itself. The concepts of *rabṭ* and *ravānī* are only the starting points for a wider poetics. What can and should be accomplished within a single two-line verse? And how did the classical ghazal poets themselves describe their achievements?

7 THE ART AND CRAFT OF POETRY

Within the larger field of rhetoric (*balāġhat*), traditional Perso-Arabic theory separated the "art of discourse" (*ʿilm-e bayān*) from the "art of poetics" (*ʿilm-e badīʿ*). The art of discourse concerned itself generally with the ways in which language could extend its descriptive range beyond the literal and matter-of-fact. Although it recognized the possibilities of implication (*kināyah*), it was chiefly concerned with the simile (*tashbīh*) and the metaphor (*istiʿārah*). These were subdivided into numerous kinds, based in part on various possible relationships between what I. A. Richards would call the tenor and the vehicle.

The art of poetics was the branch of rhetoric that analyzed the specifically literary possibilities of language. It in turn was subdivided into two branches: what might be called "figures of meaning" (*ṣanāʿ-e maʿnavī*) and "verbal figures" (*ṣanāʿ-e lafẓī*). Figures of meaning included the various kinds of rhetorical devices available to the poet, such as different types of double meanings; ambiguities; deliberately opaque utterances; claims of ignorance; quotation of proverbs and illustrations; enumerations; analytical discriminations; affirmation followed by denial; question and answer; yoking of opposites; paradox; and hyperbole.

"Verbal figures" included all kinds of nonsemantic wordplay: numerous sorts of homonyms; fully or partially rhyming words and phrases; repetition; systematic alliteration; anagrams; puns; and so on. The category also included elaborate verbal and mental games that could be played with the verse: verses in which the last word of one line was the first word of the next; verses that could be read in two different meters; cryptogrammatic verses in which names were encoded; verses with their two lines in two different languages; four-line verses that had the same meaning in whichever order the lines were read; verses divided into symmetrical phrases that could be read meaningfully in any order; and other tours de force. Some verbal figures were of even more specialized and esoteric kinds: verses in which all (or none) of the consonants were labials, for example; or verses in which all the short vowels had the same sound; or verses devoid of certain basic letters; or verses made only of letters used in Arabic. Some figures consisted of extravagant orthographic performances: verses in which all the letters were undotted; verses in which dots appeared only above the words (or only below, or in some alternating pattern); verses made up only of nonconnecting letters (or only of connecting ones); verses in which letters connected in groups of two (or three, or four); and so on. Poetry as a "game of words" had thus developed, over the centuries, a wonderfully elaborate repertoire of possible moves.[1]

Yet any such inventory of devices defined the means, rather than the ends, of poetry. Such devices played the kind of analytical and descriptive role that terms like *metonymy* and *synecdoche* played in traditional English poetics. Among poems that made use of the traditional devices, which ones were to be preferred to others, and on what grounds? When poets employed such traditional devices, what kind of effects were they seeking to achieve? The terms used to characterize these effects were of an entirely different order. Although they were widely recognized, they were never systematically arranged and defined in any one treatise. Since the poetry was almost always taught, learned, and practiced orally (in transmission from ustad to shagird) and performed orally (in mushairahs),[2] no one seems to have felt any real need to put its theoretical basis in writing.

Thus the relevant terms must be searched out: they must be picked up from hints and allusions within the poetry itself, deduced from examples in ustads' letters to their shagirds, disentangled from the "old-fashioned exaggerated language" of tazkirahs, extrapolated from traditional literary anecdotes. While the great ustads cherished the Perso-Arabic tradition on which their art was founded, they also shaped their own views as they shaped their own poetry. As classical Urdu poetry developed in North India, both the "Indian style" (*sabk-e hindī*) of Persian poetry and indigenous Indian poetic theories played a role in its evolution. The great creative period of this poetry and of its (unwritten) poetics extended for about a century and a half—roughly from 1700 to 1850.[3]

To try to recognize and understand the operative terms of classical Urdu poetry is a formidable task, but it is also absolutely necessary. Without it we cannot read the poetry rightly at all. For to read rightly is "to read it the way that the makers of this literature expected it to be read." While there is more than one way to read literature, "every way should be founded on the ideas present and current in the culture that created the literature."[4] The account I present here rests on much collaborative work with the distinguished Urdu critic Shamsur Rahman Faruqi, who makes brilliant use of his wide knowledge of Persian, Urdu, and English poetic theory.

· · ·

Each two-line verse, as we have seen, inhabits the special ghazal universe with its gardens, deserts, and wine houses. This whole universe mirrors the consciousness of the passionate lover, who longs for the presence of his inaccessible (human or divine) beloved. The ghazal universe is built up and expanded chiefly by metaphor. If "metaphor is the essence of real poetry," it is also a tool for (culturally specific) perception: "By means of metaphor, meaning is expanded." And in fact, as al-Jurjānī has noted, "the meanings in metaphors are not those of the words that we have used, but rather those of the *maẓmūn* that has been presented by means of those words."[5] Thus the metaphor-making process is called *maẓmūn āfirīnī*, which might in common usage be translated as "theme creation," but which in the case of the ghazal tends, I would argue, to mean something like "metaphorical-equation creation." The process is based on an extended, proliferating, free-wheeling use of metaphor, one that generates a constant supply of new images, thoughts, and propositions about the ghazal universe. Over time, if a particular leap of metaphor is admired and widely adopted, it undergoes a kind of concretization, becoming a well-established part of the ghazal landscape. As such, it can readily become the jumping-off point for further leaps of metaphor. The ghazal universe with all its ramifications takes as its charter what Mark Turner calls "Aristotle's metaphor": "A thing is what it has salient properties of."[6]

To take an altogether fundamental example: the beloved is overpoweringly, cruelly, even fatally beautiful. Therefore "his" beauty slays the lover.[7] It follows that the beloved's beauty is a deadly weapon. This metaphor opens up a number of avenues that have long been richly developed and concretized. (1) The beloved's glances are arrows, which lodge in the lover's body, pierce his heart, and so forth. One who shoots arrows must have a bow, so the beloved is an archer, and comments on his archery are in order. (2) The beloved's long curls are nets, in which the lover is hopelessly entrapped. Nets and snares are used by hunters, so the beloved is a hunter and the lover is the helpless prey. Nets and snares are also used by birdcatchers, so the beloved is a birdcatcher and the lover is a bird. As a captive bird, he is kept in a cage, and can comment on the world as it looks from his cage. (3) The beloved's beauty pierces the lover's heart through and through, so it is a sword. Wielding a sword, the beloved is a warrior on the battlefield whose horse wades in the blood of the lover and others whom he has fiercely and triumphantly slain. (4) Alternatively, if the beloved wields a sword, he is an executioner, ready to decapitate condemned men on the scaffold; the lover is thus a condemned man, willingly facing execution. These images have been accepted and elaborated in hundreds of thousands of Persian, Urdu, Turkish and Pashto verses,[8] so that the beloved is well known to be, if the poet so chooses, an archer, hunter, birdcatcher, warrior, or executioner, and new *maẓmūns* can be based on these identities.

Moreover, each of these new identities generates an indefinite number of further *maẓmūns*, as its ramifications are explored; such secondary propositions are derived by extention from the basic metaphor. From the basic metaphor "The beloved is a hunter," for example, come such *maẓmūns* of the hunter's life as "The hunter lies in wait for the prey"; "The hunter slaughters the prey and makes it into kabobs"; "The hunter enjoys the vain struggles of the wounded prey"; or "The hunter does not deign to pursue the prey."

A *maẓmūn,* therefore, may be understood as a proposition or statement that describes some aspect of the ghazal universe and that is derived metaphorically or logically from previously accepted propositions. Thus *maẓmūn āfirīnī* is the extension of the ghazal universe by offering new metaphorical statements or propositions—which can then be employed by other ghazal poets. Complete novelty is not required: the poet can also seek "to create some new aspect in a familiar *maẓmūn,* or to express it in such a way that the *maẓmūn* increases its scope." Moreover, everyone borrows from everyone else: *maẓmūns* circulate freely, evolving as they change hands, and this is the basis of the whole system.[9]

We have seen how this process is regulated by *iṣlāḥ* and argument: the *maẓmūn* that the wineglass is a laughing mouth is solidly based on its wide round bowl, and cannot be reversed at will to allow it to grieve instead. An unusual assertion like the claim that fire flows through rock may be publicly challenged, as we have seen, and must then be substantiated by a warrant—one drawn not from history, but from poetry. Alternatively, the poet can anchor such a claim solidly in widely accepted metaphors, as does Ġhālib: people have veins, and rocks have veins; when you strike a person, drops of blood come out, and when you strike a rock, sparks come out—thus the *maẓmūn* that rock veins are blood veins, so that sparks of fire flow in the veins of rocks the way drops of blood flow in human veins.[10] The possibility of making inappropriate or unacceptable *maẓmūns* is so well recognized within the tradition that it can be used to humorous effect:

Ġhālib says, "Don't even ask about the errors made in *maẓmūns*— / People write of laments as 'effective'!"[11]

Even if not specifically challenged, a new *maẓmūn* that found no favor would simply fall by the wayside—no one would adopt it or build on it, and it could never become known as part of the real structure of the ghazal universe. A delightful case in point is the following *shiʿr* by Ātash, which builds on the rock-solid, long-concretized *maẓmūn* of the beloved as hunter: "That nose is equal to a double-barreled shotgun / If only the beauty spots on the murderer's face had acted as birdshot!"[12] It is well accepted that the beloved's glances and eyelashes can be arrows, shot from the bow of the eyebrow, but no one seems to have taken up the new *maẓmūn* that the beloved's nostrils are shotgun barrels! Ṭabāṭabāʾī says, "Until an intellectual development has entered the language, the poet cannot use it."[13] But metaphors fail for other reasons as well; some poets' volumes bristle with bizarre, extravagant, one-time-only *maẓmūns* that never caught on.

The obsessive pursuit of novelty for novelty's sake in *maẓmūns* was a recognized tendency of certain poets: these poets were known, often in praise (for their extraordinary ingenuity), sometimes in reproach (for the extravagance and indiscriminateness of their conceits), as poets of *ḳhiyāl bandī*, "fancy-invention," or *nāzuk ḳhiyālī*, "delicate fancy."[14] Azad speaks disapprovingly of poets who "enjoy the breezes of the garden of *ḳhiyāl bandī* and *nāzuk ḳhiyālī*": they "throw away the roses and make use merely of scent without flowers." But he concedes that their *maẓmūns* show "an imaginative subtlety and delicacy" that is often quite effective (377).

The process of *maẓmūn āfirīnī* depends heavily on a close knowledge and study of earlier poetry. One must know where the jumping-off points are, and what kind of leap might trace out a successful trajectory. This is just the sort of prowess, half technical knowledge and half imagination, that years of *iṣlāḥ* from a good ustad, years of notebook keeping, years of mushairah attendance, would produce. In general, a new *maẓmūn* should be, at the least, appropriate; better yet, it should be interlocked with preexisting *maẓmūns*; best of all, it should be organically connected to earlier *maẓmūns* in as many ways as possible. Out of innumerable cases in point, let us look for the present at one particular metaphor: the basic *maẓmūn* of the beloved as a cypress, with its later corollary *maẓmūn* of the beloved's stature as a verse-line. The *shiʿrs* below have been chosen to illustrate the development of this metaphor over a span of centuries, in the hands of Persian and Urdu poets who knew their tradition well enough to build on one another's work.[15]

As far back as the earliest Persian poetry, the beloved has frequently been described as a cypress, with the points of comparison often carefully adduced. Then, as the metaphor became concretized, the beloved simply *became* a cypress, at the poet's pleasure, and could be addressed as such with no explanation necessary, as in this verse by "Sa'dī" Shīrāzī (c. 1200–1290):

sarv-e sīmīnā bah ṣaḥrā mī ravī
nek bad 'ahdī kih bī mā mī ravī[16]

Oh silver cypress, going to stroll in the countryside
You're a true false-promiser, that you're going without me!

Why is the beloved a cypress? Because "he" is slender, tall, and straight, like the trunk of a cypress, and sways gracefully while walking, like a cypress in the wind. Why a silver cypress? Because the beloved is fair, and the cypress is light-colored. Why then a cypress imagined as strolling around the countryside? Because the cypress is an evergreen, immune to the cycle of the seasons; thus part of its traditional identity in the ghazal universe is as a free, independent (*āzād*) being. (The cypress is also straight like the letter *alif*, which occurs twice in the word *āzād* and thus represents the freely wandering faqir.) An independent being is not anchored to one spot but can move around at will, and is likely to follow its own pleasure rather than that of another. All these metaphorical qualities of the cypress form the well-understood background; the real focus of this particular verse is the piquant juxtaposition of *nek* ("good") and *bad* ("bad"), rendered in my translation as "true" and "false."

But if the beloved is a cypress, "he" is also, according to Muḥsin Tāṡīr, a supreme one whom the "real" cypress tree tries in vain to emulate:

garchih yak sarv bah ra'nā'ī-i āñ qāmat nīst
chūñkih taqṭī' kunad miṣra'-i mauzūñ gardad[17]

Although not one cypress has the beauty of that stature [of the beloved]
Since it does *taqṭī'*, it becomes a *mauzūñ* verse-line.

Here an act of *maẓmūn āfirīnī* produces a new and striking proposition—new, that is, to this series of *shi'rs*. Absolute newness is hard to establish, and also irrelevant: *maẓmūns* were always being reinvented as well as borrowed. Borrowing from a well-known poet was a form of either homage or challenge; borrowing from an obscure poet showed one's knowledge of the tradition; and inventing enabled one to display ingenuity. The interlocking network of *maẓmūns* was thus a shared world that belonged to everybody—a world that *had* to belong to everybody, for the poetry to remain intelligible.

Within Muḥsin Tāṡīr's verse, the word *mauzūñ* means "suitable, proper"; literally, it means "having been weighed" and is derived directly from an Arabic root meaning "to weigh." Thus it also means "metrical," since a verse-line is carefully weighed and balanced to make it scan. The word *taqt̤īʿ* is derived from a root meaning "to cut" and means: (a) to scan; (b) to prune and shape; (c) to decorate. The verse rests on the idea of the beloved's *mauzūñ* stature: this stature, being just what it ought to be, is ideally suitable and proper, something that has been carefully "weighed" and arranged to perfection. While the cypress can never rival the beloved's ideal form, it is evergreen and thus (so to speak) "spruce" in appearance; moreover, it is constantly performing *taqt̤īʿ*—pruning and decorating itself—in a vain attempt at emulation. These feats of *taqt̤īʿ*—scansion—turn it finally into a "metrical verse-line" (*miṣraʿ-i mauzūñ*), which is a thing of beauty in its own right. Three quite disparate things—the shape of the cypress, the stature of the beloved, the form of a verse-line—are all *mauzūñ*, all suitable, proper, perfect, weighed and balanced. An audacious, witty use of *maẓmūn āfirīnī* has given us the new *maẓmūn* of the cypress as a line of verse.

The tradition continues into Urdu, with Shamsuddīn Valī Muḥammad "Valī" Dakanī (1667–1720/25). For if the cypress is a line of verse, only the beloved's stature can teach it that supreme metrical fluency needed to please a real connoisseur.

hai pasand-e t̤abʿa-e ʿālī miṣraʿ-e sarv-e buland
jab sūñ gulshan meñ tirā qad dekh kar mauzūñ hu'ā[18]

The verse-line of the tall cypress has been pleasing to a lofty mind
Ever since, in the garden, it saw your stature and became *mauzūñ*.

A connoisseur with a sophisticated, elevated, "lofty" taste is hard to please. If he finds the verse-line of the "tall" cypress pleasing, it is surely because the cypress has had the best example to follow: the cypress is a shagird, the beloved an ustad. The cypress is straight like a verse-line—now. For the verse records a change in state: there was an earlier time when no real connoisseur could have enjoyed the sight of the clumsy, unmetrical, non-*mauzūñ* cypress. That was the sterile, unimaginable time before the beloved first entered the garden. The world of the ghazal can never begin with an Eden, for the beloved has never yet been possessed as fully and lastingly as the heart of the lover demands. If there is hope, it is directed toward the future, or else entirely transcendent, or else founded in renunciation. But in the ghazal world it is always the beloved who creates the beauty of "nature," rather than the other way around.

If the beloved's stature can outdo that of the cypress, it can even, when scrupulously weighed, surpass that of the glorious Tree of Paradise, which is traditionally supposed to resemble a cypress. "Shākir" Nājī (1690?–1774?) envisions the beloved as supreme not merely over "natural" beauty but over the (supernatural) heavenly realm as well.

> *mauzūñ qad us kā chashm ke mīzāñ meñ jab tulā*
> *ṭūbā tab us se ek qadam adh kasā hu'ā*[19]

> When his *mauzūñ* stature was weighed in the scale of the eyes
> The Tree of Paradise turned out to be one foot less tightly constructed.

The idea that the eyes are a scale is a classic *maẓmūn*, for the eyes resemble the two identical round weighing-pans suspended from the central pivot in a balance scale. Such a balance scale compares the weight of two items, one of which is placed in each pan. Here the beloved's stature is "weighed" or measured against that of the very Tree of Paradise itself—which is found to be lacking by "one foot." The word *qadam* has somewhat the same range of meanings as does "foot": it can refer either to a unit of physical length (the steps or paces used for measuring distance) or to a unit of metrical length, the "feet" (*afā'īl*) that measure a line of verse. The verb *kasnā* means "to draw tight" and refers also to the careful fitting of a word into a metrical line, so that the word is "drawn tight" in its correct place without redundant syllables or flabbiness; another appropriate meaning of the verb is to "try, prove, test, examine"—and another is "to weigh."

This verse offers other sources of enjoyment as well. There is the apt wordplay between *qad* ("stature") and *qadam* ("foot"). There is also the *jab tab* ("when-then") clause structure, which emphasizes the source of the judgment being made: it is when the weighing is done by the lover's eyes that this seemingly objective measurement is reached. But the verse achieves most of its piquancy through its use of *maẓmūns*. By now, a century after Muḥsin Tāṡīr, the *maẓmūn* of equating the cypress's *mauzūñ* stature with a line of verse has been concretized, so that it can be assumed without being freshly justified within the verse itself. The beloved's stature, even more *mauzūñ* than that of the cypress, thus becomes an even more perfect verse-line. The wordplay with the verb *kasnā* and the noun *qadam* would otherwise remain unintelligible. Moreover, since the cypress is nowhere mentioned in the verse, the reference to the Tree of Paradise would be fully meaningful only to a reader who knew it as a kind of glorified cypress.

Soon afterward, Mīr (c. 1780) carries the *mazmūn āfirīnī* a step further, by identifying the garden itself as a literary "notebook."

> *sair kī rangīñ bayāẓ-e bāġh kī ham ne bahut*
> *sarv kā miṣra' kahāñ vuh qāmat-e mauzūñ kahāñ*[20]

> I wandered long in the colorful notebook of the garden,
> Where is the verse-line of the cypress—where is that *mauzūñ* stature [of the beloved's]?

The garden is a notebook (*bayāẓ*) because it is the proper place to find vivid, colorful verse-lines—such as the cypress and the beloved, with their *mauzūñ* stature. The common Urdu sentence pattern "where is A, where is B" is a powerful interrogation: it implies that A and B are so far apart, and one of them is so incomparably superior to the other, that they cannot even be mentioned in the same breath. So the second line can be read most naturally as an implied assertion: "The beloved's *mauzūñ* stature is incomparably superior to the verse-line of the cypress." But formally the line consists of questions: "Where is the cypress, with its (*mauzūñ*) verse-line stature? Where is the beloved, with his *mauzūñ* stature?" Since both the cypress and the beloved are free and independent, they may be strolling in some other part of the garden, and the lover must wander long in search of them, hoping to enjoy the sight of their beauty.

This verse also offers a particularly elegant instance of wordplay when it juxtaposes *rangīn*, "colorful," with *bayāẓ*, literally "whiteness" (only by extension does the word come to mean a blank "white" book for use as a notebook). But the verse's real delight is its mapping of one domain onto another, its conflation of images: the lover wandering through the colorful garden, longing to see the graceful cypress and the much more graceful beloved; and the poet browsing through his "white" notebook, looking for certain colorful verse-lines of especially graceful and "metrical" effect. This equation of the garden with the notebook is a fine example of sophisticated *mazmūn āfirīnī*: it invokes our knowledge of several *mazmūn*s already concretized within the tradition, and unfolds itself out of them with seeming simplicity and ease. For there even exists, as we have seen, a kind of tazkirah called a "bouquet" (*guldastah*).

But the process does not stop there. The *mazmūn* now develops a further refinement: by comparison with the beloved's stature, as Mīr (c. 1790) notices, the cypress is actually a defective, "nonmetrical" verse line.

> *sarv to hai sanjīdah lekin pesh-e miṣra'-e qadd-e yār*
> *nāmauzūñ hī nikle hai jab dil meñ apne toleñ haiñ*[21]

The cypress is *sanjīdah,* but before the verse-line of the beloved's stature
It proves to be non-*mauzūñ* when I weigh it in my heart.

The adjective *sanjīdah* is a past participle of the Persian verb *sanjīdan* ("to weigh"), so that it literally means "weighed, measured"; but in Urdu it is used to mean "weighty" in the sense of "serious, grave." Both meanings are elegantly invoked here: neither the cypress's measuredness nor its stateliness enable it to stand for direct comparison "before the verse-line" (*pesh-e miṣra'*) of the beloved's stature. Since the term *pesh miṣra'* also refers to the first line of a two-line *shi'r,* we see that the poet already has his *mauzūñ* second line (the beloved's stature) and is trying to find a suitable first one in the same meter, as in the exercise of *miṣra' lagānā* (the kind of challenge that we saw Ẓafar fling out to Żauq). But when he weighs the two lines, he finds the cypress, alas, unmetrical; he must reject it, and where will he ever find another suitable verse-line? Plainly he never will, since even the supremely suitable cypress has failed him. The beloved's stature must remain a unique, peerlessly *mauzūñ* verse-line, never to be integrated into a *shi'r,* never to find a fitting equal or rival or term of comparison. Which is an elegantly paradoxical result, for the formal precision of Urdu meter makes it absolutely impossible that a line could be metrical and yet no other line could be found in the same meter to go with it. But after all, the lover is weighing the metricality of these verse-lines in his *heart.*

The accusation against the cypress becomes even more radical, however, as the earlier *maẓmūns* are concretized: Nāsiḳh has a different jumping-off place for the leap of imagination.

ġhazab hai sarv bāndhā us parī ke qadd-e gul gūñ ko
yih kis shā'ir ne nāmauzūñ kiyā miṣrā'-e mauzūñ ko[22]

What a disaster—[someone] called that Parī's rose-colored stature a cypress!
Which poet made this *mauzūñ* verse-line non-*mauzūñ*?

Nāsiḳh here takes a stance of high indignation: as an ustad, he is denouncing an instance of entirely unsatisfactory, indefensible, technically incompetent workmanship. He actually demands the offending poet's name, implying that the perpetrator should be drummed out of the next mushairah. The equation of the beloved with the cypress appears to be faulty on several counts: the beloved—or rather, somewhat elusively, his stature—is "rose-colored," while a cypress would be, as we know, silver, or in another sense green (evergreen). Moreover, in a classic *maẓmūn,* the beloved is a Parī (=fairy). The Parī race, known for its superhuman beauty, is well established in Persian and Urdu story literature: Parīs are made of fire, so that rose-red is a natural color for them, while cypresses (and mortals) are made of earth; and Parīs fly through the air, rather than walking as the cypress is imagined to do. But the really grievous fault is to identify the beloved's *mauzūñ* stature with the (by comparison) non-*mauzūñ* stature of the cypress. To make such an equation is, in effect, to ruin a line of verse: in a general sense, to make a suitable, perfect (*mauzūñ*) line unsuitable or imperfect (*nāmauzūñ*); in a specific technical sense, to make a metrical line unmetrical. In fact, the real charm of the verse lies in its wit: its tone of righteous indignation ("What a disaster!"), its outrage at such flagrant, inexcusable incompetence in a poet.

Eventually, however, a given line of development seems, with most *maẓmūns*, to be worked through to its end in terms of *maẓmūn āfirīnī*. It is almost as though a certain vein of poetic ore had been mined out—though of course fresh deposits are often discovered later in the same fields. There is a slight falling off in the achievement of the following verse of Nāsiḳh's, a slackening of tension.

bāġh meñ taqṭ̤īʿ us sarv-e ravāñ kī dekh kar
sarv kā miṣraʿ mirī naẓ̤roñ meñ nāmauzūñ huʾā[23]

When I saw the *taqṭ̤īʿ* of that *ravān* cypress in the garden
The verse-line of the cypress became non-*mauzūñ* in my eyes.

The beloved is well known to be a "walking cypress" (*sarv-e ravāñ*), and as we have seen, a fluent line of verse is called *ravāñ* ("flowing"). But apart from this smallish point, the idea of the "walking cypress" doing *taqṭ̤īʿ*—adorning itself, pruning its branches, scanning its syllables—must bear all the weight of the *shiʿr*, and it can hardly sustain the burden. The phrase "in the garden" appears to be mere padding, since the garden setting is not exploited within the verse. In fact, the phrase actually seems to limit the effects of the beloved's beauty: when I saw the beloved "in the garden" I had a certain reaction, but who knows whether he would have appeared as impressive in another setting, outside the garden? The verse is apparently borrowed from Muḥsin Tāṡīr's—but Nāsiḳh does not improve on his predecessor's work. The verse lacks energy and concentration, and somehow feels a bit flat.

Even without new *maẓmūns*, however, imagery can be effectively deployed. A good measure of success can be achieved, as in this *shiʿr* by Ātash:

pahuñchtā use miṣraʿ tāzah o tar
qad-e yār sā sarv mauzūñ nah niklā[24]

A fresh green verse-line would have reached him—
[but] no cypress turned out to be *mauzūñ* like the
beloved's stature.

The basic line of thought here is the same as that of Mīr's *shi'r* above. The beloved's stature is a verse-line, and if a line could be found to match it the result would be a complete *shi'r*. The lover would like to bring the beloved such a verse-line, as a tribute: instead of flowers he would offer a "fresh green" cypress. But alas, no cypress could be found that was quite as *mauzūñ* as the beloved's stature: no cypress could "reach" the beloved in the sense of coming up to his level—and therefore no cypress could "reach" the beloved in the sense of being offered to him. The real work of the verse is done by *tāzah o tar*, a phrase with a range of meanings centering on freshness, moistness, greenness, newness. Both adjectives are used for poetry as well. A vital, "fresh, new" verse-line (*miṣra'-e tāzah*) is an excellent achievement, while new and fresh growth is just the quality one would expect to find in the (evergreen) cypress. Similarly, a "rich, verdant" verse-line (*miṣra'-e tar*) is as lush as foliage still wet with dew.

Successful verses can rely not only on simplicity and freshness, but also on complexity and abstraction—as in the case of Ġhālib (c. 1816), the example par excellence of a "metaphysical poet" in Urdu.

tire sarv-e qāmat se ik qadd-e ādam
qiyāmat ke fitne ko kam dekhte haiñ[25]

Because of your cypress-stature, by one Adam-height
I see the mischief/turmoil of Doomsday to be less.

Muslims know that Doomsday (*qiyāmat*) will bring terrible trials and disasters upon the sons of Adam. The literal meaning of *qiyāmat* is "to rise": the dead will "rise" again from their graves to experience that day, and the various kinds of mischief and turmoil expressed in the noun *fitnah* are always spoken of as "arising." Here the lover seems somehow to measure the height of the beloved against the "height" of the disaster of Doomsday.

The lover speaks as a firsthand observer, addressing the beloved intimately and making a comparative judgment: "I see the mischief of Doomsday to be one Adam-height less (than it would otherwise have been), because of your cypress-stature (which has been taken away from it)." The beloved's beauty is so fatal, and his use of it so devastating, that the lover experiences it as a portion of Doomsday come upon him in advance. Since the beloved is made of pure *qiyāmat*, the remaining supply of disaster yet to come must be that much less. The measurement seems to be made in terms of height. Since the lover has known a certain amount of Doomsday already, the final Doomsday rises, in his eyes, to less of a height; its height is less by the stature of one human—who is, surely, the beloved. Moreover, if the two lines are read separately and sequentially, as they should be, a further effect emerges. The concreteness of the first line, which speaks of the beloved's (slim, straight, swaying) "cypress-stature" as measured in precise "man-height" units, sets us thinking in terms of physical measurement. Thus the second line comes as a jolt, since the lover still pretends physically to "see" a comparison in height—of which one term is the altogether abstract and nonlinear "mischief of Doomsday." The linking of *qāmat* and *qiyāmat* is delightful wordplay—and another fine source of *rabt̤*.

In the twentieth century, *maẓmūn āfirīnī* has, for a number of reasons, radically diminished. While modern poets may achieve other effects, their use of *maẓmūn*s would never have satisfied a classical audience. Sulaimān "Arīb" (1922–1969) writes:

> *ay sarv-e ravāñ ay jān-e jahāñ āhistah gużar āhistah gużar*
> *jī bhar ke maiñ tujh ko dekh to lūñ bas itnā t̤hahar bas itnā*
>   *t̤hahar*[26]

> Oh walking cypress, oh life of the world, pass slowly, pass
>   slowly
> Let me look at you to my heart's content—only stop that
>   long, only stop that long.

Here the complexities of the *maẓmūn*s have been entirely disregarded. The verse gets the most out of its *ravānī* and sound effects: it has some internal rhyme, it makes creative use of repetition, its semantic units correspond to its metrical feet. Thus the verse sounds hypnotic, it flows swayingly and beautifully—the way the "walking cypress" moves. But it does not do anything more. The poet has stopped short: he has achieved something that is emotionally provocative but intellectually very limited. Perhaps he is not aware of the possibilities; perhaps, for all we know, he disdains them. The world of traditional poetry may be partially lost to him.

Yet that world is always available for rediscovery. A single word can give rise to a new *maẓmūn*: we have seen what a pivotal role was played by the word *mauzūñ* in generating ideas about the beloved, the cypress, and the verse-line. "A word that is fresh (*tāzah*) is equal to a *maẓmūn*," as Shāh Jahān's poet laureate Abū T̤ālib "Kalīm" put it.[27] Mīr praised the appropriately named poet "Maẓmūn" for his constant "search for a fresh word."[28] Sometimes, in fact, *maẓmūn*s can bear more weight than the poet nowadays even realizes: "It often happens that we, in imitation of the ancients, use *maẓmūn*s we have found in their work, and when connoisseurs praise our verses we realize we didn't know that this verse had these virtues."[29]

In short, if there is any activity central to classical ghazal poetry it is the making and using of *mazmūns*. The concretization of successful *mazmūns* meant that the ghazal universe was always expanding—or perhaps developing would be a better term, since mined-out fields of metaphor were sometimes (temporarily or permanently) abandoned. The smallest possible poem, the two-line *shi'r*, could thus inhabit an indefinitely large and sophisticated universe. But this universe had to be *brought* to the poem; it had to live first of all in the minds of the poet and the audience. A difficult *shi'r* can be the most demanding poem in the world and can remain, without the requisite background knowledge, utterly opaque. (In this respect—as in a number of others—it resembles the classical Japanese haiku.)[30]

Because of the centrality of *mazmūn āfirīnī*, of all genres of poetry the ghazal has surely the least interest in the "natural" world, in wildflowers and birdsongs and sunsets and rambles through the countryside. The ghazal world creates its own flowers, birds, and suns according to its own laws of metaphor, and these have only the most abstract resemblance to their namesakes in the "natural" world. Mīr was archetypally correct when he never bothered to open the shutters of his study—his own ghazal garden was much more absorbing than the "real" one outside. The fascination of the ghazal can prove overpowering: "Its pleasure so grows on the poet that he often remains ignorant of other genres of poetry."[31] Dr. Leitner maintained that "Persian poetry . . . has an almost intoxicating effect on the native mind." (Thus it was "sternly prohibited to be heard or read by most respectable females"; still, "poetesses were by no means scarce, especially in the higher Muhammadan families.")[32]

With its radical completeness and self-referentiality, the ghazal universe in fact metaphorically generates the physical universe, as well as the other way around. We have seen the tribute that Ṣābir addressed to the verses of his emperor, the poet Ẓafar:

> The colorfulness of festive meaning is the glistening of wine; in martial verses, the wetness of the ink is blood and perspiration. In mystical verses, the circular letters are seeing eyes; and in romantic verses, tear-shedding eyes. And in spring-related verses, [the decorations] between the lines are flowerbeds; and in sky-related verses, the Milky Way. The breath, through the floweringness of the words, is the garden breeze; and vision, through the freshness of the writing, is the vein of the jasmine. The verse-line has the stature of a cypress; the verse is the eyebrow of the beautiful women of Khallukh and Naushad.[33]

Mazmūn āfirīnī thus comes full circle: just as we have seen that the cypress's stature is the stature of a verse-line, we now see that "the verse-line has the stature of a cypress." And meaning *is* wine, and ink *is* blood and perspiration, and rounded letters on the page *are* eyes. Metaphor *is* reality. The ghazal poets claim, as a matter of course, omnipotent creative powers within their own universe—and also, it seems, beyond it.

Ġhālib uses the stature-as-verse-line metaphor to praise the power of *maẓmūns* within the verse: "Asad, the rising of those of devastating stature at the time of adorning [themselves] / Is the growth of lofty *maẓmūns* in the dress of a poem."[34] The beloved's tall stature is a *maẓmūn*: the rising up of beloveds to their full devastating height, their adorning themselves to display their beauty, is the development of "lofty" *maẓmūns* within the dress or "guise" of the verse they occupy. In fact, *maẓmūns* were so admired that at times they were even perceived as overvalued. The great Indo-Persian poet "Ṭ̤ālib" Āmulī, of the court of Jahāngīr, poked fun at certain boastful poets: "Observe how the masters of meaning have written / They have abandoned words and have written *maẓmūns*!"[35] But still, *maẓmūns* were invaluable. Azad recognized that while Mīr and Mīr "Soz" shared a similar style, the former was a superior poet because he "introduced *maẓmūns*," while the latter used "merely words and more words" (198). Words must be used not just for their own sake, but to enhance and deepen *maẓmūns*. For *maẓmūns* are far more potent than words: "As *maẓmūns* are increased, meanings too are increased; as words are increased, meaning is diminished."[36]

8 THE MIND AND HEART IN POETRY

"As *maẓmūns* are increased, meanings too are increased," said Ṭabāṭabā'ī. Urdu poets of the eighteenth and nineteenth centuries "mention *maẓmūn* and meaning (*ma'nī*) again and again"; Momin, for example, boasts, "Although Momin indeed composes poetry extremely well [in general] / [Above all] where is there a meaning-maker and *maẓmūn*-achiever like me?"[1] Like *maẓmūn āfirīnī, ma'nī āfirīnī,*[2] "meaning-creation," is a fundamental goal of the ghazal poet. "The ghazal was also invented for the practice of putting meanings into ever-new forms."[3] At the very start of the tazkirah tradition, Mīr uses *tah dārī* (depth-possession) and *pech dārī* (complexity) as terms of praise; over and over he emphasizes the creation of meaning.[4] He boasts of these subtle qualities in his own poetry: "A single utterance has any number of aspects, Mīr / What a variety of things I constantly say with the tongue of the pen!" And again: "Every verse is curled and twisted like a lock of hair / Mīr's speech is of an extraordinary kind."[5]

Much later, near the end of the tradition, one of Ġhālib's letters offers a famous dictum on the subject: "My friend, poetry is the creation of meaning (*ma'nī āfirīnī*), not the measuring out of rhymes."[6] In *Water of Life*, Azad praises Ġhālib's prowess as a "lion of the thickets of *maẓmūns* and meanings" (495); both Azad (485, 522) and Hali use *ma'nī āfirīnī* as a technical term to describe effects produced not only by Ġhālib but by other poets as well.[7] Faruqi goes so far as to argue that "the greatest achievement of the 'Indian style' poets, and then of our classical poets, is that they investigated the difference between meaning (*ma'nī*) and *maẓmūn*."[8]

What is it, then, to "create meaning"? Essentially, since almost any line of poetry will have at least one meaning, *ma'nī āfirīnī* lies in the multiplication and enrichment of meaning: it is the art of creating a single verse that will elicit two or more different meanings and/or will trail along with it many strands of implication (*kināyah*).[9] Urdu has been endowed by its own grammatical and literary development with remarkable potential for *ma'nī āfirīnī*. Mīr says, for example:

kyā dilkash hai bazm jahāñ kī jāte yāñ se jise dekho
vuh ġham-dīdah ranj-kashīdah āh sarāpā ḥasrat hai[10]

Let us retain the key word for purposes of discussion:

Kyā, the gathering of the world is attractive; whomever you see
going away from here
he is sorrowful, grief-stricken—ah, he is utterly full of regret.

There are three different ways to interpret the first clause, all generated by the various senses in which *kyā* can be used. First: as an inquiry, since *kyā* at the beginning of a statement signals a yes-no question. "Is the gathering of the world attractive (or isn't it)?" (We wonder why those who are leaving the party all weep.) Second: as an exclamation of wonder, with *kyā* meaning something like "how much." "How attractive the gathering of the world is!" (Those who are leaving the party thus weep at having to depart.) Third: as an exclamation of scornful challenge, with *kyā* meaning something like "What!" "What!—[Do you think] the gathering of the world is attractive?!" (Those who are leaving thus weep over the sufferings they've endured.) The charm of the *shi'r*—virtually its only charm, since it is not one of Mīr's masterpieces—lies in these multiple interpretive possibilities, such that the mind swings back and forth among them with no help from the poet in selecting any one over the others.

While *kyā* is the most versatile, Urdu has other interrogatives as well—for example, *kaisā* ("what kind"), *kitnā* ("how much"), *kahāñ* ("where")—that can be either genuinely interrogative or (positively or negatively) exclamatory. Classical ghazal was never punctuated, which of course helped to retain such multiple possibilities. The tendency of some modern editors to insert Western-derived punctuation into *shi'rs* is thus an especially unfortunate barbarism, since it destroys certain kinds of *ma'nī āfirīnī*; in fact, it is one more symptom of the large cultural and literary problem with which the present study is concerned. Even classical Urdu prose was punctuated only very lightly, and not at all in the modern Western way.

At the heart of many instances of *ma'nī āfirīnī* is *inshā'iyah* (noninformative, nonfalsifiable) speech: speech in the interrogative, exclamatory, imperative, subjunctive, or vocative mode.[11] By contrast, speech in the *ḳhabariyah* (informative, falsifiable) mode, which makes what purport to be factual assertions about the world, is less richly endowed with multiple possibilities. The differentiation of these modes has a long history within the Islamic literary-critical tradition, and has recently been analyzed in English poetry by John Hollander.[12] Within the Urdu tradition, moreover, no poetic utterance need be irrevocably *k̤habariyah,* for it can always be read as a yes-no question from which the introductory *kyā* has been omitted—an omission very common in colloquial speech.

Another grammatical feature of Urdu is also particularly fruitful for *maʿnī āfirīnī*: the versatile and indispensable *iẓāfat,* one of the most valuable treasures Urdu appropriated from Persian. The *iẓāfat* is a construction that connects two words—the first usually a noun, the second either a noun or an adjective—with a small linking vowel. The two words connected by an *iẓāfat* can have a variety of relationships. Noun-adjective *iẓāfat*s, for example, are relatively straightforward: *kitāb-e nau* ("book"-*e* "new"), "the book that is new." But the far more common noun-noun *iẓāfat*s offer multiple interpretive possibilities: *kitāb-e dil* ("book"-*e* "heart"), the book "of"[13] the heart, may mean the book about the heart, or the book that belongs to the heart, or the book that is the heart. As can well be imagined, with a string of two or three noun-noun *iẓāfat*s in a row the interpretive possibilities multiply rapidly—with the help, furthermore, of the normal Hindi/Urdu possessive postpositions *kā/ke/kī,* which themselves have an equally wide range of meaning.

Here, for example, is Ġhālib being ostentatiously Ġhālibian, with one noun-adjective *iẓāfat* and either four or five noun-noun ones:[14]

> *nishāṭ(-e) dāġh(-e) ġham-e ʿishq kī bahār nah pūchh*
> *shiguftagī hai shahīd-e gul-e k̤hizānī-e shamʿa*[15]

Here is a literal rendering, with the noun-noun *iẓāfat*s shown as "= of =" and the noun-adjective one in brackets:

> Springtime of ecstasy (= of =) wound (= of =) grief = of =
> love, don't ask
> Flourishingness is martyr = of = [rose autumnal] = of =
> candle.

In the above verse, the parentheses show *iẓāfat*s that, formally speaking, may or may not be there. For in addition to their multivalence, *iẓāfat*s have a further gift for the poet, and it is often the greatest gift of all: they can be used in such a way that they may or may not be present. In classical ghazal, *iẓāfat*s ideally are not shown by any written marker, so that the poet's opportunities for *maʿnī āfirīnī* remain as fully open as possible. In some metrical situations, an *iẓāfat* must be present, or must not be present, to make the line scan. But in others, the line will scan either way—with of course two (or more) different meanings. In this verse, the interpretive possibilities for the first line alone include: with all possible *iẓāfats*, "Don't ask about the springtime of the ecstasy of the wound of the grief of love"; with one optional *iẓāfat*, "Oh ecstasy of the wound, don't ask about the springtime of the grief of love"; with another optional *iẓāfat*, "Oh ecstasy, don't ask about the springtime of the wound of the grief of love." With all the different internal possibilities of meaning for each *iẓāfat*, it is clear that the verse is indeed remarkably multivalent—in Mīr's words, "curled and twisted like a lock of hair."

But the most wonderful effects of *ma'nī āfirīnī* are often achieved by seemingly simpler means. Here is one of Mīr's most elegantly enigmatic *shi'rs*:

> *mīr(-e) gum-kardah chaman zamzamah-pardāz hai ek*
> *jis kī lai dām se tā gosh(-e) gul āvāz hai ek*[16]

Now here is—not a translation, but a set of literally equivalent English words, preserving all the possibilities:

> Mīr (= of =) lost garden song-performer is one
> of whom song from snare to ear (= of =) rose voice is one.

Here are several interpretations, all of which are defensible readings of these two lines:

> Mīr who has lost the garden is a unique singer
> whose song reaches undiminished from the snare to the ear
> of the rose.

The lover is a captured bird, who has been snared and has thus lost his access to the garden—but whose song still reaches the ear of the rose. The song should be diminished by distance—but it isn't. Moreover, in the ghazal universe, the rose has ears (in the form of petals), but is deaf—which raises the interesting question of how the song reaches the rose's ear.

> Mīr, the singer who has lost the garden is only one—
> the same one whose song can be heard from the snare to the ear
> of the rose

The poet is counting up the sources of the song he hears, and concludes that there is really only one singer, not two—although the range of his powerful voice is so great that there at first seem to be two singers. Perhaps the source of his power is his unique suffering: there is only one singer who has "lost the garden," and so only one who can sing so spectacularly.

> Mīr, he whom the garden has lost is one singer;
> he whose song reaches from the snare to the ear of the rose is
> one (other) singer.

The poet is counting up the sources of the songs he hears, and concludes that one and one make two different singers. Do they sing two different songs—the first a song of absolute failure, of having been "lost" by the garden (through the garden's carelessness, or jealousy, or perhaps hostility?), and the second a song of success, since even in the snare one can sing with confidence right to the ear of the rose? Or do they, in their different situations, nevertheless sing the same song? (This interpretation involving two singers can be challenged, but it can also be defended.)

> Mīr who has lost the garden is a unique singer
> whose song, from the snare to the ear, is entirely a rose-voice.

Does the fact of losing the garden, of being enmeshed in the snare, somehow confer upon the captured bird a new, deep affinity with the garden? Now that he can never sing directly to the rose again, does he sing with the rose itself wholly present in his voice?

And so on—for we are still far from exhausting the possible permutations of meaning that can be enjoyed in this single brilliant *shiʿr*. The creation of multiple interpretations is one of the glories of *maʿnī āfirīnī*.

But it is by no means the only effective strategy, for implication (*kināyah*) is also a basic technique. Hali asserts that "implication is always more eloquent than straightforwardness."[17] Here is a verse in which Mīr exploits the possibilities of implication: he says something very simple, and lets its suggestions and ramifications unfold.

> *yūñ gaʾī qad ke ḳham huʾe jaise*
> *ʿumr ik rahrav-e sar-e pul thā*[18]

> It went when the stature became bent, as if
> Age were a traveler on the bridge.

Unlike the verse about the singer(s) in the garden, this one is extremely easy to translate—and to translate in one straightforward way. The piquant first line withholds meaning; under actual performance conditions, it might be recited several times, with interludes, giving time for curiosity to develop before the second line resolved the mystery. But if the statement itself is simple, its implications are rich and subtle. There is, of course, the physical basis for the metaphor: the bent back of old age resembles the curved shape of a bridge. But that is only the beginning.

Bridges are places of transition, confined movement, and possible peril: travelers traditionally hurry across them. And since travelers do not linger in the middle of a bridge, they may well pause for a time at the near end, preparing to make the crossing; or they may press on and stop only at the far end, after the crossing has been made. After a long leisurely trip on a straight road (while the young man's posture was erect), "Age" has now made a rapid final crossing over a curved bridge. The primal metaphor "Life is a journey" is obviously and powerfully invoked—with its corollary, "Death is arrival."[19]

Moreover, Mīr is invoking the long-established associations of the Persian/Urdu phrase *sar-e pul* ("on the bridge"). For example, *yārān-e sar-e pul,* "on-the-bridge friends," are casual companions, not intimate or trusted ones. And a *va'dah-e sar-e pul,* an "on-the-bridge promise," is one made lightly, one that will not necessarily be kept. "On the bridge" was a temporary meeting place where travelers formed relationships soon to be broken. The attitude shown by "Age" toward us humans is of exactly this kind. Such suggestive use of "on the bridge" may be called wordplay, but it is really meaning-play and *ma'nī āfirīnī* as well: it creates in a small space rich and dense verbal textures, surrounded by a penumbra of suggestion.

Or consider one more example of Mīr at his (deceptively) simplest, in what to me is one of his most beautiful verses:

āvāragān-e 'ishq kā pūchhā jo maiñ nishāñ
musht-e ġhubār le ke ṣabā ne uṛā diyā[20]

When I asked for a sign of the wanderers of love,
the breeze took a handful of dust and flung it into the air.

One might naturally ask such a question of the breeze, which is itself a tireless wanderer. And what is the meaning of its response? Faruqi suggests a remarkable number of possibilities: the breeze may be implying that the wanderers of love (1) end up after death as mere handfuls of dust; (2) are as nameless and unknown as handfuls of dust; (3) are, in their essence, handfuls of dust; (4) are perpetual wanderers, as restless as handfuls of dust. Or (5) the breeze may be conveying total ignorance of their fate, as in the Urdu idiom "I know dust (= nothing)" (*ḳhāk ḳhabar hai*); or (6) the breeze may be expressing total lack of interest in their fate, so that it merely flings dust into the air instead of responding to the question. Or (7) the breeze may intend to fling dust into the inquirer's face as a sign of contempt: "Who are you to presume to ask about them?" Or (8) the breeze may be flinging dust on its head as a sign that its grief for the wanderers of love is beyond words. Or in fact (9) the question may not be addressed to the breeze at all: the inquirer may be asking some other, unresponsive third party, or merely thinking aloud—and receiving no answer except the ceaseless, indifferent movements of the breeze. "This is hardly a verse—it is a carved, faceted jewel."[21]

The elegance of *ma'nī āfirīnī,* its ability to make powerful meaning out of seemingly farfetched conceits, can be seen to special advantage in three of the following five verses; in the remaining two, its vulnerability will become equally apparent. Four of the five *shiʿrs* invoke the same traditional inhabitant of the ghazal universe, the auspicious Humā bird—the best of birds, the bird who might land on your head and make you a king. The verses start with the well-known fact that the Humā lives on a diet of nothing but bones.

Here is Mīr, in a verse that works obliquely, resting on the *maẓmūn* that love is fire. The consuming power of the lover's passion, its glory, its fatality, its obsessiveness, are all the more strongly suggested for being kept at several removes from the surface meaning.

in jaltī haḍḍiyoñ ko shāyad humā nah khāve
tab ʿishq kī hamārī pahuñchī hai ustuḳhvāñ tak[22]

These burning bones—perhaps the Humā might not eat them
The fever of my love has reached to the bone.

The lover appears to be speculating—in the *inshāʾiyah* mode, of course—quite detachedly about the fate of his bones after his (imminent?) death, and expressing only a kind of clinical observation. Traditional Indian medicine recognized a "fever of the bone," which was more or less a name for tuberculosis. The lover describes his passion as a kind of physical disease—yet one of more than physical potency, since the fiery heat in his bones will persist after his death. It is a natural disease, "fever of the bone," yet it takes him into nonnatural realms—for his bones will be scrutinized not by physicians but by the legendary Humā bird.

There is not an ounce of self-pity or sentimentality in the verse. But what exactly is the tone? It can be read with melancholy (the lover recognizes that his bones may be of no use), with pride (the lover savors the depth of his passion), with curiosity (the lover wonders whether, in fact, the Humā will eat the bones), with a reflective thoughtfulness (the lover realizes that his passion has now transcended the merely human realm and become the indestructible essence of his being). Eliot, who knew that "No contact possible to flesh / allays the fever of the bone," would have understood.

Ġhālib, in one of his Persian verses, uses the same *maẓmūn*—love is fire, the lover's bones are glowing coals—with less sensibility and more wit. He relies even more heavily on the power of implication; and he uses the *inshāʾiyah* mode, issuing a command:

dūr bāsh az rezahhā-e ustuḳhvānam ay humā
kīñ bisāṭ-e daʿvat-e murġhān-e ātash-ḳhvār hast[23]

Stay far from the fragments of my bones, oh Humā
for this feast is spread for the Fire-eater birds.

In this verse we know that the lover's bones are desirable; in fact they are a "feast." Pulverized into small, glowing fragments, spread out in utter disintegration, they look so delicious that the lover—who seems somehow to be present, with undiminished vitality and spirits, to preside as host—has to keep a sharp eye out for gate-crashers. Thus he warns off the Humā—perhaps out of consideration, since it will not be able to digest the burning fragments of bone; or perhaps out of snobbery, since only the Fire-eater birds are worthy of such a uniquely radiant offering. Of course, he never tells us explicitly that the bones are burning; we know this only by way of implication. Nor does he tell us that they are burning with love; we know this only because we carry the ghazal universe with us in our heads.

By introducing the Fire-eater birds (*murġhān-e ātash-ḳhvār*), Ġhālib heightens the whimsical quality of the verse. Some birds are regular denizens of the ghazal universe, like the Humā and—even more integrally—the *ʿanqā*, the "imaginary bird" defined by the fact that it is not really there, so that no nets of awareness can ever ensnare it. By contrast, the Fire-eater birds are only casual visitors; their appearance adds a gratuitous, playful note. (One of them, named Mūsīqār, or "Musician," burns alive while singing through the one thousand holes in its beak.) The wit of the verse rests on the vision of the lover, simultaneously dead and alive, proudly holding a feast with a very select, strictly monitored guest list—a feast consisting of his own fragmented, dispersed, and still burning bones. In this verse the lover may be speaking wryly or with resignation, but the buoyancy of his spirit is still irresistible. And, of course, he may be speaking with the exhilaration of one who has somehow triumphed in his love, who revels in it, who finds joy and pride in it even beyond death.

"Nasīm" Dihlavī (1794–1864), a shagird of Momin's, takes the idea a step further: perhaps the fire of love will destroy the lover's bones entirely.

tan shuʿlahhā-e ġham se huʾā ḳhāk ay nasīm
dekheñge ustuḳhvāñ nah hamāre humā ke nāz[24]

My body was turned into dust by the flames of grief, oh Nasīm
my bones will not see the coquetries of the Humā.

The untranslatable *nāz* can include coquetry, caprice, disdainfulness, sulking, pouting, an affectation of anger, and all manner of consciously flirtatious airs and graces. The lover admires it in the beloved, and would much rather receive it than receive no attention at all. Here the suggestion is that the lover not only has failed to receive true love from the beloved, and not only has failed to receive even coquetry—but even after death will still be ignored completely. His bones will not only be denied the fine destiny of being accepted and eaten by the Humā—they will be deprived even of the Humā's show of *nāz,* of the chance to be picked over with fastidious disdain. The bones are dust already, and so can receive no such attention. The lover seems to speak from a sort of limbo on the verge of death: his body has already become dust, but the (non)-event of the Humā is still in the future. The lover's low expectations are clearly suggested: he doesn't say that his bones will not be eaten by the Humā, but that his bones will not be picked over (and possibly rejected) by the Humā.

Once again we have a verse devoid of sentimentality, one that can be read in several tones: pride (that my passion has been so extraordinarily powerful); neutral self-examination (that this is simply the truth of the case); melancholy (that my bones will not experience even in death the kind of coquetry I longed for in life); relief (that I will be able to escape this world cleanly, leaving no trace behind). The verse turns on the many suggestions carried by the word *nāz;* applying this term to the Humā sets up a resonance between the Humā (the bone-eater, the king-maker) and the beloved (who can utterly destroy the lover, who can raise the lover to unimagined heights). The suggestions continue to unfold as the reader savors the verse; this is *ma'nī āfirīnī* of a fine order.

But how jarring it is to bring the Humā, denizen of the ghazal universe, down into something more like the real world. Sayyid Muḥammad Ḳhān "Rind" (1797–1857), a shagird of Ātash, in the same generation as Nasīm, says:

> *paṛā hangāmah hai shāyad hamāre ustuḳhvānoñ par*
> *hu'ā jhagṛā humā meñ aur sagān-e kū-e dilbar meñ*[25]

> There's perhaps been a turmoil over my bones—
> A quarrel took place between the Humā and the dogs of the beloved's street.

The ghazal universe certainly contains the possibility that the lover might die of his passion in the beloved's street, which he constantly haunts, alone and unattended. In that case, it would be possible that the dogs of her street would devour his bones, just as real dogs in a real street would. But imagine the lofty, legendary Humā actually fighting on equal terms with such dogs! "The Humā is a street dog"—an amazing *maẓmūn,* capable of various kinds of piquant development. But here, unfortunately, nothing much is made of it. Since the meaning of the verse is simply, flatly, all on the surface, the *ma'nī āfirīnī* is almost nonexistent.

The *maẓmūn* of the lover's bones as scraps has also been used with reference not to the Humā at all, but simply to "real" dogs. "Siṭvat" Lakhnavī, shagird of "Laṭāfat" Lakhnavī, says:

talkhī-e furqat thī jo beḥad nah hargiz khā sakā
haḍḍiyāñ merī sag-e jānāñ chabā kar rah gayā[26]

The bitterness of separation was so extreme that he couldn't possibly eat them
The beloved's dog merely gnawed a bit on my bones, then left them.

The beloved's own dog is, of course, a privileged creature—although even the dogs of her street are privileged, compared to all the other dogs in the world. Here the lover has had the happiness of dying at least within the beloved's courtyard, so that either the beloved's own dog finds the body, or the beloved has even deigned to order the body thrown to the dog. Here the *maẓmūn* is not of the bones as glowing coals but of the bones as scraps—with a pun on the double meaning, both culinary and mental, of "bitterness" (*talkhī*). The possibility of rejection is no longer merely speculative: here the dog actually starts to gnaw the bones, then abandons them as inedible. The *ma'nī āfirīnī* is minimal, while the *maẓmūn āfirīinī* has become crude and grotesque. The ghazal universe seems to collide in a damaging way with the "real" world.

Yet the very vulnerability, the subtlety, the refinement, of *ma'nī āfirīnī* is part of its endless fascination. The Empson of the *Seven Types of Ambiguity* would have been overjoyed to have the chance to explore it. Ġhālib is usually compared to Donne; but many others of the finest Western poets would also have been at home in the ghazal world. It would be hard to find a more perfect example of *ma'nī āfirīn* than Yeats's lines, "O body swayed to music, O brightening glance, / How can we know the dancer from the dance?"

· · ·

The ghazal could accommodate the most cerebral and "metaphysical" poetry; but it always had ample room for poetry of quite a different sort. It was famous for speaking both to the mind and to the heart. Around 1750, Mīr composed a *shi'r* that not only identified the two great poets of the day (and envisioned, tongue in cheek, a grim future for the language when they were gone), but also specified the qualities that marked their greatness:

nah ho kyūñ reḳhtah be shorish o kaifiyyat o ma'nī
gayā ho mīr dīvānah rahā saudā so mastānā[27]

Why shouldn't Reḳhtah [= Urdu] be devoid of *shorish* and *kaifiyat* and *ma'nī*
Mīr has gone mad, and there remains Saudā—who's drunk.

In addition to the quality of *ma'nī*, or meaning, Mīr names the two qualities of *shorish*, which may be roughly rendered as "passion," and *kaifiyat*,[28] which may be perhaps even more roughly translated as "mood."

The term *shorish* has a range of meanings involving tumult, turmoil, disturbance, and bitterness; it can even be used to refer to a political insurrection. But here the reference is to inner turmoil, so that "passion" or "passionateness" might be a reasonable English counterpart. A variant form of the term, also common, is the adjectival *shor angez*, "passion-arousing," which has been used occasionally by Ġhālib and repeatedly by Mīr.[29] Mīr boasts, for example, "On every page, on every leaf, is a *shor angez* verse / The aspect of Doomsday is the aspect of my volume as well"; and again, "Wherever you look, a *shor angez* verse turns up / A turmoil like Doomsday is everywhere in my volume."[30] Azad speaks of a "writhing" verse (198).

A verse with *shorish* is a powerful, emotion-charged expression, usually not narrowly personal, of the lover's experience of life. The form of the expression is unsentimental, and we are invited to experience it as deeply true. The verse conveys a state of strong feeling on the part of the lover and implicitly (though not directly) invites us to share it. The lover's simplicity, authenticity, and passion make his voice authoritative. In a verse of *shorish* the lover speaks with a sudden surge of power that instantly comes through. Azad writes approvingly of poetry that is "as full of impact as a fingernail jabbing into the liver" (376). The appeal of *shorish* is immediate: the lover is the one real voice of the ghazal world, and that whole world suddenly opens to us in his speech.

For just these reasons the power of *shorish* is extremely hard to convey in translation. It is something that must almost be demonstrated ad hominem. If you feel it, you feel it strongly and unmistakably, but it does not lend itself readily to the kind of analysis possible in the case of *maẓmūn āfirīnī* or *ma'nī āfirīnī*. There is much work yet to be done here. For the present I offer only a few examples, knowing that they cannot manage to be as powerful in translation.

Here is a verse of Mīr's that is not only a masterpiece of *shorish* but also contains the word itself:

zindāñ meñ bhī shorish nah ga'ī apne junūñ kī
ab sang mudāvā hai is āshuftah sarī kā[31]

Even in prison, the *shorish* of my madness didn't go—
now stone is the cure for this distraction.

The lover, who sometimes behaves like a self-destructive madman, is liable at such times to be chained up in a prison cell. If the tumult and bitterness of passion cannot be controlled even by confinement, the only remaining remedy is "stone"—a stone wall to beat his head against, a stone to crush his head with, or the stones thrown by taunting boys when they see a madman. In the lover's head is a tangle of confusion and distraction; stone is simple. The lover's mental processes are overwhelmed by emotion; stone is unfeeling. The lover is tormented by his consciousness; stone could be used to render him unconscious. The lover suffers, ultimately, from the disease of life; stone, a means of death, a symbol of lifelessness, represents the final "cure." All this—without a trace of self-pity—is conveyed by the lover's own brief, stark, powerful diagnosis of his case.

Mīr's contemporary Dard conveys instead a passionate urgency of inquiry, in a verse of doubly *inshā'iyah* form:

mujh par bhī to yih 'uqdah tū khol ṣabā bāre
ẕulfoñ ne kise bhejā yih nāmah-e pechīdah[32]

For me, too, open this knot at last, oh breeze!
The curls have sent this convoluted letter—to whom?

The verse is entirely in the *inshā'iyah* mode and addresses the breeze, which is bearing the scent of someone's wonderful dark, twisting curls. The breeze has carried the scent from afar, conveying a hint of it to many people in passing, but ultimately what is its message, and for whom is it destined? The breeze knows, and the word "too" (*bhī*) suggests that others might already know, while "at last" (*bāre*) suggests that the lover himself has long been desperately eager to find out. To "open the knot" is a common Persian and Urdu image for what we might call unraveling a knotty problem; it also evokes the act of loosening tied-up curls of hair. The letter sent by the curls is *pechīdah,* literally "twisted" and thus by extension "convoluted" and hard to understand; and the lovely sinuous letters of the Urdu script curl on the page like locks of hair. A *nāmah-e pechīdah* is also a "fancily folded letter," carefully creased into some elaborate shape; and something *pechīdah* is "complex" and has many meanings. This convoluted letter, sent not even by the beloved but by the "curls" themselves, is both thoroughly mysterious and infinitely desirable. It arouses a longing that is apparently doomed to frustration, since the verse is full of uncertainties that the lover has no means of resolving: all he asks of the breeze (which may well refuse to respond) is the name of the addressee—who is likely to be someone else entirely.

Or here is Ġhālib, imagining the lover as a wild bird who has been captured and caged in a particularly cruel manner:

pinhāñ thā dām saḳht qarīb āshiyān ke
uṛne nah pāye the kih giriftār ham hu'e[33]

The net was hidden hard against the nest
I hadn't managed to fly—when I was trapped.

The adverbial phrase *saḳht qarīb*, "extremely near," I have translated as "hard against"; the archaic "hard by" would have been another possibility. For the literal meaning of *saḳht* is "hard," and when used adverbially it means "very, extremely, excessively"—but with negative overtones that leap at once into the mind: "severely, violently, harshly, painfully, cruelly." The lover makes a matter-of-fact statement, and permits himself only the most indirect, the most marginal comment on his fate: the secondary overtones of a single adverb. The vision of passion under such provocation, yet under such restraint, creates a classic effect of *shorish*.

If Ġhālib's indirectness can be subtle, it can also be violent in its imagery of passion:

abhī ham qatl gah kā dekhnā āsāñ samajhte haiñ
nahīñ dekhā shināvar jū-e ḳhūñ meñ tere tausan ko[34]

I still think it will be easy to see the killing-ground—
I haven't seen your horse swimming in a river of blood.

In the early stages of love, the lover underestimates the ordeals ahead of him. He expects that to die of and for love, to die at the beloved's command or even by the beloved's own hand, will be pure joy. He does not realize the deadly absoluteness, the grim extravagance, of the spectacle that awaits him. He is not fated to be the only victim. The carnage will be unimaginable: blood will flow in the streets, the beloved's horse will literally swim in it. Even the first stage, even to behold the *qatl gah* (place of killing), will not be an easy thing. The lover depicts himself as emotionally naive and unprepared—yet in another sense he is not, for he knows what's in store for him. Still, knowing what he knows, he gives not the slightest hint of fear, of second thoughts, of a wish to back out while there's still time. The lover makes wry fun of his own naïveté—but his eyes are wide open. With no illusions, no heroic posturing, he goes on.

It is clear that the love of *shorish* remains powerful right into the twentieth century, when other classical possibilities of the ghazal have been all too little remembered—and even less valued. Examples of modern *shorish* are easy to find, such as this from the early-twentieth-century poet "Jigar" Murādābādī (1890–1961):

ay muḥtaṣib nah phenk mire muḥtaṣib nah phenk
ẓālim sharāb hai are ẓālim sharāb hai[35]

Oh Officer, don't throw it out—my dear Officer, don't throw it out!
You tyrant, it's wine!—oh you tyrant, it's wine!

The public-morals patrolman (*muḥtaṣib*) is a stock character in the ghazal world; his chief role is to detect the forbidden act of wine drinking and to destroy the wine. Here the lover makes an altogether passionate appeal to him to refrain. The appeal is urgent, even desperate; its language is entirely colloquial. And the nature of the appeal? It is purely ad hominem: how can the wretch not see that it's *wine* that he's wasting? In one sense the *muḥtaṣib* knows very well that it's wine that he's pouring off—but in another sense he obviously doesn't know at all. The lover's urgency and passion testify to the marvelous qualities of the wine: its power to intoxicate, to bestow visions, to bring escape from the self. Yet these qualities are conveyed only by suggestion, and only through the lover's *shorish*.

The following verse, which we have already examined in another context, is also a fine example of *shorish*. Even in translation it retains something of its power:

ay sarv-e ravāñ ay jān-e jahāñ āhistah guẓar āhistah guẓar
jī bhar ke maiñ tujh ko dekh to lūñ bas itnā ṭhahar bas itnā ṭhahar

Oh walking cypress, oh life of the world, pass slowly, pass slowly
Let me look at you to my heart's content—only stop that long, only stop that long.

· · ·

If *shorish* is hard to describe in English, *kaifiyat*, or "mood," is even more elusive. The term *kaifiyat* has a central meaning of "state" or "condition," with a tendency to mean a desirable state: an exquisite, inwardly flourishing, even ineffable mood, sometimes with mystical overtones. While *shorish* is a quality of passion shown by the lover, who is the protagonist of the ghazal world, *kaifiyat* is a quality of response located in the hearer or reader of the poetry; it is a mood evoked by the verse as a whole.[36] Azad reports that on one occasion a young poet recited a most successful verse, and its hearers repeated it again and again. Even on the following evening they were still reciting it: "In the mood (*kaifiyat*) of his *shiʿr*, the night passed with an extraordinary pleasure" (113). On another occasion, Mīr didn't even notice a visitor's arrival. He was pacing obliviously back and forth, apparently absorbed in the mood (*kaifiyat*) of a single line which he kept repeating: "This time too the days of spring have somehow or other passed" (211).

In a verse of *kaifiyat*, meaning is almost irrelevant; on the first hearing the meaning may hardly even register, yet a certain mood pervades the hearer's mind. In English poetry, mysterious lines like Nashe's "Brightness falls from the air" evoke a similar response. The mood of *kaifiyat* is usually a melancholy one, but always one to be savored and enjoyed. A verse of *kaifiyat* often has a very simple vocabulary and an air of innocence—with depths behind it, but generally not ones accessible to rational analysis. As the great Indo-Persian poet ʿAbd ul-Qādir "Bedil" (1644–1720) put it, "a good *shiʿr* has no meaning."[37] Ṭabāṭabāʾī has said of Bedil himself, "I agree with Hali's statement that 'you may not understand Bedil's poetry, but it still sounds good.'"[38] Eliot spoke of a certain poem as "delightful," while admitting that he could not at all explain what it meant, and he doubted that the author could either. What he admired was the mood it evoked: the poem had "an effect somewhat like that of a rune or charm," it produced "the effect of a dream."[39]

Ġhālib, in a letter to a close friend, contrasts one poet's work that is *shor angez* with another's that is *taṣavvuf kī chāshnī se labrez*, "overflowing with a mystical flavor."[40] The word *chāshnī* ("flavor"), with its suggestions of a sweet/sour taste, a relish, a rich syrup, combines with the adjective *labrez*, "overflowing, enthusiastic," to convey the immediacy and power of *kaifiyat*. This is just how, according to Azad, Żauq responded to certain verses: "He used to smile, and show his joy on his face, as if he was established within the *kaifiyat* of the *shiʿr*" (494).

Giving examples of *kaifiyat* is of course next to impossible in translation, for the verses lose most of their magic persuasive power. But a few attempts can be made. Here is Mīr's epitaph for the lover, which speaks in a voice absolutely simple and quiet:

nāmurādānah zīst kartā thā
mīr kā ṭaur yād hai ham ko[41]

He used to live without hope—
I remember what Mīr was like.

In this short and seemingly plain verse, *nāmurādānah* (hopelessly, without hope) glows like a fine jewel in a simple setting: it is the first word, an unusually long word (while all the other words are unusually short), and it occupies fully a quarter of the syllables of the whole verse. It defines the whole memory that a friend might have of Mīr—and lingers in the hearer's mind with a wonderful *kaifiyat*. Mīr provides another epitaph for the lover, in what has been called a "verse of pure *kaifiyat*":

āʾī bahār o gulshan gul se bharā hai lekin
har goshah-e chaman meñ ḳhālī hai jā-e bulbul[42]

Spring has come, and the garden is full of roses, but
in every corner of the garden, the nightingale's place is empty.

How many nightingales had been there, to have left empty places in "every corner" of the garden—or does the one nightingale's absence echo so persistently? The new spring renews the roses—but where has the nightingale gone?

In a verse of *shorish* cited earlier, Mīr's contemporary Dard asked the breeze about the "convoluted letter" sent by the beloved's curls. Here he addresses the breeze in a verse-sequence of pure *kaifiyat*:

yahī paiġhām dard kā kahnā
gar ṣabā kū-e yār meñ guẓre
kaun sī rāt ān milī'egā
din bahut intiẓār meñ guẓre[43]

Deliver this message from Dard
if, oh breeze, you ever pass through the beloved's street:
Which night will you come and meet me?
So many days have passed in waiting.

The breeze is once again an uncertain messenger: it may or may not pass through the beloved's street—because the beloved lives so far away, or is so inaccessible that even the breeze is denied entry. But the message is the stubborn simplicity of longing: it is patient, humble, yet importunate in the way that love must be. The meeting is, after all, presented not as a question of "if," but merely of "when," and it is clearly to take place by night rather than day. But as for "which night," the expression permits uncertainty to linger (*kaun sī* is much vaguer than the alternative *kis*). The lover does—and doesn't—and does—have hope.

Sometimes a verse of *kaifiyat* may have little apparent meaning, as in this famous one of Muṣḥafī's:

chale bhī jā jaras-e ġhunchah kī ṣadā pih nasīm
kahīñ to qāfilah-e nau bahār ṭhahregā[44]

Keep moving along to the sound of the opening of the bud, oh
breeze
Somewhere the caravan of the new spring will halt.

What does it mean exactly? It is hard to say. Buds are indeed thought to open with a tiny but audible click. It is not the verse's meaning that appeals, but the evocative quality of the images. And what do they evoke? A promise of rest, a threat of death, an alluring melancholy—above all, a feeling of the mysteriousness of things.

Even more remarkably, a verse of *kaifiyat* may have an illogical meaning that somehow fails to mar its effect. Here is one of the best-known verses of Faiẓ:

nah gañvā'o nāvak-e nīm kash dil-e rezah rezah gañvā diyā
jo bache haiñ sang sameṭ lo tan-e dāġh dāġh luṭā diyā[45]

Don't waste the half-drawn arrow—I've laid waste to every
fragment of my heart
Save the leftover stones—I've caused my wound-covered body
to be despoiled.

There are at least two serious problems with the imagery of this verse. A heart that has been riddled with arrows, so that one more arrow is unnecessary, might look like a pincushion, but it would not be in the kind of tiny fragments (*rezah rezah*) that suggest a cannon shot or an explosion. Even more problematically, *dāġh dāġh* normally means "spotted, speckled" rather than "wound-covered" as I have (by courtesy) translated it above. And has the speaker really caused his own body to be "looted"? The second line is merely a weaker echo of the first, and thus anticlimactic. The verse ought to seem at least clumsy, if not somewhat ludicrous. Yet it does not. One must make a mental effort to break out of its spell and raise rational objections. The verse seduces directly, without detouring through the brain. If it succeeds, a wave of emotion flows through the reader or hearer. The contrast is traditionally drawn between complex, sophisticated verses, which evoke an exclamatory *Vāh!* of admiration—and verses, including those full of *kaifiyat*, which evoke an *Āh*, a sigh. (Azad praises Żauq for creating such multifaceted poetry that it evokes both responses [455].)

Basic concepts like *rabṭ, ravānī, maẓmūn āfirīnī, ma'nī āfirīnī, shorish,* and *kaifiyat* are perhaps as close as we can now come to the poetics inherited by Azad and Hali. These terms deserve much more critical attention than they have yet received. Shamsur Rahman Faruqi's work, and my own dialogue with his work, have not yet gone as far as we both intend. There is much more to be said about these terms; but on the basis of extant materials from the period, there is not nearly as much more to be said about them as we would wish. The task remains frustratingly inferential. A great deal was lost when, in the generation after 1857, the direct heirs to the classical oral tradition were unable to claim their patrimony. Instead, they had to sell their birthright for a mess of all too realistic Victorian pottage.

Part Three

LIGHT FROM ENGLISH LANTERNS

Those with new-style educations, whose minds
are illumined by light from English lanterns,
complain of our tazkirahs.

AZAD, *Water of Life*

9 THE CYCLES OF TIME

The classical vision of poetics inherited by Azad and Hali aspired to timelessness. Poetry in any age was to be deeply interwoven with earlier poetry; poets of the present were to know, memorize, admire, and emulate the poetry of their predecessors. The rules of the prestigious "game of words" had to be constant over time, to permit comparison and competition—or else how could the game be played at all? Any changes must take the form of adjustments or refinements, mediated by a consensus of senior ustads. Poets of the present were proud to inherit the superb achievements of the whole Persian and Urdu past, and to play the great game of words through the same time-honored "elegant encounters."

Thus the tazkirah tradition had no special concern with time. As we have seen, people organized their "notebooks" and tazkirahs however they pleased: several tazkirahs discuss poets in almost entirely random order, while others adopt idiosyncratic methods (special categories for the writer's personal friends, and so on). Tazkirah writers generally preferred a synchronic, alphabetical arrangement, because they experienced the poetry as a unified whole. When it came to their own work, individual poets shared this preference: rather than dating their poems, they arranged them first by genre and then alphabetically (by the last letter of the refrain). They did this not only in a single volume but even in their complete works (*kulliyāt*), so that their lifelong oeuvre became all of a piece.[1] Thus, as Azad laments, we usually cannot say of a poet "which work was written when, and how his temperament inclined from time to time" (153). The whole Persian and Urdu literary tradition, stretching back for centuries, was directly available.

All this cultural security broke down, however, in the aftermath of the

Rebellion. The political, economic, and intellectual organization of society was drastically changed. Azad and Hali had seen an "instructive reversal" in their world; the nature of time, and its power to inflict change, became a lifelong problem for them both.

· · ·

In *Water of Life,* Azad began with a long historical and linguistic introduction, and then proceeded to divide Urdu poetry into five *daurs*. The literal meaning of *daur* is "going around" or "circle," and he imagined the poets of each *daur* as constituting a kind of mushairah: the table of contents introduced, for example, "the first *daur* of *Water of Life,* in which Valī and his excellent contemporaries are seated in assembly" (5). In his preface to the first *daur,* Azad continued the imagery—"Look, the mushairah is resplendent with the aristocratic and the elite"—and went on to describe the appearance and demeanor of those present (81). Each later *daur* had its own mushairah as well, introduced in an equally visual style. But the word *daur* also means "period," and Azad used the chronological sequence of *daurs* to organize his great tazkirah-cum-history.

For the *daurs* are soon revealed as stages in a clearly marked sequence of development. The poets of the first *daur* write simply and naturally: "Whatever they see before their eyes, and whatever thoughts then pass through their minds—this is what comes to their lips." They use no "convoluted ideas, far-fetched similes, subtle metaphors." Such spontaneity is characteristic of every language and its poetry "as long as it is in a state of childhood." Although their *maẓmūns* are often "light and commonplace," these early poets have a "simplicity and informality" that give their work an "inborn beauty" and "natural excellence" (82).

The second *daur* is "the springtime of the natural beauty of the language," the time when "the flowers of *maẓmūns* in the garden of eloquence are in their natural youthful prime" and show an "inborn grace" that shuns all artificial adornment (106). "In what clear language, and with what simple expressions, these poets conveyed their thoughts!" Moreover, "the mood they expressed in their poetry pervaded their heart and soul." This is why every verse you look at is "overflowing with 'movingness' (*tāṡīr*)." Such genuineness and sincerity are "just what the Europeans (*ahl-e firang*) are seeking today" when they say that poetry "should show the real condition of each thing" (122).

Trouble begins in the third *daur.* When its poets "entered the garden of speech" and strolled about in it, they saw the earlier *daurs'* "flower of eloquence, which was showing its inborn, natural, youthful prime in a natural springtime." But now "they too had to make their names," so they "wanted to go beyond their elders." Although they "ran around a great deal in the surrounding fields, all the flowers had already been used." Thus, "when they found nothing before them, having no choice, they raised their buildings high." Azad promises his readers a wonderful show: "Just look—they won't [merely] use *maẓmūns* of height, they'll bring down the stars from the sky. They won't merely get praise from connoisseurs—they'll get worship!" In the process, these poets used a certain amount of "elaborateness"—but only, Azad says in their defense, "like the dew on roses, or a mirror held up to a picture," so that it added pleasure, and did not obscure what lay behind. Still, the damage was done: their "high-flying temperaments" caused them to turn their faces "upwards." Alas, "if only they had gone forward, so that they would have emerged from the limited field of beauty and love, and galloped their horses into fields that knew no bounds, and that were free of wonders and refinements!" (123–24).

The fourth *daur* carries the process a step further. The poets of this period are frivolous; they are wits and jesters who will "make you laugh until your jaw grows tired." But they "will neither take a single step to move forward, nor raise earlier buildings higher." Instead, they will "wander among them, leaping and bounding" and "use one house to decorate another." They will keep changing the color of everything they show. "Taking the same flowers and dipping them in perfume, they will sometimes weave a garland, sometimes adorn curls of hair, sometimes make flower-balls and fling them around to create a Holī festival" (221).

By the time of the fifth *daur,* exhaustion is setting in. The poets in this *daur* are of two types. Some use "old branches and yellow leaves" to make "new colors and new types of bouquets." Others are of such "lofty imagination" that they employ "vapors of thought to send the breezes of invention flying through the air—and use them, like towers made of fireworks, to reach a high level." Rather than exploring the limits of the terrain around them, they fly so high that some reach an altitude at which "the sun becomes a star," and some "fly up and just keep on flying." They call their practice *ḳhiyāl bandī* and *nāzuk ḳhiyālī,* but in fact "poetry is their magic, and they are the master magicians of their time." Their artistry cannot be doubted, but it is only of a certain kind: when they notice a "flower of *maẓmūn*" swaying in the breeze in the garden of eloquence, "they will take its buds, and use the point of a pen to make drawings on them that can't be seen without glasses" (325). They face a fundamental problem: "Earlier poets had already made use of every single leaf in the gardens around them—now where could they get new flowers?" They are trapped: they find "no road onward, and no equipment for making a road."

The problem is not theirs alone, but appears in Persian and Arabic also, and in other languages as well. Even English is not exempt: "Although I don't know English I do know this much—that its later generations too complain of the same difficulty" (326).

Among the various metaphors Azad uses to describe the *daurs*, the ubiquitous one is that of flowers as *maẓmūns* and poetry as a "garden of eloquence." The primal action of the poet seems to consist of picking flowers, in a state of springlike, flourishing innocence and youthful vigor. This state seems, ideally, to be shared by the language, the poetry, and the poets alike; it is a "natural" state and is "just what the Europeans are seeking today." And it is a state that, by definition, cannot endure; later poets cannot recapture it, and whatever else they do is less satisfactory. The problems of loss of direction, of being trapped in exhausted fields of dead leaves, are seen as universal. The very achievements of earlier generations create painful difficulties for their successors.

Of course, the real flow of Azad's narrative constantly violates this deterministic scheme of *daur*-based growth and decay. Early in his history, after all, Azad tells us the emblematic story of how thoroughly Mīr preferred his inner garden—the crumpled drafts of ghazals lying on the floor—to the real, outer garden all around him. No flower picking for him! As this anecdote shows, Mīr's ghazals were not "natural" and spontaneous outpourings of emotion, immediately reflecting the poet's feelings, but were the product of struggle, of many reworkings, of old versions crumpled and tossed on the floor. Azad's anecdotes about ustads, shagirds, *iṣlāḥ*, mushairahs, and so on, don't by any means reveal a steady decline in poetic satisfaction, achievement, or "naturalness" as the *daurs* progress—much less a sense that all the available poetic material has been "used up" by earlier poets. Moreover, the revered Żauq is a member of the fifth *daur*—yet he emerges as a universal genius, the culmination of the tradition, and none of the supposedly inevitable difficulties of his exhausted *daur* seem to trouble him for a moment.

Creating so many *daurs* within such a narrow span of time posed chronological problems as well. For Azad chose to begin the classical poetic tradition proper with Valī (1667–1720/25), largely ignoring the several centuries of fruitful literary development in the Deccan from which Valī's poetry had emerged.[2] Within the brief one-and-a-half-century period between Valī and Ġhālib, there was, of course, much overlapping of generations and of individual poets' lives. In several cases Azad actually put shagirds in the first *daur*, and poets whom he declared to be their ustads in the second and even third *daurs*.[3] Shāh Ḥātim (1699–1783), whom Azad put in the second *daur*, outlived four of the seven poets in the third *daur*.

The life spans of two important poets of the fourth *daur*, Jur'at (1748–1810) and Mīr "Ḥasan" (1727–1786), were completely contained within the life span of Mīr (1722–1810)—whom Azad put in the third *daur*. Mīr, who lived to be eighty-eight, wrote poetry all his life and produced six separate volumes; his work spanned more than half of the whole historical period about which Azad was writing. How could Mīr be so firmly assigned to a single *daur* in the first place? Such difficulties arise from the vexed question of how, and on what basis, Azad drew his dividing lines between *daur*s.

While the *daur*s were roughly chronological, they were not—and could not be—perfectly so; and in any case Azad made no effort to assign them beginning and ending dates. Each *daur* appears in fact to be defined, as well as constituted, by the particular group of poets assigned to it. Thus to make the *daur* system intelligible, we have to believe that these groups of poets differed from one another in coherent, consistent, adequately describable ways. But is the third-*daur* poetry of Mīr, for example, really one level more "natural" than the fourth-*daur* poetry of Mīr Ḥasan, and two levels more "natural" than the fifth-*daur* poetry of Żauq? (And what, of course, does it mean to be "natural"?)

The overgrown fifth *daur* poses particular problems, for it contains no fewer than eight poets—Nāsiḳh, "Ḳhalīq," Ātash, Shāh Naṣīr, Momin, Żauq, Ġhālib, and "Anīs"—of whom almost all are strong, important ustads who loom large in Urdu literature and have their own distinct and recognizable styles. It is impossible to think of *any* rubric—much less one of generalized "exhaustion" or "high-flying" tendencies—that would adequately draw them all together as a *daur* over against other *daur*s. For since the poets from adjacent *daur*s were often virtual contemporaries, and knew each other's work intimately, and were trained in the same way by the same ustads, and sought to please the same audiences, it is hard to believe that *daur*-based differences among them could actually be well marked and consistent. Certainly the burden of proof rests heavily on Azad to convince us that this is the case.

But Azad not only fails to convince us—he hardly even tries. Beyond the minor linguistic changes over time that he occasionally adduces as evidence, he never sets forth the (presumably special) literary characteristics of each *daur* with any cogency. His few metaphorical images at the beginning and end of his account of each *daur* do not serve even to differentiate the *daur*s in theory, much less to persuade us that the poets in each *daur* really share those special qualities. Visions of a whole *daur* picking flowers together or leaping from building to building or flying up to the sky do not suffice. In fact his vision of each *daur* as a single mushairah only serves to remind us how many different mushairahs poets attended in their lives, and how contentious and controversial even a single mushairah could be. Why, for that matter, should there be exactly five *daur*s, rather than four or six or some other number? Azad never provides any rationale for the system as a whole. He lays down the law for each *daur* with a firm, though mostly metaphorical, introduction; then, once he is safely launched into the *daur* itself, he seems to heave a sigh of relief and forget his own framework almost entirely.

Azad's real vision of the poetry is in fact so much more complex than his "official" vision that again and again he undercuts his own *daur*-based approach. From the introduction to *Water of Life,* for example, we learn that the poets of even the first *daur,* rather than being simple and natural, made a practice of using elaborate wordplay:

> At the beginning of [the account of] Urdu poetry, it is worth mentioning that in Sanskrit one word has quite a number of meanings. For this reason, in it, and in its offshoot Braj Bhasha, wordplay with double meanings and punning (*īhām*) was the foundation of verses. In Persian, this figure exists, but less commonly. In Urdu, at the very first, the foundation of poetry was laid on it. And among the poets of the first *daur,* this edict remained constantly in force. (75–76)[4]

Later he laments this fondness for wordplay: "God knows how the elders of his [Valī's] time became so enthusiastic for this! Perhaps the style of *duhrās* [= *dohās*], which were the wild native foliage of the language of Hindustan, lent its color" (81). So much for the alleged simplicity of the first *daur!* (And of Braj Bhasha, a point on which Azad is equally contradictory.)

It has been argued that Azad's *daur*s are so arbitrarily defined and poorly explicated that he perhaps borrowed the scheme blindly from English sources.[5] In specifically literary terms, the outlines of the idea were available no further afield than Wordsworth's "Appendix on Poetic Diction," which he added to the *Lyrical Ballads* in 1802: "The earliest poets of all nations generally wrote from passion excited by real events; they wrote naturally, and as men." But then, Wordsworth notes with regret, things changed: "In succeeding times, Poets, and men ambitious of the fame of Poets, perceiving the influence of such language . . . set themselves to a mechanical adoption of these figures of speech, and . . . frequently applied them to feelings and thoughts with which they had no natural connection whatsoever."[6] The emphasis on "natural" as a term of praise, and on an inevitable temporal progression downward from emotion toward artifice, is just what lies at the heart of Azad's scheme of *daur*s.

However, Azad had no need to look even as far as Wordsworth. The Islamic side of his own culture offered a powerful paradigm in Ibn Ḳhaldūn, with his vision of hardy warriors coming in from the desert, taking over the city, and gradually, irresistibly, being softened and transformed by urban luxury over several generations—until they fall prey to some new band of hardy warriors from the desert.[7] And the Indic side of his heritage of course offered the traditional system of *yugs*, in which the virtue, health, and natural order of the universe decline over time during four long ages, culminating in dissolution—followed by eventual renewal (though only after an inconvenient number of eons have passed). But we need not rely too much on such speculation, for in fact many particulars of Azad's *daurs* seem to have been borrowed without acknowledgment from two earlier Urdu writers who had devised similar—and equally problematical—temporal divisions.[8]

The *daurs* were, literarily speaking, new bottles into which Azad poured the old wine of traditional anecdote. But their rigid temporal determinism made them very awkward containers. They were shaped not by the poetry itself, but by Azad's paradoxical double vision. Azad the progressive needed to show that the old poetry was moribund anyway—through no one's fault, but by the laws of its own internal history, by the decree of Time itself, so that leaving it behind and moving on to fresher fields was both absolutely necessary and entirely desirable. And Azad the lover of the past needed to exalt earlier times, to mourn for the lost world, to give scope to his lifelong nostalgia; even the fifth *daur*, the terminal one, could contain the magnificent Żauq. Consigning the old poetry irrevocably to the past, proving that its life span was over, allowed Azad to depict it as a lost Paradise—while also condemning it, and endorsing a very different sort of poetry for the present and future.

Azad places his faith in the tremendous power of poetry. Urdu in particular owes all its expressive capability, all its creativity, all its beauty and vividness, in fact everything it has, to its poets (27). The necessary breakthrough into a new poetry can and must be made. No doubt the process of adjustment will be painful, but Urdu is fortunate to have English as a source of stimulation and technical help, continually "giving *iṣlāḥ* to our literature."[9] It is time to look ahead, time now to begin creating poetry for today and tomorrow. Dividing the old poetry so carefully and rigorously into temporal *daurs*, measuring out its life with coffee spoons, is a way of putting it into storage forever.

Whatever their psychological value, for critical purposes the *daurs* are worse than useless. Instead of highlighting the real qualities of real poems, they impose a framework that is arbitrary, misleading, and hostile. They impose a framework designed first to kill the poetry—and then to prove that it died of old age. The remarkable thing is not that Azad invented a badly flawed system, but that almost everyone since has faithfully carried it on. Azad's scheme of division into *daurs* has become the foundation of Urdu literary history: it has been "extremely widely accepted" for the whole past century. "From Hali to the *ḥāl* (present), the effects of this division can be seen everywhere."[10]

· · ·

Hali's famous *Introduction to Poetry and Poetics* was published in 1893, but he had been working on it at least since at least 1882, which means that he must have started it, at the latest, fairly soon after reading and reviewing *Water of Life*. For in 1882 he wrote to a friend about his plan "to set forth means for the *iṣlāḥ* of Urdu poetry, which has become extremely corrupt and injurious," and "to make clear how much benefit poetry, if it is founded on excellent principles, can bring to the community."[11] His methodology, like Azad's, included charting the movement of poetry over time. Not surprisingly, he shared Azad's general vision: he too saw an inevitable development from a desirable simplicity toward an unfortunate artifice, ending in some sort of decay or death. But while Azad was chiefly concerned to demarcate the stages of Urdu poetry over the previous century and a half, Hali painted with broader strokes, and on a larger canvas. His interest in Islamic history led him to emphasize the workings of a similar temporal progression within Arabic poetry. He maintained that Arabs, and Muslims in general, have more poets than any other group, and love and reward them more.[12] Early Arabic poetry was full of fervor, enthusiasm, and genuine feeling (78–80). Poets wrote about the events of the day; or the qualities of their favorite camels and horses; or their own families (36–37). They considered lies and exaggeration to be poetic vices (100–101); even their odes were generally realistic and accurate (190).

"But unfortunately, from the time of the [eighth-century] ʿAbbāsid caliphate, this true fervor began to grow less, and finally imitation spread through all the genres of poetry"; real beloveds were replaced by fake names, real towns by imaginary ones (80). Both poetry and society entered an age of decline (37). Although real love is always unique to each individual, "when description becomes entirely false and love only imitative, then poets are forced to repeat forever the things that have been written before" (38). Thus "from the time of the ʿAbbāsids till today, falsehood and exaggeration have been making constant progress"; by now they are not only permissible, but are considered an adornment. And once falsehood and exaggeration entered the poetry, "from that time its decline began" (100).

The same blight can be seen in Persian as well. "It is certain that the first [Persian] ghazal poets must have adopted as the property and domain of love, in a manner entirely natural[13] and straightforward, the beloved's face, beauty, glances, airs and graces, and so forth." But change was inevitable: "After them, people used these things in ornaments involving representation (*majāz*) and metaphor." For example, they described the beloved's beauty as a sword, and "from this novelty and freshness, the *maẓmūn* became more subtle and enjoyable." But the problem worsened over time: "When later generations fell upon this *maẓmūn*, and no other metaphor came to hand that was better than the metaphor of the ancients, and the desire for novelty seized them, they ignored the representational meaning of the sword and began to take it as a real, particular sword" (106). Hali gives a number of examples of this process of imaginative elaboration over time, and concludes: "In this way later generations took every *maẓmūn*, which the early poets had used in a natural way, beyond the limits of nature into another world" (109).

Hali, like Azad, saw this process as a universal problem. "In every language natural poetry has always been the portion of the early poets" (105). Later poets, by contrast, face grave risks. If they don't do anything but imitate, "if they remain within the limits of this narrow circle of thoughts that the early poets have expressed," then "their poetry gradually declines from a natural state—so much so that they end up very far from the straight road of nature" (105–6). This bleak prospect is not quite unrelieved. Hali does recognize that later poets can sometimes improve on the work of earlier ones; he gives examples, including a personal anecdote in which someone with "a correct taste in poetry" finds a verse of Ḥāfiẓ's inferior to a similar verse of Ġhālib's. "Sometimes some deficiency remains in the work of earlier poets, which later ones supply"; sometimes, for example, "earlier poets consider some *maẓmūn* to be expressible in only one given style" and then "later ones create a new style for it" (147–48). Later poets build on the work of earlier ones, as "one lamp is lit from another" (150). There can, it seems, be exceptions to the process of decline—but only local and limited ones. As Azad somehow in practice leaves room for Żauq, Hali leaves a bit of room, even in theory, for Ġhālib.

The general view set forth by Azad and Hali, however, seems to imply a series of cycles throughout history, with "natural" poetry arising in a culture, losing its naturalness over time, declining, and finally dying, as the culture makes some radical breakthrough that leads to a fresh poetic start. English too is subject to this process and provides individual (good) examples; it is a special case, as we will see, and is not discussed very systematically. But the languages Azad and Hali use as their main case studies—Arabic, Persian, and Urdu—all seem to be in the stage of decline, facing an uncertain future. Neither Azad nor Hali gives any example of a real poetic breakthrough, a successful restoration of naturalness after the collapse of a worn-out tradition. Hali, reviewing *Water of Life*, criticizes Azad for this omission: he notes that the introduction contains an "extremely fine" history of Urdu poetry, but that "in it no mention has been made of 'natural poetry,' the foundation for which the author himself laid in the Anjuman-e Panjāb." But then, Hali reminds himself wryly, it could be argued in Azad's defense that "up to the present this type of poetry can barely be said to exist."[14]

For Azad, the birth of the new poetry is a matter merely of time and creative energy. But Hali sees a more ominous future. Poetry is threatened not only from within, in a cyclical way defined by its own evolution, but from without, in a linear way: civilization itself has "a bad effect" on poetry, and this effect is steadily increasing.[15] "Poetry Makes Progress in Uncivilized Times," as one of the *Introduction*'s chapter headings informs us; and as long as society is no more than half-civilized, the imagination still rules,[16] and life still "appears as a story." But as knowledge becomes more subject to research and verification, "to that extent imagination, on which poetry is founded, wastes away." For "the habit of investigation, which goes hand in hand with the progress of knowledge," is "fatally destructive" to poetry (25). If even a plain, unvarnished story is told to a half-civilized society, the story arouses "sometimes fear and sometimes surprise and sometimes fervor, and on these things poetry is founded." But when civilization makes further inroads, "these fountains dry up—and if somehow they don't dry up, then they are stopped up with extreme care, to preserve their flavor" (26). In the next chapter, a single paragraph called "The Example of Firdausī," Hali argues that the old magic is indeed losing its hold, and the great Persian hero Rustam himself is on his way to being considered "no more than an ordinary man" (26).

But Hali wants to have it both ways. For next comes a chapter called "Poetry Can Remain Established in Civilization" (26), which begins: "Although the opinion about poetry that was mentioned above is true to some extent, we ought not to adopt it without careful consideration." Some people, Hali says, argue eloquently that the advance of science opens up new and inexhaustible fields of imagery; that eternity, human emotions, personal experience, patriotism, and the constantly occurring events of life provide ample raw material for the imagination; and that man can never be alienated from a poetic relationship to the natural world.[17] But he himself is not convinced: the manifest features of nature have already been used by earlier poets, and the initial wonder that they aroused can never be surpassed by anyone (27).

By now, we feel that poetry is on the wane, if not actually dying. But Hali wants to have it a third way, too. He launches abruptly into a hymn to poetry, with a long quotation from an unnamed "European scholar" who praises the unworldly influence, soothing power, and other God-given capabilities of poetry, and finally concludes that "poetry is virtue, or leads toward virtue" (28). Then, if poetry is dying, will virtue die too? Apparently not, for Hali now provides a number of chapters about the relationship between poetry and society: both influence each other, for good or for ill; both need each other.

Clearly, Hali is less than entirely consistent. As he goes along, he keeps changing the basis on which he defines and discusses poetry. But behind all his clarion calls for reform and reinvigoration, the note of pessimism, based on a sense of general literary deterioration, is sounded again and again. Thus we are not surprised to be told that nowadays in Urdu, the level of poetry is steadily falling. "Artificialness of language, and weakness and thinness of thought, are increasing from day to day" (129). Only great masters can really innovate: "The kind of innovations that poets in our country usually create" are such that "from day to day, poetry grows more and more low, base, and stupid" (151). Poets may try to practice "self-help" (*silf hilp*), but they know that they are working against the current of the times—"especially in a time when the poetry of languages far more lofty and sophisticated than Urdu is subject to the disease of decay (*zavāl*)." Thus Hali can only say bleakly that "the struggles of animals being slaughtered, and the hopes of sick people, endure till their last breath—so whatever I write, it is not to say 'this will be' but to say 'if only this were!'" (97). For Hali, it is all too possible that poetry will gradually wither away, no matter what kind of modernizing breakthrough is achieved.

Since Hali adopts the same basic framework as does Azad, he is vulnerable to many of the same counterarguments. As compared to Azad, he writes with less color and passion, but a more painstaking concern for the reality of disagreement and debate. Hali recognizes opposing viewpoints, and seeks to accommodate them by qualifying or amplifying his statements. But this intellectual breadth is not achieved without a price. He can often be seen to contradict himself in theory; even more often, he can be seen to violate in practice his own theoretical rules. Sometimes he uses his own basic terms with an unabashed flexibility, so that their meaning slips and slides considerably from one passage to another.

Hali has been plausibly accused of trying to incorporate the views of too many authorities at the same time, and of mingling bits of the old poetic values with bits of the new in a thoroughly inconsistent way. Thus, as one critic wrote, although "the flame of intellectual brilliance flares up here and there, he was not able to turn it into a continuous fire."[18] Or rather, as a more recent critic has put it, "It is not lack of intellectual brilliance that is Hali's failing. His problem is that his soul is full of conflicting desires."[19] And, of course, there is the redoubtable Westernizer Kalīmuddīn Aḥmad, who maintains that any real understanding of English literature and poetics was quite beyond the powers of someone as superficial as Hali—someone with "mind and perceptions commonplace, thought and reflection inadequate, discrimination of a low standard." With such a poor opinion of Hali, Kalīmuddīn finds that having to recognize the *Introduction* as still "the best work of criticism in Urdu" is "extremely dispiriting."[20]

Critics have argued that the *Introduction* is organized in a way that positively encourages Hali's tendency to self-contradiction. Formally speaking, the *Introduction* is simply divided into eighty-three chapters, ranging in length from a few lines to a number of pages; each of these chapters has its own title. At a higher level, however, the organization is roughly tripartite: the first section presents a historical study of poetry and discusses the general relationship between poetry and society; the second section sets forth the three qualities of good poetry, which are—as we will see—simplicity, truth, and fervor; while the third section introduces the famous idea of "natural poetry." Although these three large sections seem never to have been formally demarcated by the author, their boundaries are so conspicuous that they are generally agreed upon.[21] Yet the three sections show, just as conspicuously, a tremendous overlapping of ideas.

Laurel Steele, discussing this casual, point-by-point structure, notes that Hali never "organizes his statements with a view to their overall progression" and that his conveniently loose structure "allows him to contradict himself and change his approaches to the problems as he moves along." In fact, as she concludes, the segmentary organization of the *Introduction* actually makes it resemble a ghazal. And just as a ghazal is not, in one sense, "about" nightingales and roses, the *Introduction* "is not about the specific statements that are in it." Rather, she finds that it is built on one underlying idea: "that poetry, as a reflection of society, must change and must reflect the new forces loose in India."[22] Hali himself might have concurred—but he would have maintained that the "must" is imposed not by any practical necessity or external coercion, but by the irresistible power of time itself.

Sometimes Hali in fact became almost superstitious about the omens given by time. In his review of *Water of Life* he wrote pessimistically, "It seems that the movement of Urdu poetry was so haphazard right from the start that the more it developed, the further it got from the desired goal." Perhaps, he mused, Urdu was born at an ill-omened time: "It's a strange coincidence that the beginning of Urdu poetry and the decline of the Mughal empire start from just the same time—as though its seed had been sown in ground that could no longer sustain growth."[23] Perhaps Urdu was doomed even from its infancy.

In *Water of Life,* Azad had a much more hopeful image for the situation: Urdu was an orphan child who had already come much farther than his casual, marginal past would have made likely. "I was astonished—that a child should be found wandering in the bazaar of Shāh Jahān, that the poets should take him up, that they should nurture and raise him in the land of speech, and that in the end he should go so far as to seize control over the country's writing and composition!" (1). Urdu was fortunate in being the language of Delhi, with the prestige of its cultivation at the royal court; then it was fortunate in finding patronage in Lucknow when Delhi's political fortunes declined (62–63). Now, of course, times are changing, and "knowledge and its forms of communication take new directions with every day's experience." Some languages have sought to escape the necessary changes: "In Arabic and Persian, this progress and *iṣlāḥ* have been blocked for many years." But Urdu, unlike Arabic and Persian, will change with the times, for it has that special, infallible talisman: "The English language is a magic world of progress and *iṣlāḥ*" (4).

Time would tell. Time itself was, to Hali, the "great reformer" (*greṭ rifārmar*).[24] And its verdict on the house of classical Urdu poetry seemed all too clear. As Hali put it, "The times are saying, in a loud voice, that either the building will be repaired, or the building itself will not exist" (128).

10 FROM PERSIAN TO ENGLISH

"Although the tree of Urdu grew in the soil of Sanskrit and [Braj] Bhasha, it flourished in the breezes of Persian" (49). Azad traces the earliest development of Urdu back to the first great Indo-Persian poet, Amīr Ḳhusrau, who receives—for his folk poetry—the supreme accolade: "Look at these words and ideas, how they are immersed in nature (*nechar*)!" (69). In his more sophisticated work Amīr Ḳhusrau used "the salt of Persian" to season his Urdu (67); in fact, he and other early poets used Persian and Bhasha "like salt and pepper, such that the language makes you smack your lips" (72). Sometimes the mingling was less successful: in the poetry of Valī and his generation, Persian was added to Urdu "as if someone had put sugar in milk, but it had not yet been well dissolved: one sip is particularly sweet, one absolutely flavorless; then in another, the teeth crunch a sugar crystal" (31). Persian brought into Urdu "the coloring of metaphors and similes." If such a coloring "had come only like oil rubbed into the face, or like collyrium around the eyes, it would have been both attractive and beneficial for vision. But alas—its intensity caused severe harm to the eyes of our power of expression" (49). "The eyes of our power of expression"—what an image! Azad himself, with his uninhibited love for metaphors and similes, would have been quick to acknowledge his own share in this Persian heritage.

Persian gave to Urdu "many lofty thoughts" and also "exaggeration of *maẓmūns*," so that it became alienated from the straightforward temperament of Braj Bhasha; Bhasha and Urdu became "as different as earth and sky" (49). Bhasha remained so simple and clear, of course, only because all the elaboration went into Sanskrit (56).[1] Persian groomed Urdu and "adorned it with metaphors and similes, so that it advanced beyond Bhasha in the subtlety of its thoughts, the tautness of its constructions, the force of its speech, its swiftness and sharpness; and many new words and new constructions created breadth in the language as well" (57). Azad had provided a kind of epitaph for this relationship in *The Wonder-World of Thought*: Urdu "flew with the wings of Persian, it mounted to the sky through verbal and rhetorical power; then, when it fell, it was buried beneath a layer of metaphors and disappeared."[2]

Alas, Azad laments, that the price of the Persian heritage was so high. When Urdu poets gave up realistic poetry, they casually flung away a "natural flower" that had its own color and scent (57), in favor of the artifices of Persian. "They didn't understand that this unreal coloring destroys our true temper." And then Azad continues, most remarkably, without a moment's pause, "This is the reason that today we are very deficient in writing in the style of English and in translating its *maẓmūns* quite fully" (58). How extraordinary that the cure for an overdose of Persian should be—not some sort of literary self-exploration, but an equally powerful dose of English!

Azad can certainly be accused—as in fact he often was—of uncritical Anglophilia. In general, he never has a bad word to say about the British. Even when he registers harsh judgments made by "civilized nations" about his own country, he has nothing to say against them. "Everyone knows," he observes neutrally, that "India has long been notorious for cowardice and laziness" (6). In *Water of Life*, when poets encounter Englishmen, most of their experiences are unexceptionable. Mīr is courteously invited to call on the governor general—and haughtily declines: "My lineage [as a Sayyid] is of no interest to the Sahib, and he does not understand my work. Certainly he will give me some reward; but that kind of visit can produce nothing but humiliation" (211). By contrast, the uninhibited Inshā introduces himself to John Baillie, the resident at Lucknow, by secretly making faces in his direction from behind the nawab's chair. The resident is amused, and he and Inshā are soon engaged in friendly banter (277–78).

Still, one long anecdote surely gives us a look into Azad's heart. It is not even identified as the usual "anecdote" (*naql*) or "jest" (*laṭīfah*), but as a "chance encounter" (*ittifāq*), a label Azad almost never uses. This incident is narrated in the first person—by the uniquely authoritative Żauq. It is reported as a word-for-word conversation, and by Azad's normal narrative standards it is uncharacteristically exact and detailed. Azad recounts Żauq's precise words:

> One day the king gave me a draft of a ghazal and commanded, "Fix this one up too and give it to me." It was the rainy season. Clouds

> were forming. The river was at its height. I went into the Hall of Private Audience and sat down to one side, looking out on that view. And I began to work on the ghazal. After a little while, I heard footsteps. When I looked, I saw a learned European Sahib standing behind me. He said to me, "What is you writing?"[3] I said, "It's a ghazal." He asked, "Who is you?" I said, "I praise His Majesty in verse." He said, "In which language?" I said, "In Urdu." He asked, "What languages does you know?" I said, "I know Persian and Arabic also." He said, "Does you compose poetry in those languages too?" I said, "If it's some special occasion, I have to compose in them too; otherwise I compose only in Urdu, since it's my own language. What a man can do in his own language, he cannot do in someone else's language." He asked, "Does you know English?" I said, "No." He said, "Why hasn't you studi-yed it?" I said, "My mouth and voice are not suited to it, it just doesn't come to me." The Sahib said, "Well (*vil*), what is this! Look, I speaks your language." I said, "In old age, a foreign language cannot be learned, it's a very difficult thing." He then said, "Well, I has learned your three language after coming to India. You cannot learn our one language. What is this?" And he went on and on about it. I said, "Sahib, I consider learning a language to mean that one should write and speak on every matter the way educated native speakers (*ahl-e zabān*) themselves do."—He says, "I 'as learned your three language"! Why, what kind of language is that, and what kind of learning! I don't call it learning and speaking a language—I call it ruining a language! (475–76)

Apparently the Englishman went off secure in his smugness, since it seems unlikely that he was crushed by Żauq's parting shot. Żauq was left fuming—muttering offensive bits of the conversation to himself, venting the anger he had suppressed. That is, if the "chance encounter" ever took place at all, which seems on the face of it unlikely.

But what a set of colliding values the "chance encounter" depicts! The old Mughal patronage relationships (Żauq respectfully obeys the king's command) are challenged by the new English ones (the Englishman saunters insolently around the palace). The old sensibility (Żauq enjoys the beautiful sights of the rainy season) is challenged by the new pragmatism (the Englishman ignores the scene entirely). The old courtesy (Żauq is impeccably polite and self-deprecating throughout) is challenged by the new arrogance (the Englishman is unabashedly rude and domineering). The pursuit of quality (Żauq polishes sophisticated poetry) is challenged by the pursuit of quantity (the Englishman boasts of his three languages). The lifelong immersion in one's own, uniquely known, supremely valued language is challenged by the casual annexation—and consequent devaluation—of the languages of others. Here we have a small, perfectly constructed jewel of implicit social commentary; and it does sound like a cri de coeur from Azad's own deeper self. If Persian overcomplicated Urdu, the English were all too capable of ruthlessly oversimplifying it.

Yet this very plainness and directness, this disdain for literary niceties, this concern with the real world, is part of what Azad wants from English. To him, English is valuable because it provides a correct and liberating poetics—one that enables literature to break the confining bonds of tradition, to cut through all artifice and self-reflexivity, to reach the eternal nonverbal bedrock of Nature itself. We have seen that the lucky, uncorrupted poets of the first two *daur*s simply write down whatever is in their hearts, and this makes their poetry wonderfully moving and effective. "English writing" values this effectiveness, and Azad holds its poetics up for emulation. "The common principle of English writing is that whatever thing or inner thought you write about, you should present it in such a way that you arouse the same state—of happiness, or grief, or anger, or pity, or fear, or fervor—in the heart as is aroused by experiencing or witnessing the thing itself" (58). This is almost word-for-word the same creed Azad had advocated at that memorable meeting of the Anjuman-e Panjāb in 1874, but now he makes it even clearer that for him this view is at the heart of "English writing." English shows us how to use language instrumentally, how to short-circuit the play of words, how to get from feelings in the poet's heart to feelings in the reader's heart with a minimum of fuss in between. Mere words may be suspect, the autonomous "game of words" may have been discredited—but feelings are reassuringly real and irreproachably "natural."

Despite his official rejection of the "game of words," however, Azad himself is a very clever and slippery writer. Prose really does turn to poetry in his hands. To make his ideas persuasive he uses not simple, straightforward exposition or step-by-step reasoning, but his own inimitable literary skills. As a master of wordplay he has no peer in Urdu, and his style has always been held—with good reason—to be untranslatable. Azad so often tends to "send the breezes of invention flying through the air," and to build sustained metaphorical "towers of fireworks," that he in fact resembles his own vision of the fifth *daur*—of which he was, chronologically, a member in good standing. Between one lively, engaging sentence and the next there may lie a tremendous chasm; but the reader is often seduced into leaping easily over it, allured by the sentence on the far side. Azad can be at his most delightful when he is being persnickety and prejudiced. Although he sometimes sets forth opposing points of view with a show of judiciousness, his real interest is always in placing a dexterous thumb on his preferred side of the scales.[4] His "unofficial" ideas about poetry, which underlie many of his shrewd remarks and observations, are always suggestive, and often full of insight.

But when Azad expounds his official, Westernized poetic ideology, he rarely achieves his finest effects. His views are merely set forth, loudly if not clearly, as self-evident; they obviously arouse strong emotion in him, but the emotion is not in itself persuasive. Rather than analyzing or defending his views, he reiterates them, and drapes them in fresh imagery, and heaps passionate scorn on the old poetry. He has to persuade himself as well as us: as we have seen, he feels himself ultimately a stranger in the world of the "New Light" people (328), his heart sadly unmoved by the "new civilization" (297). He flogs himself into flogging his views; remembering how he was situated, who can blame him?

Of course, it is absurdly easy to question the assumptions of Azad's official poetics. He assumes that expressing one's own immediate and "natural" feelings is the most effective way to arouse the same feelings in a reader or hearer. He assumes that arousing such "natural" feelings in the reader is the single great goal of all literature. He assumes that all of "English writing" has a common poetics—and that it is the one he describes. He assumes that to be, like Amīr Ḳhusrau and other early poets, "immersed in nature," is not only a self-evidently desirable condition, but a self-explanatory one that requires no further definition or discussion. If these crucial assumptions are challenged—as of course they must be—his work is incapable of responding to the challenge. Azad is simply not a coherent or systematic thinker. His officially declared poetic ideas are so sweeping, imprecise, and metaphorical that it is almost impossible even to pin them down, much less to defend them.

The same vagueness makes it difficult to decide where Azad got these ideas. The principle of Occam's razor would suggest that he got them from the people who had thrust them vigorously into his face: perhaps he merely combined Colonel Holroyd's forceful contempt for poetic "decadence" with Sir Sayyid's emphatic ideal of bringing poetry as "close to nature" as possible. Certainly he didn't get his ideas from Johnson and Addison,[5] the two English writers with whom we can be sure he was at least somewhat familiar (since he had transcreated—without acknowledgment—a number of their essays in *The Wonder-World of Thought*). In *Water of Life* Azad does not mention the name of a single English theorist;[6] he hardly does so elsewhere in his writing either. Views are attributed to "English writing" or "Europeans" or "civilized nations," even in the rare case of individual mention: "A wise European (*firang*) says that the poet brings his poetry with him when he is born" (83). He uses relatively few English words.[7] Azad perceives not merely the English but Europeans in general as a collective group with a single, powerful point of view.

Their authoritative language, English, is equally powerful. The young language Urdu, with its "limited scope," far from equaling English, is not even capable of expressing the full range of English ideas in translation. But at least the work of translation is well under way, and "now we can hope that perhaps one day Urdu too will attain some standing in the ranks of learned languages." After Azad has duly expressed his official, optimistic point of view, however, his mood changes with characteristic speed. Such a happy day will not come soon, for even "Arabic, Persian, Sanskrit, Bhasha, and so on, which are Urdu's elders," do not have in their treasuries the right words to translate everything from English. It should not surprise us if "poor Urdu" cannot yet succeed where its elders have failed. Especially, Azad concludes somberly, since Urdu is not the only one at fault—"especially since Hindus and Muslims both have let their inheritances from their ancestors slip through their hands" (25).

· · ·

Azad never ceased to grapple with the question of Persian, the heritage he loved so much yet denounced so fiercely. The importance of Persian in *Water of Life* was made clear in Azad's three-part preface: first came "The History of the Urdu Language" (6–25); then "When Persian Entered into Braj Bhasha, What Effects It Created, and What Hope There Is for the Future" (25–63); and finally "The History of Urdu Poetry" (64–80). The middle section—the one about Persian—was longer than both the others put together. The discussion was chiefly historical and linguistic, however; if Azad knew anything of the many sophisticated Persian literary theorists, he did not make his knowledge evident. When Hali reviewed *Water of Life*, he praised the preface as "extremely useful and full of insight," as one that "mirrors the reality of the language"; he noted approvingly that in it Azad had "with much effort" used English sources. His only real complaint was that Azad had neglected to mention Sir Sayyid's reformist journal, *Tahżīb ul-Akhlāq*.[8]

But when Hali came to write his own *Introduction*, he did not mention Persian in a single one of his eighty-three chapter headings.[9] For him, with his interest in Islamic history, Arabic poetry and Arabic theorists (including Ibn Khaldūn) were a more useful case in point. But the people with whom Hali was most obviously concerned were neither Arabs nor Persians, but Europeans. While Azad saw Western poets and theorists as a single harmonious chorus, Hali was very much aware of their individual identities. Not for nothing had he spent those four years in Lahore, editing the translations of English works into Urdu. Hali's *Introduction* mentions by name: Plato (14, 29); Byron (16, 19); Solon (17–18); Byron's "Childe Harold's Pilgrimage" (19); the "Marseillaise" (21); Shakespeare (21, 69, 72); Goldsmith (41–42); Macaulay (46, 70, 113); Homer (46, 68, 72); Dante (46); Sir Walter Scott (56–57); Scott's *Rokeby* (57); Virgil (60); Ariosto (60); and Milton (61, 68–70, 113).[10] These references generally occur in the first third of his book; once Hali is well launched in his own arguments, he no longer needs such Western examples and authorities.

Moreover, Hali clearly knew a certain amount of English and was not averse to displaying it. Or rather—to do him justice—he was inclined to retain English words that he felt were impossible to translate. English words crop up, carefully transliterated, in all his mature critical writing. The English words that appear in the *Introduction* include: actor, Asiatic, blank verse, civilization, copyright, despotic government, dictionary, grammar, imagination, immoral, introduce, judge, literature, magic lantern, material, moral, moralist, natural, nature, novelist, organ, poetry, point, political, public, publisher, science, second nature, self-help, simple, social, society, supernatural, unnatural, and verse. It is a list that says a lot already about his concerns.

At times, however, Hali shows a surprising coyness (or even ignorance?) about his English borrowings. The very first image he offers for poetry is that of a "magic lantern" (*maijik lenṭarn*) that glows more brightly as the room—or the age—grows darker (14). Later, continuing to develop his argument that poetry declines as civilization advances, he presents the magic-lantern image more elaborately, in the form of a quotation:

> A great supporter of this opinion says:
>
> Poetry puts the same sort of curtain over the heart as a magic lantern puts over the eyes. Just as a magic-lantern show reaches its full effect in an entirely dark room, in the same way poetry shows its full fascination only in a dark age. And just as the moment light comes, all the displays of the magic lantern vanish, in the same way when the limits of the physical world gradually become visible and the curtains of possibilities are raised, to that extent the magical manifestations of poetry disappear, because two incompatible things—that is, reality and illusion—cannot be combined. (26)

Who is this "great supporter" whose words are so carefully set apart from Hali's own, but whose name we are not told? Hali leaves us to wonder.

It turns out to be Macaulay, in his essay on Milton; Hali uses a somewhat simplified but quite recognizable translation of his words.[11] Elsewhere in the same essay Macaulay had made his point even more clearly, declaring that Milton himself from his height of civilization "looked back with something like regret to the ruder age of simple words and vivid impressions." To Macaulay, this was no cause for surprise. "We think that, as civilisation advances, poetry almost necessarily declines. . . . We cannot understand why those who believe in that most orthodox article of literary faith, that the earliest poets are generally the best, should wonder at the rule as if it were the exception."[12]

Here, in a nutshell (where perhaps it properly belongs), is the seed of the naturalistic poetics Azad and Hali both advocated: "that most orthodox article of literary faith, that the earliest poets are generally the best." Scholars who play find-the-sources for Azad and Hali soon discover that most of their ideas floated in the Victorian air. A cyclical view of time, for example, was common among a number of Victorian thinkers, including Mill and Carlyle; they often saw their own age as part of a period of doubt and dissolution preceding the next rebirth at a higher level of progress.[13] Hali may thus have encountered some of his favorite ideas in more than one writer; and, conversely, even when he quotes directly from a writer, he may have known his work only partially or inadequately, through brief or poorly translated excerpts. The game of find-the-sources thus becomes even more complex.

About Hali's sources Vaḥīd Quraishī concludes: that Hali knew Macaulay only through two essays ("Milton" and "Moore's *Life of Lord Byron*"); that he drew much material from Johnson's *Lives of the Poets*; that he was "probably quite unacquainted with Mill and Carlyle," although they were widely known in his circles; that he borrowed a single half-phrase from *Biographia Literaria* but did not know more of Coleridge, or else "perhaps his view of poetry would have been different from its present form"; that he did not know Matthew Arnold at all, or else he would surely have made use of his essay "Literature and Science"; and, most intriguingly, that he knew Wordsworth's poetry but not his famous "Preface," because "if this essay had fallen into his hands, he would at once have translated the whole essay and included it in his book," since it could have provided him with "a wonderful foundation for his notion of 'simplicity.'"[14] By contrast, Iḥtishām Ḥusain maintains not only that Hali did know Wordsworth's "Preface," but that its influence was probably what caused him to write a similar *Introduction* to his own poems in the first place.[15] Similarly, Mumtāz Ḥusain concludes that Wordsworth's "Preface" seems to be the source for the whole of "whatever Hali has written in the *Introduction* about the *iṣlāḥ* of poetic language."[16] Other scholars have lined up on one side or the other, especially with regard to Wordsworth.[17]

This kind of argument from personal judgment may or may not help us identify Hali's exact sources, but it serves to bring home the extent to which Hali was operating within a larger Victorian literary milieu, in which possible sources were legion and influences and parallels even more so. Cultural transmission from England to India was actively promoted (for different reasons) by various parties in both countries; while it did not always keep up with the latest fashions, it became a powerful intellectual force. Certain elite groups in the larger Indian cities in fact came to have access to a highly sophisticated English literary education. As early as 1852 the *Calcutta Review* sarcastically noted the frequency with which "young Babus undertake to reveal to the admiring world beauties in Milton which Macaulay never perceived, and archaisms in Shakespeare which Halliwell never detected."[18]

At the time of the Lahore mushairah series in 1874, a "Muslim from Amritsar" seems to have actually imported Macaulay into Indian traditional lore when he wrote to a newspaper: "'To the extent that education progresses, poetry declines,' one says proverbially in India; and indeed, things turn out thus."[19] By the last two decades of the nineteenth century, literate Urdu speakers indeed had many opportunities to become familiar with English theorists of the early and middle decades of the century. Wordsworth's "Preface" is an obvious, plausible, well-known source that Hali could have, should have, or even—many critics feel—must have, used. But how do we account for the fact that Hali, who mentions so many other names, never once mentions Wordsworth's?

With all this possible or probable borrowing, Hali remains perforce an original thinker; for just as Azad had feared, the linguistic and cultural barriers through which English ideas had to pass proved only semipermeable. The supreme example, one discussed by dozens of Urdu critics, is Hali's explicit borrowing from Milton of his three criteria for poetry. In the "Tractate of Education," Milton had spoken of teaching schoolchildren "a gracefull and ornate Rhetorick" based on classical texts: "To which Poetry would be made subsequent, or indeed rather precedent, as being less suttle and fine, but more simple, sensuous, and passionate."[20] Coleridge extracted these latter three adjectives from their casual, comparative, descriptive context, made them absolute and normative, and then defined them according to his own lights. Other writers discussed them as well. What Milton actually meant by these three adjectives remains ultimately uncertain. What concerns us here is what Hali thought—or chose to think—Milton meant.

According to Hali, Milton said, "The excellence of poetry is that it should be simple (*sādah*), filled with fervor (*josh se bharā hu'ā*), and founded on truth (*aṣliyat par mabnī*)" (68). Since Hali probably read the original passage at second hand, in a discussion by someone else—or rather at third hand, through a translation of a discussion—the changes are not surprising. Indeed, he immediately presents just such a discussion of Milton's words, attributed to an unnamed "European scholar" (68–70). This passage has been identified as a very free transcreation and expansion of the words of Coleridge—another writer whose name Hali never once mentions.[21]

Here is what Coleridge, taking his own liberties with Milton, originally wrote. It is very intricate, and the whole thing turns out to be a single long sentence:

> For the first condition—simplicity,—while, on the one hand it distinguishes poetry from the arduous processes of science, laboring towards an end not yet arrived at, and supposes a smooth and finished road, on which the reader is to walk onward easily, with streams murmuring by his side, and trees and flowers and human dwellings to make his journey as delightful as the object of it is desirable, instead of having to toil with the pioneers, and painfully make the road on which others are to travel,—precludes, on the other hand, every affectation and morbid peculiarity;—the second condition, sensuousness, insures that framework of objectivity, that definiteness and articulation of imagery, and that modification of the images themselves, without which poetry becomes flattened into mere didactics of practice, or evaporated into a hazy unthoughtful day-dreaming; and the third condition, passion, provides that neither thought nor imagery shall be simply objective, but that the *passio vera* of humanity shall warm and animate both.[22]

The prospect of turning such a sentence into Urdu would undoubtedly give a translator pause. No reader could possibly expect—nor could any translator produce—a perfectly literal rendering.

Still, no one would expect what Hali has produced, either. He has really taken inexcusable liberties—or perhaps excusable ones, since he never identifies his source. Hali's version brings in nature, Homer, Shakespeare, and magnetism; it is much plainer in diction, and something like three times as long.

> Simplicity does not mean merely simplicity of words, but rather that thought, too, ought not to be so refined and subtle that ordinary minds would not have the capacity to understand it. To walk along the highway of the emotions, not to turn aside from the simple, straightforward road of informality, to keep the intelligence

> away from a show of quickness—this is what is called simplicity. The road of knowledge cannot be so clear for its seekers as the road of poetry ought to be for its hearers. Seekers of knowledge have to traverse depths and heights, caves and peaks, pebbles and stones, waves and whirlpools, in order to arrive at their goal. But the readers or hearers of verse ought to find such a level and clear road that they will walk on it easily. Rivers and water channels ought to flow on both sides, and fruit and flowers, trees and houses, should be present all along to lighten their journey. Those poets who have become famous in the world have produced works that have always been seen or heard in just this way. Every mind finds such a work congenial, and every heart has room for it. Homer, in his poetry, has everywhere captured such a picture of nature that old and young, and nations who live at opposite poles from each other, can equally understand it and take the same pleasure in it. His poetry has moved over every inch of the world of emotions, and its light has spread out like the sun. It impartially illumines inhabited areas and wastelands, and has the same effect on the learned and the ignorant. Shakespeare, too, has the same quality as Homer. They both, unlike most poets, do not claim any exceptional status, but always choose the common share. They don't want to make people infatuated with their special capabilities by displaying extraordinary sights and unique events.
>
> The second thing that Milton said is that a poem must be founded on truth. This means that thought should rest on something that really exists, rather than the whole *mazmūn* being like a spectacle in a dream: one moment it's everything, and when you open your eyes—it was nothing. Just as this ought to be true of the *mazmūn*, so it ought to be true of the words also. For example, the kind of similes and metaphors that seem to be based on abstractions ought not to be used.
>
> The third thing was that a poem should be filled with fervor. This does not mean merely that the poet should have written the poem in a state of fervor, or that the style of the poem should express his fervor, but rather that it must also arouse fervor in the hearts of the people to whom it is addressed. And for this purpose their hearts must be wrung, and to attract their hearts the poem must have a magnetic pull in its expression. (68–70)

This passage is so different from its putative source that it might even be a translation from some other source entirely—from some imitator or popularizer of Coleridge who has not yet, even after a century of zealous Urdu scholarship, been identified.

But to a person who has read a lot of Hali, what it really sounds like is pure Hali. It is adjusted suspiciously well to the kind of Urdu structures Hali used, and straightforwardly advocates exactly the ideas that Hali was in the process of presenting. Thus we might take the passage to be not so much a translation as Hali's own meditation on Coleridge meditating on Milton.[23] For after all, attribution to an unnamed "English scholar" was a fine convenience; it offered the necessary prestige, without the risk of having anyone challenge the translation. But on the other hand, perhaps Hali himself in this case had some kind of imperfect access to some actual text. For he then continues: "The 'magnetic pull' that this European scholar has mentioned in his commentary on Milton's words is one that Lord Macaulay says is found in Milton's words alone," and he offers a quotation in which Macaulay attributes to Milton "magical" powers of speech (70–71). And now suddenly the Urdu translation of Macaulay's words is so accurate, so perfectly faithful to the original, that it could hardly be improved upon.[24]

We cannot say how well Hali controlled his English sources, and how much he was at the mercy of translators. But certainly he knew what he wanted to say, and went looking for English writers who would help him say it. For consider the actual outcome: Hali first invokes Milton, whose three adjectives are thoroughly ambiguous; he next quotes an anonymous "English scholar" who turns out to write, most cooperatively, almost exactly the way Hali writes himself; and finally he cites a passage from Macaulay that eulogizes Milton in such particular terms that it expressly denies to itself any wider critical relevance. Then, with his English credentials duly established, Hali proceeds to turn Milton's adjectives into nouns, and do as he pleases with them. His next three chapters are called "What Is Meant by Simplicity (*sādagī*)?" (71), "What Is Meant by Truth (*aṣliyat*)?" (73), and "What Is Meant by Fervor (*josh*)?" (76). In them he uses the "English scholar" passage as a starting point, explicates the three concepts at greater length, and provides Persian and Urdu examples. By now, however, the concepts are unabashedly Hali's own and are made to undergo various convolutions as his arguments develop.

Hali is not only his own man but also manifestly, as his pen name ("Contemporary") proclaims, a man of his own time. In the *Introduction* almost all his real English sources are from the nineteenth century. Shakespeare, like Homer, Dante, and others, is no more than a name. Although Hali speaks with great respect of Milton, he obviously sees him through the eyes of Macaulay and (to some extent) Coleridge. Even when he claims to find in Goldsmith (?1730–1774) an exemplary eighteenth-century poet, he cannot really make use of him. Hali seeks to identify Goldsmith's literary aims with his own reformist efforts. He gives Goldsmith a tiny little chapter all to himself, called "Goldsmith's Poetry," and says of him, "When Goldsmith, in the very beginning, abandoned the practice of the early poets of his country—a practice that was based on falsehood and exaggeration, and on *maẓmūns* of love and desire—and adopted true natural poetry, these same difficulties [of innovation] confronted him. Thus he described this situation in a poem; addressing the poetry of his new path, he says,"—and there follows a careful prose rendering, including even explanatory annotation for place names, of the conclusion to "The Deserted Village" (41–42).

But if Goldsmith is so favorably contrasted with earlier English poets and their apparently false or overly romantic poetry, what of Shakespeare and Milton, whom Hali also officially admires? Moreover, in the course of "The Deserted Village" Goldsmith has earlier described the meretricious effects of "luxury" on an original simplicity of character: "Thus fares the land, by luxury betrayed, / In nature's simplest charms at first arrayed; / But verging to decline, its splendours rise, / Its vistas strike, its palaces surprise." Ignoring this and other obviously congenial passages, Hali cites only the poem's conclusion—which is not nearly so much to the point.[25] Then, without a word of discussion, he immediately begins a fresh chapter, never to mention Goldsmith's name again. It is hard to escape the conclusion that Hali knew little more of Goldsmith than the end of "The Deserted Village," which he perhaps found excerpted in a textbook.

The only other Westerner to be honored with a chapter of his own is Sir Walter Scott (1771–1832). Yet here too Hali's discussion is perfunctory—and even here it is drawn not from a real analysis of Scott's work but from unidentified contemporary secondary sources. The chapter begins: "Sir Walter Scott is a famous poet of England, and it has been written about him that . . . " According to Hali, everyone agrees that Scott's best poems are based on reality and on seeking new ways to express genuine meanings. Then Hali offers an unattributed anecdote ("They say that . . . ") about how Scott once carefully noted down the appearance of some tiny wildflowers, telling an inquirer, "In the whole universe there are no two things that are exactly the same." Hali concludes by emphasizing the importance of paying close attention to reality, rather than relying on one's own mind, "which is an extremely limited supply of some commonplace similes or illustrations" (56–57). (Although it would seem to follow that if each tiny wildflower is unique, each mind should be much more so.) Beyond a few secondhand comments and a single anecdote, it is not clear that Hali knew anything at all about Scott and his work.

Hali's relation to his English sources in the *Introduction* is thus a kind of swamp, with some patches of clear ground, some muddy places, and some areas in which the English original (if any) is completely submerged. And above the swamp, it should be remembered, certain ideas float freely in the air of the time. If we leave aside all the speculative find-the-sources games, however, one plain fact emerges: it is above all Macaulay on whom Hali chooses to rely. From Macaulay he borrows an (unattributed) account of the idolatry accorded to Lord Byron (16–17),[26] the (unattributed) magic-lantern passage (26), the description of Milton's poetic "magic" (70–71), and the argument that people can truly learn and create only in their mother tongue (113). This is far more borrowing than can be established in the *Introduction* for any other single Westerner.

Macaulay was certainly a safe and respectable choice. When the viceroy wished to honor Sir Sayyid Aḥmad Khān for his educational work, he presented him with a gold medal—and a copy of Macaulay's works inscribed "in his Excellency's own handwriting."[27] It is intriguing to wonder how well Hali really knew Macaulay. Did he know of the famous "Minute on Education" (1835)? In it Macaulay reasoned from a single sweeping postulate: "All parties seem to be agreed on one point, that the dialects commonly spoken among the natives of this part of India contain neither literary nor scientific information, and are, moreover, so poor and rude that, until they are enriched from some other quarter, it will not be easy to translate any valuable work into them." Even the natives' classical languages fared no better: Macaulay maintained that "a single shelf of a good European library" was "worth the whole native literature of India and Arabia."[28]

On the strength of these arguments, Macaulay concluded that it was necessary to create a class of people capable of being "interpreters between us and the millions whom we govern"; these people were to be "Indian in blood and color, but English in taste, in opinions, in morals, and in intellect."[29] Did Hali know this aspect of Macaulay's thought—and would he have objected, if he had known? Perhaps he would not have objected very strongly. Hali's hero Sir Sayyid Aḥmad Khān, who initially found fault with Macaulay's views, later came to accept them, at least as far as they pertained to English-language educational policy. Sir Sayyid in fact deliberately echoed Macaulay's words: the aim of the Muhammedan Anglo-Oriental College he founded at Aligarh in 1875 was "to form a class of persons, Muhammedan in religion, Indian in blood and colour, but English in tastes, in opinions, and in intellect."[30]

Macaulay was an early advocate of what became known as the "filtration theory": an English education was to be given to a small Indian elite, and these chosen few were then to "act as teachers and translators of useful books, through which they would communicate to the native literature and to the native community 'that improved spirit' they had imbibed from the influence of European ideas and sentiments."[31] Even without having received an English education, Azad and Hali performed exactly the task that Macaulay envisioned. While Sir Sayyid sought to reform and Westernize many aspects of Indo-Muslim life, Azad and Hali were among the first to devote themselves chiefly to reshaping literature—and they were incomparably the most influential.[32] They did their work well. Today, after more than a century, the influence of "that improved spirit" is still clearly to be seen in Urdu literature and criticism.

11 "NATURAL POETRY"

Azad was always ready to celebrate the unique powers of poetry. "In the workshop of the world poetry is an extraordinary craft, which comes from the divine Craftsman." But the powers of poetry depend, it seems, largely on *maẓmūns*. How amazing that a *maẓmūn* can appear as an ordinary line of prose—and "then when you look at the same *maẓmūn*, with only some words shifted around, it achieves another state entirely." It develops rhythm, the "power of the writing increases," and "such sharpness comes into the *maẓmūn* that the razor of its effect abrades the heart" (64–65). Even the ghazal, with its long-cherished formality of structure, entered the poetic repertoire of Urdu through the appeal of its *maẓmūns*: "By means of romantic *maẓmūns*, that series of verses came into our hands that we call ghazal" (72). Through its romantic (*'āshiqānah*) *maẓmūns*, the ghazal found its way to the heart of Urdu. But by now, Azad argues, romantic themes have taken over the whole cultural heartland—and to a markedly unhealthy degree.

For while the ancient poets of Iran "extracted pleasure from every type of *maẓmūn*," later Persian poets generally "relied on the ghazal alone." Urdu poets too, "considering it an easy task, and wanting to please the common people, took up the *maẓmūns* of beauty and love, and so on." Azad concedes that "there is no doubt that what they did, they did very well" (79). But the very success of these *maẓmūns* arouses Azad's indignation:

> These are the same fixed ideas! Sometimes we move the words around, sometimes we make some modifications and keep using them. As though they're morsels that have already been eaten—or rather, have been chewed by other people. We chew on them, and

> we're happy with them. Think about it—what relish do they still have left? Beauty and love—marvelous!—very good! But for how long? Whether she's a Houri or a Parī, when you put a garland [of marriage] around her neck, she makes you sick. How long can it be till you get fed up with beauty and love? And by now she's a hundred years old! (79)

Here Azad can be seen vigorously trying to kill off the old poetry, trying to persuade his readers that—contrary to appearances—they are really in fact tired of all this romantic twaddle. Making effective use of an Urdu idiom, he urges them to think of the classical *maẓmūn*s as bites of food that have already been chewed by others, but that we latecomers are still content to chew on in our turn.

This kind of attack is developed at great length in the introduction to *Water of Life*. Azad adopts a hectoring tone; he seems to preach to an audience who will (he strongly suspects) be unreceptive. Again and again he reproaches the classic *maẓmūn*s for their success in shaping the Indo-Muslim mind, not only in poetry but in prose as well:

> It is an unhappy thing to note that our poetry became ensnared in the nets of a few commonplace meanings: that is, romantic *maẓmūns*, intoxicated drinking of wine, creating imaginary colors and scents without the rose and garden, lamenting the pain of separation, delighting in imaginary union, feeling alienated from the world, experiencing thus the hostility of the heavens. And the amazing thing is that if we want to speak of some real matter, we express this idea in metaphors. The result of which is that we can do nothing. (77)

The problem is that "our ancestors left us the instruments—words and meanings, metaphors and similes—for expressing these ideas" in poetry. "And by now they come so fluently to our tongues that everybody can, after a little thought, compose something or other" along classical lines (79).

A strange reproach to level against one's culture—that it gives "everybody" a poetic voice, enables "everybody" to participate in making and enjoying poetry! But this, one of the special glories of the old culture, is in Azad's view a problem indeed: it makes the poetry much harder to kill off. Urdu knowers find that "the wretched *maẓmūn*s of beauty and love" are "built into their mouths and tongues." Thus radical action is necessary: "If we want to say something, first we have to forget these things, then after that we can create, in their proper places, novel metaphors, new similes, innovative constructions, and excellent verbal inventions." But this will not be easy: it is "a matter that demands much sweat and desperate toil" (79).

Azad devotes many pages to developing an absolute—and of course, as we have seen, highly overdrawn—dichotomy between the foreign complexities of Persian and the indigenous simplicity of Braj Bhasha. "Bhasha doesn't, even by accident, take a step toward metaphor. Whatever enjoyable sights you see with your eyes, and whatever pleasant sounds you hear, or whatever perfumes you smell, are exactly what it very clearly describes in its sweet language, without elaboration, without exaggeration" (56). For the process of metaphor making is, despite its beauties, suspect from the start: it destroys the innocence of our natural feelings. "The result of those imaginary elaborations and invented refinements is that even things that are spontaneous and apparent to the feelings become enveloped in coil after coil of our similes and metaphors, and they too enter into the world of the imagination." The fundamental error is that "in describing our thoughts, we first of all suppose lifeless things to be alive—or rather, we suppose them to be humans." Because of this anthropomorphic fallacy, "we endow those lifeless things with the properties suitable to living and intelligent creatures, and generate the kind of fancies that are mostly the special national and religious characteristics of the lands of Arabia, or Iran, or Turkestan" (51).

Urdu thus inflicts a terrible fate on "spontaneous" things that are "apparent to the feelings": these emotional realities become enmeshed in "coil after coil" of metaphor and are then dragged into "the world of the imagination." As we have seen, this world is a den full of stale false imagery, unnatural "invented refinements," and repulsive scraps of chewed-over food. It is a world obscured by ever-increasing heaps of metaphor upon metaphor, a world doomed to grow ever "narrower and darker" (54).

· · ·

In *Water of Life* Azad sought to use words visually: he wished to create not *maẓmūn*s but pictures. He declared that he wanted to paint "living pictures" of the poets, so that "speaking, moving, walking pictures of their lives should come and stand before us, and should attain immortal life" (4). Once he had hit upon this literary credo, his own emotions were steadied and focused: "Thanks be to God, that in a mere matter of days my anxious and disorderly thoughts became collected; for this reason I gave this collection the name *Water of Life* (4).[1] Azad's pictures are to evoke genuine emotion: "Where can I find the words with which to show you living, alert, speaking pictures of these people, such that respect cannot even lift its eyes to their firm images, and the eye of love cannot tear itself away from their precious forms?" (81).

For Azad, this attempt was bound up with his own deepest emotions: nostalgia, grief, longing, fear, hope, foreboding. He maintained, in fact, that real, natural-born poets cannot help but base their work on emotion. "We know from experience that when the feeling of happiness or grief and anger, or some kind of passion and enthusiasm, agitates the heart, and it runs up against power of expression, then rhythmic speech spontaneously falls from the lips" (65). True poets use words simply and unpretentiously, to "make pictures stand before us"—and it is the pictures that move our hearts (106). Mīr is ranked above other poets because "in a number of places it seems as if he is capturing a picture of nature" (202). Moreover, if words can paint pictures, why should they not aspire to reproduce photographs? Azad praises Ġhālib's letters for showing photographs (*foṭogrāf*) of his friends and their gatherings (491).[2] Poetry should be natural, emotional, spontaneous, pictorial—poetry should, it seems, be based on anything rather than "the game of words," and drawn from any source other than the imagination.

Hali admired Azad's cultivation of the dramatic, visually evocative possibilities of language. Reviewing *Water of Life*, he praised it for its pictorial style: "The way the special character of that amazing age can be seen pictured in this tazkirah—of such pictures the pages of history are blank." Hali then described his own strong reaction: "At a number of places, reading about these things makes the heart fill with emotion, and a picture of the past age moves before the eyes."[3] Hali's response has been echoed again and again through the decades, to the present. The one absolutely obligatory cliché about *Water of Life* seems to be its "living, speaking pictures" and their deep emotional power. Hardly a single Urdu critic has written about Azad without ritually invoking such "pictures" as the supreme achievement of his narrative art. After duly marveling over these pictures, sympathetic critics generally move on to other kinds of (equally impressionistic) praise, while hostile critics proceed to impugn Azad's historical accuracy. How thoroughly Azad has succeeded in imposing his vision! It is hard to think of another writer who has caused critics, decade after decade, to form into a kind of chorus, collectively describing his work exactly as he himself described it.

The pictorial method itself is seen as resting on an especially Western poetics. Hali, reviewing *Wonder-World of Thought*, praised one of the essays for its evocative power. "When you read it, the aspect [of the subject] comes before your eyes. All the other essays have been written on this principle; by seeing them and reflecting on them, an estimate can be formed of the loftiness and breadth of Western poetic thought."[4] To some extent, Hali is right: Western writers have indeed praised and emphasized the pictorial possibilities of language. It has been observed that most works of literary criticism written between the middle of the sixteenth and the middle of the eighteenth century make approving mention of the classical Latin saying that "painting is mute poetry, and poetry a speaking picture." Johnson, for one, found the parallels between poetry and painting "literal and real."[5] Among the Victorians, this emphasis continued. "The power of Poetry," said Coleridge, "is by a single word to produce that energy in the mind as compels the imagination to produce the picture."[6] Hali's own favorite authority, Macaulay, maintained that the poet should aim "to portray, not to dissect." Macaulay even made this idea part of a definition of poetry: "By poetry we mean the art of employing words in such a manner as to produce an illusion on the imagination, the art of doing by means of words what the painter does by means of colours."[7]

Macaulay's definition itself, however, suggests some of the problems Azad and Hali faced when they called for the realistic depiction of nature. We have seen that for Macaulay poetry was a "magic lantern" that operated best in darkness and was threatened by the bright light of rational inquiry. If poets can in any case create only an "illusion on the imagination," why should they confine themselves to imitating the natural, daylight world? Why should poets not use words to evoke whatever they want to imagine, just as painters use colors to depict whatever they want to see? In fact Azad and Hali can only cling, in times of trouble, to their great fetish-word, Nature. All dimensions of poetic creation must be natural: the true, natural-born poet must react to the real, natural world with spontaneous, natural emotions, which he must then depict for his readers or hearers in the most direct, vivid, natural manner possible, so that they too can naturally come to share them.

But why? Only because the semantic dice have been loaded so heavily that the game is over before it starts. Because anything not "natural" is, by definition, in one or another inherently negative state: it is affected, distorted, artificial, inauthentic, derivative, decadent, perverted, false. Anything not natural is, ultimately, "unnatural." Consider, for example, the classic list of vices provided by the censorious Ram Babu Saksena in his *History of Urdu Literature* (1927). Saksena charges Urdu poetry with (among other sins) showing a "servile imitation" of Persian poetry that has led to its "debasement" and has made it, according to his own enumeration of the charges: (1) unreal; (2) rhetorical; (3) conventional; (4) mechanical, artificial, and sensual; and (5) unnatural, for Persian poetry was often "vitiated and perverse."[8] And unnatural things are of course doomed, if not already dying—for Nature is busy creating their fresh and natural replacements. It is actually kinder (as well as more prudent) to put them out of their misery, and to turn one's attention from morbid death to healthy rebirth.

· · ·

Azad maintained, as we have seen, that using the same old romantic *maẓmūns* used by earlier poets was like chewing on bits of food that had already been chewed on by others. His argument was that *maẓmūns* are exhaustible: they only have a certain amount of juice or flavor in them, and once that is gone they are mere worthless bits of gristle. Hali too uses images based on food and flavor to make the same point. In Arabic poetry, he says, after a certain point the earlier romantic *maẓmūns* became "like bones that had been licked and sucked dry, with no more relish left in them"—so that both poetry and society gradually succumbed to crude, vulgar, decadent tastes (37). Or the use of *maẓmūns* is like cooking: the first cook who discovers salt delights everybody; the second cook adds other "suitable" spices and wins much praise; the third cook has no other way of showing his own mastery except by adding "more than the proper amount" of hot peppers and other powerful seasonings (106). We should remember that poetry is not as necessary as food: people will eat one kind of food for a lifetime if they have to, but will grow bored with only one kind of poetry. And by now ghazals are in danger of becoming entirely predictable, like "a box of English sweets—their shapes are different, but they all taste the same" (141–42).

But Hali goes further: he offers a literary account of the way such poetic decadence comes about, and once again the real villain is time itself. He postulates an inevitable development of certain basic elements of ghazal imagery from naturalness to unnaturalness. The lover's heart, for example, first metaphorically "given away" to the beloved, gradually becomes a separate physical object that can be lost, found, sold, auctioned, or whatever. And the heart is far from the only such case:

> Or, for example, earlier poets described the beloved metaphorically as a hunter, because it was as if he hunted down people's hearts. Later poets gradually equipped him with all the genuine attributes of a hunter. Now he sometimes sets a snare and traps birds, sometimes shoots them down with arrows, sometimes confines them alive in a cage. He sometimes pulls out their wing-feathers, sometimes slaughters them and leaves them writhing on the ground. . . .

> He makes hundreds of birds into kabobs and eats them up . . . all the birdcatchers are amazed by his feats. (107–8)

Similarly, while earlier poets described the experience of divine or human love as a form of intoxication, later ones took the idea of wine literally, developed it further, and described drunken behavior in undesirable detail.

> Or, for example, ancient poets considered the wasting away of the body a necessary result of the sorrow of love or the shock of separation, and described it in some moving fashion. Later poets gradually brought it to the point that when the sweeper wields his broom, along with the sticks and straws he sweeps up the afflicted lover too and bears him off. When the beloved wakes up in the morning, the lover is so emaciated that he cannot find him on the bed; in desperation, he shakes out the bedding to see whether anything falls to the floor. Death wanders around looking for the lover, but he is so thin that Death cannot spot him. (108–9)

There are other examples as well: the beloved's mouth and waist, always small, become over time so minute that they vanish entirely. And so on, and so on, as Hali provides a parody-pastiche thoroughly entertaining to read.

Moreover, this kind of satirical account—an argument ad hominem of sorts—has apparently influenced a number of Urdu critics, right up to the present day. Western readers will encounter it, borrowed without attribution (but with many of the same examples), in Sadiq's history of Urdu literature.[9] Rather than offer reasoned argument, the account really does no more than point a scornful finger: Look what silly poetry this is!

Several obvious weaknesses in such a critical approach can, of course, be noted. Any poetic genre that has enjoyed widespread and long-standing popularity will accumulate a substantial amount of mediocre poetry, and a certain quantity of genuinely bad poetry. But no amount of weak poetry can discredit the genre's achievements. Genres are not judged by their weaker moments, but by their best. Moreover—and much more important—the classical ghazal was by no means devoid of humor, and pushing *maẓmūns* to implausible limits was one way to create a witty, ironic, or simply comic effect. An occasional playful, baroque, self-mocking verse, interspersed as it was among other verses of widely varying moods and tones, made a fine addition to a ghazal. The most extravagant verses were appreciated by classical audiences in a much more sophisticated way than Hali is prepared to acknowledge.

Through such extreme examples, Hali holds some of the ghazal world's more bizarre fancies up to ridicule as though their very existence were sufficient to discredit the process that produced them. This process, a form of collective metaphor making that I have called, for want of a better term, concretization, is the process by which the whole ghazal universe grows and develops. And this process indeed takes place over time. Azad and Hali to the contrary, however, it does not move in historical lockstep from the plain to the fancy. All stages of it are always present and coexistent. Azad and Hali themselves, in their less doctrinaire moments, know this perfectly well. As soon as they move into the realm of practical criticism, their official ideology seems discreetly to fade into the background. They recognize that metaphorical extravagance and complexity can be found very early—and, conversely, that simplicity and straightforwardness can be found very late. Individual poets, and particular metaphors, always had full latitude for movement in any direction.

For within the medieval Persian ghazal tradition, there has always been verbally complex, subtle, elaborate, fanciful poetry. Alongside the tradition of Saʿdī and Ḥāfiẕ, Azad acknowledges another tradition that includes Jalāl "Asīr," "Qāsim" Mashhadī, Bedil, Nāṣir ʿAlī, and others. Although he slants his arguments markedly in favor of the former tradition, he cannot deny that in the latter one "those who enjoy the breezes of the garden of *ḳhiyāl bandī* and *nāzuk ḳhiyālī*" are able to "develop many subtleties and delicacies such that if you think carefully about them you get extreme pleasure." Such poets may indeed "throw away the roses and make use merely of scent without flowers"—but Azad concedes that "these *maẓmūns*, through an imaginative subtlety and delicacy, create freshness in the poem" (377). Elsewhere, Hali too divides Persian poetry into the simple and the complex: over against Saʿdī, Ḳhusrau, Ḥāfiẕ, and Jāmī he places Ẓahūrī, Naẕīrī, ʿUrfī, Ṭālib, Asīr, and others. Hali acknowledges that even though this latter tradition is nowadays falling into disfavor as people in India turn to "natural poetry," changing fashions over time can never alter these poets' masterfulness or their serious importance.[10]

Moreover, in the Urdu ghazal itself, the idea of a development over time from straightforward simplicity to verbal complexity cannot be sustained. Azad complains, as we have seen, that wordplay was present from the very start of Urdu poetry: "The foundation of poetry was laid on it," and "among the poets of the first *daur*, this edict remained constantly in force" (75–76). While, conversely, Azad's fifth-*daur* hero Żauq not only uses literary devices like similes and metaphors but can also create a simplicity that cuts like a razor, so that the hearer sometimes says *Vāh!* in admiration, and sometimes sighs (*Āh!*) in sheer emotion (455).

Hali in fact acknowledges (on occasion) that the gradual development of *maẓmūns* over time—the very process he has ridiculed so scathingly—sometimes enables later poets to improve on earlier ones; he gives several examples in which his own hero, Ġhālib, has done so (147–50) and names no fewer than five other late poets who have developed—and even in some cases "purified"—their art and language, reaching new heights of accomplishment (112).[11] He recognizes that *maẓmūns* can and must be reused, for even in very early Arabic poetry the inevitability of repetition—either of others or of oneself—is affirmed. "Thus, when 1,350 years ago poets held this opinion, how can we say that we can dispense with the insights of earlier poets, or that we have the power to use some *maẓmūn* once and then not repeat it?" In fact, Hali notes two contradictory Arabic sayings on this subject: "Earlier poets have left a great deal for later poets," and "Earlier poets have left nothing for later poets." From these two sayings we should conclude, he says most interestingly, that "earlier poets have left many incomplete things, so that later poets can complete them, but they have left for later poets nothing of which no example is already present" (146).

· · ·

As we have seen, Hali also argues in his less reasonable moments that "later poets took every *maẓmūn,* which the ancient poets had used in a natural way, and brought it beyond the boundary of nature into another world" (109). But if the ghazal universe does not develop linearly over time from simplicity to extravagance, neither does it start from any primal, authentic place "within" the boundary of nature and later transgress that boundary. All poetry, being made of words in the first place, is irrevocably cut off from the external, natural world; the immemorial chasm between word and thing, between signifier and signified, has in our century become an object of intense fascination, with a river of critical ink flowing through it. And if this is true of all poetry—even of poetry that does aspire to represent the world—how much more is it true of the ghazal, which explicitly does not. Practices like the use of *iṣlāḥ,* the invocation of the warrant, and the holding of patterned mushairahs all fly in the face of any naturalistic poetics: they remind us that the ghazal has always aspired to move not from nature to art, but from art to art.

In short, if there was ever a genre of poetry that made and inhabited its own world, that genre was surely the classical ghazal. We have seen how Ṣābir put it: "The sequences of lines, through the reflection of *maẓmūns,* are lamp-wicks for the bedchamber of the page. The circular letters, through the effect of meaning (*ma'nī*), are the wine-mark on the flagon in the festive gathering of pages."[12] In this world made of lines and letters, pages of poetry have such potent and substantial lives that they sleep, wake, drink, and gather for parties. And why not? They have no need to look outside for validation. They have good cause to celebrate the matchless creative powers they command within their own world.

When Ṣābir described the lives of pages of poetry, he attributed their powers to the active effects of *maẓmūns* and *ma'nī*. The classical poetic terms we have discussed—*maẓmūn āfirīnī, ma'nī āfirīnī, shorish, kaifiyat,* and the ubiquitous and fundamental *rabṭ* and *ravānī*—are well able to appear as powers in their own right, as presences that loom large in the poet's practice and give effective guidance to the discourse between ustad and shagird. They are analytical indeed, but so intimately and helpfully so that they are also in a sense creative. Without such concepts, how could the fundamental back-and-forth, creative-and-critical process of *iṣlāḥ* ever proceed?

By contrast, "natural poetry" is a term of general after-the-fact approval that provides very little guidance for the practicing poet. Hali means it to suggest a sort of haunting simplicity; he praises above all a description by Ibn Rashīq: "When it is read, everyone thinks, 'I can compose such poetry'; but when he tries, his inventive powers fail him." It is hard to imagine ustads and shagirds using such a criterion in their work. Hali is aware of the problem. He attempts to meet it by falling back on his three terms borrowed (after a fashion) from Milton: simplicity, truth, and fervor. He claims that these three terms provide the key not only to recognizing, but also to composing, fine poetry. Although they are not infallible, "the poet who keeps those three requirements in mind will find that here and there in his poetry those flashes of lightning will be seen" (95). Still, even the finest poets produce uneven work, for only God is perfect. Hali acknowledges that he has not said enough on this subject, but says he hopes to return to it on some later occasion (96).

The logic of his own argument, however, requires him to take a more radical step as well. If he cannot produce terms that can guide the process of *iṣlāḥ*, that is because his view of poetry tends to discredit the whole notion of *iṣlāḥ*—and with it the ustad-shagird relationship itself. Hali advises, first of all, that only a person who has an inborn gift and a suitable temperament should even think of writing poetry. (Azad agrees: "The poet brings his poetry with him when he comes out of his mother's womb" [231].) Only someone, says Hali, who has for poetry the same instinct that leads a weaverbird to build a nest, or a spider to spin a web, should attempt to create poetry (97). And that person needs only minimal outside help—just as a weaverbird needs only straw and twigs, while the ability to shape the nest comes from within (98). "The custom of choosing an ustad for poetry, and always showing work to him for *iṣlāḥ*, has come down through the ages in our country; but there is no hope of any substantial advantage systematically accruing to the shagird." For what can the ustad do for the shagird, Hali asks scornfully, except correct his faults of grammar or meter?[13] "In order to become a poet, the first thing is a previously existing capability; and then, the examination of nature." Only tertiarily should one read and study (rather than memorize) earlier poetry, and seek the company of those with "a true taste" for poetry—whether or not, Hali adds pointedly, they are poets (99).

Hali thus insists on the poet's direct "examination of nature" as a firm and fundamental principle. But, as usual with Hali, there seems to be a bit of leeway as well. For the poet has a power that "frees him from the bonds of time and space, and brings the past and the future into the present age for him." The poet "describes Adam and Heaven, Doomsday and the rising of the dead, as though he has seen all these events with his own eyes," and makes his descriptions as moving to others as real accounts would be. Nor is his power confined to religious visions: the poet can depict even Jinns and Parīs, the *'anqā* or imaginary bird, the Water of Life, and other such "imaginary and nonexistent things" so skillfully that "a picture of them appears before the eyes." It is as if "when the heart rises to some extent above its normal level," the poet is no longer bound by the rules of logic: "sometimes a single word of his makes a magic army stand before us" (51).

Of course, this imaginative power must be used with discrimination. Otherwise, its movement is as dangerous as that of an extremely swift horse with no bit in its mouth. "The freedom and unbridledness of this power have led thousands of promising poets astray." The imagination is most "high-flying and reckless" when the poet's mind fails to provide it with its proper food of "realities and events." Then it creates "improbable ideas devoid of all truth," and forcibly carries the poet off in a mad dash over hill and dale. Such a misfortune is quite avoidable, however, for "the treasury of nature is always open to the poet," so that there is no shortage of true food for the imagination. Thus, rather than sitting at home and making paper flowers, the poet should contemplate the power of creation as manifested in "mountains, forests, and his own inner self," for thus he will find an undecaying treasury of real flowers (67).

But if imagination is to be held in check by judgment and focused on nature, this does not mean that it has no scope at all. It means rather that poetry must be founded on something that is present "in reality, or in people's belief, or only really in the poet's own opinion—or it should appear that it is really present in his opinion," at least while he is writing.

The poet need not hold himself slavishly subject to reality, but there must be "a preponderance of truth" in his endeavor; if by his own choice he "emphasizes or de-emphasizes" things, that's quite permissible (73). He may even indulge in outright "exaggeration"—provided he either stays within hailing distance of reality, or shows an especially convincing degree of fervor. When one is writing odes, for example, there is a difference between praising people lavishly for qualities they possess to only a modest degree (which is acceptable, though risky), and praising them for qualities of which they are completely devoid (which is not acceptable) (75–76).

The barrier that separates good, natural poetry from bad, overimaginative poetry is thus a porous one. Or rather, it is a firm one pierced by a certain number of loopholes—loopholes that Hali can enlarge or shrink according to the rhetorical needs of the moment. He can often be seen to give back with one hand what he has just taken away with the other. Thus, since the poet inherits a world of Devs, Parīs, the Water of Life, and so forth, which "the progress of human knowledge" has shown to be false, he ought not to wash his hands of these entities entirely but ought rather "to describe realities and events and true and natural ideas in the guise of these false and baseless things." The poet should not by any means allow the enchantment (*ṭilism*) created by his elders to be broken—"otherwise he will immediately see that the very parts of his magic spell that bring hearts into subjugation have slipped his mind" (161). The poet is to undermine the powers of the old imaginative world and subvert that world from within; he can thus win people over gradually to the new poetry without breaking the spell of the old.

But the goal is very clear, and all the rest is merely tactical: "realities and events and true and natural ideas" are to be the stuff of poetry, and "examination of nature" the source from which they are to be drawn. The new poet will be almost literally a "naturalist," a close observer of nature. In the classical tradition, by contrast, the poet does not observe nature but somehow himself becomes a natural force. As Ṣābir puts it, "The breath, through the floweringness of the words, is the garden breeze; and vision, through the freshness of the writing, is the vein of the jasmine."[14] The poet's mouth and eyes make their own world—out of an irreducibly, inexhaustibly creative element: words.

· · ·

Azad and Hali's whole relationship with their own heritage is haunted by the invisible presence of Wordsworth and his poetics—"or 'prosaics,' as they might more correctly be called."[15] Neither Azad nor Hali so much as mentions his name; but Hali in particular seems to be writing in the *Introduction* an Urdu counterpart to the "Preface." Wordsworth claimed, as we have seen, that the "earliest poets of all nations generally wrote from passion excited by real events"; unlike later mechanical imitators, "they wrote naturally, and as men." Wordsworth sets himself up in the "Preface" as a champion and paradigm of such "natural poetry," and more than one of his junior contemporaries saw him in this light. Matthew Arnold, for example, says, "Wordsworth's poetry, when he is at his best, is inevitable, as inevitable as Nature herself. It might seem that Nature not only gave him the matter for his poem, but wrote his poem for him. He has no style."[16] (No style—what an appalling compliment!)

This line of thought was sometimes carried so far as even to be turned against Wordsworth himself. Mill found Wordsworth not nearly natural enough, for the only truly natural poetry is pure, unmediated emotion: it is "Feeling itself, employing Thought only as the medium of its utterance." Natural poetry is thus expressive, overflowing, unrelated to the external world. For Mill, Shelley's poetry is the ideal, while that of Wordsworth "has little even of the appearance of spontaneousness."[17]

It was the fashion of the time. During the early decades of the nineteenth century a kind of literary "Naturalism" was "so powerful in England" that it permeated "Coleridge's Romantic supernaturalism, Wordsworth's Anglican orthodoxy, Shelley's atheistic spiritualism, Byron's revolutionary liberalism, and Scott's interest in the past," influencing "the personal beliefs and literary tendencies of every author."[18] In the latter half of the nineteenth century as well, naturalistic views were common enough in both England and India.

But then, in due course, such views lost their currency in the West and were displaced by new sets of critical assumptions. Wordsworthian views are so archaic now in Western literary criticism that they appear quaint; the idea that there should—or even could—be something called "natural poetry" would be incomprehensible to most contemporary critics. In Urdu criticism, however, this paradigm shift never took place. On the contrary: the demand for natural, realistic poetry was reinforced from the 1930s onward by the proletarian sympathies and nationalist concerns of the Progressive movement—and it persists in one form or another right down to the present. A "large part" of Urdu criticism rests on the underlying assumption that "poetry should be the expression of emotions. If the emotions are genuine then that's very well; but anyway they should at least be emotions."[19]

Thus the icon of "natural poetry," so long enshrined, so variously and vaguely interpreted, has never been decisively dislodged from its niche.

With the patina of time, it has now taken on a hallowed air, and most critics would still rather (explicitly or implicitly) reinterpret it, or dodge delicately around it, than question it in any radical way. The icon of "natural poetry" stands as a monument to a time in the late nineteenth century when the English owned nature, and thus had a monopoly on naturalness. The icon does not entirely block the road to the future; but it blocks the road to the past. It traps the classical ghazal within a historical bubble, like the snow scene in a glass paperweight. It makes some of the richest achievements of the Indo-Muslim tradition virtually inaccessible to their rightful heirs.

Yet, ironically enough, in our own century Western literary criticism has generally embraced visions of literature much closer to the autonomous, intertextual "game of words" of the classical ghazal than to the "natural poetry" of the reformers.[20] For much of the twentieth century, concepts like *ma'nī āfirīnī* (ambiguity, complexity, overdetermination,) and *maẓmūn āfirīnī* (metaphor, intertextuality, imagery, symbolism, allegory) would have been intelligible and interesting to most Western critics; the work of I. A. Richards on imagery and metaphor and the New Critics' emphasis on close reading come particularly to mind. And conversely, Urdu critics could have made excellent use of the work of such Western theorists. But not nearly enough such connections have been made, and not in nearly enough depth.[21] All too many Urdu critics have continued either to reproach the classical ghazal for its unnaturalness, hewing generally to the line of Azad and Hali, or else to defend the ghazal as best they can against such accusations of unnaturalness—internally generated accusations that Western critics would no longer make.[22]

What can we call this situation except part of the colonial legacy? It is understandable that Azad and Hali threw the baby out with the bathwater; but how remarkable that almost no one has yet gone back to reclaim the baby! And the few who have tried have often found themselves denounced for their trouble.[23] It is high time that we start to appreciate the ghazal on its own complex, compelling terms. For the ghazal glories in its own creative powers. The ghazal flaunts its artifice.

12 POETRY AND MORALITY

"The literature of a nation corresponds to its conditions," Azad tells us. "As was Indian education and civilization, as was the taste of the kings and nobles—so too was its literature." But above all, "everything in a country advances to the extent that it is connected with the government." European governments know how to use literature politically: "By the force of speeches and writings they make hundreds of thousands of men change in concert from one opinion to another." The difference between their literature and ours is "that of heaven and earth." Still, Azad notes optimistically, "the good fortune of Urdu, and its good prospects, are enviable." It has survived what should by rights have been its doom: "Urdu emerged from Delhi—and its lamp ought to have been extinguished with the kingship of Delhi." However, just the opposite happened: "If you stand in the midst of India and call out, 'What's the language of this land?' then you'll hear the answer, 'Urdu'" (60–61).

But Urdu is the national language of an India that has entered a bewildering new era, full of technological wonders, in which the new rulers seem to control even the forces of nature:

> Now the sun is the symbol of our Queen [Victoria] of the Horizons, and it has not been permitted to stray outside the margins of her written page. The postal service and the railroads, running from Europe to the east, have confined all kinds of animals in one cage. Delhi is destroyed, Lucknow desolate. Some of their authoritative people are under the ground, some wandering helplessly from door to door. Now Lucknow is like other cities, Delhi is like other cantonments and bazaars—or rather, even worse. No city remains whose people are capable of authority over language.

Most of the elders and ustads are dead. Even the occasional survivor is "like a dying autumn leaf on a tree," his voice unheard amidst "the clamor of committees and the drumrolls of newspapers." Azad concludes, as usual, on a somber note: "We are in a ship without a pilot, and we confide tomorrow to God" (63).

Azad has little to say, beyond general endorsement, about the use of language for political discourse and national opinion shaping; his own inner dislike for "the clamor of committees" is quite apparent. But other kinds of linguistic and literary reform concern him more closely. The Victorian attitudes taking shape in India in his time required a moral cleanup of the poetic tradition, the imposition of strict literary standards of decency to accompany the new, much more puritanical attitude toward sexual behavior. Azad, who attacks the classical tradition so forcefully for its "romantic *maẓmūns*" and excessive interest in love, might be expected to welcome this development. In a way, he does; but in an even deeper way, it seems that he does not. However strongly he attacks the old poetry on literary grounds, he is ambivalent about attacking it on moral grounds—and in fact he often turns to protect it against attacks from others.

One whole genre singled out for particular Victorian disapproval was the satire or insult-poem, which could often be obscene, or scatological, or both. This disapproval was a new and systematic importation of moral judgment into the literary realm. For early in the tradition the word *qaṣīdah* meant not just an ode but any poem with a purpose (*maqṣad*). Thus Mīr describes Saudā as composing a *qaṣīdah dar ḥajv*, a "*qaṣīdah* of satire." Praise and insult, ode and satire, were two sides of the same literary coin. Mīr describes Mīr Jaʿfar "Zaṭallī" (c. 1659–1713) as going to a patron's house to dine, equipped with both an ode and a satire—ready to recite the one or the other according to the degree of deference he was shown by his host.[1] Neither praise nor insult was expected to be objectively true. At the most, a tiny kernel of fact might be useful: if someone could ride a horse, he might be magnified into the cavalier of the age; if someone was a bit tight with his money, he might be depicted as a ridiculous miser. Everyone knew that a good effect demanded not factuality but extravagance, hyperbole, wordplay, wit, and literary skill.

Azad, however, begins by loudly joining the Victorian chorus. "I want to make it clear that the satire is a thorny branch of our poetry that is full of unpleasantness from its fruit to its flowers." Its "impurity of temper" has helped to make Saudā "notorious." Azad refers, among other examples, to the incident we have earlier discussed, in which Saudā is said to have composed a vulgarly insulting quatrain (the "ass with his mouth full of excrement" one) against Makīn. This said, however, Azad springs at once to Saudā's defense: "But the truth is that whatever came from his lips was due either to mere mischief, or to some feigned burst of anger." Moreover, once "the words were committed to paper, his heart was cleared" of ill will. Azad even goes over to the attack, saying sarcastically, "Our age is adorned with such civilized and refined people that they consider the words of a satire to be abuse. But God is the master of hearts" (138).

Inshā was an even more conspicuous culprit than Saudā; he wrote satires too "extremely obscene" to be recorded, but his excellent work in other genres is worthy of praise (260). The satires that he and Nāsiḳh composed against each other are so funny that every line can make you burst out laughing—but "if anyone should write such things today, he would be culpable in the eyes of the courts and the law" (272). Muṣḥafī too, competing with the newcomer Inshā for the patronage of Mirzā Sulaimān Shikoh, composed satires that were unfortunately "sullied" with "the most extreme kinds of obscenity and insults." But as Azad reflects on this kind of competitive mutual abuse, he finds extenuating circumstances. One factor was the mushairah atmosphere, in which poetic boasting was expected, every encounter was publicly and immediately won or lost, and quick, witty ripostes were much admired. Certainly the results could seem "very bad"; but it is necessary to judge carefully. "Those who pursue the art of language have a different opinion about this matter." Such people understand that "ordinary ideas" tend to have only a "weak" effect. By contrast, satire wakes people up: "When it unites with power of expression, it makes a little tickle within sleeping hearts." Azad even advises, "If you want to learn to create heat, quickness, and clarity of speech, studying such poems is an excellent tool for sharpening your language." After all, we should settle, like honeybees, on the sweet flowers, and simply ignore the dirty leaves (301–2).

But future students of language will have trouble profiting from the liveliness of satires, for many satires are known only within the oral tradition, and Azad finds some of these too obscene to be recorded. Although, he says, he "wanted to create a garden" from the colorful doings and sayings of Muṣḥafī, Jur'at, Mirzā Muḥammad Ḥasan "Qatīl," and their circle, "many of the flowers are so entangled with the thorns of obscenity that they keep shredding the paper they're written on. For this reason, I'm afraid to spread them out openly on paper" (254). The indecent exchanges between Inshā and Muṣḥafī included verses not fit to be known even within the oral tradition: "In my memory are some verses of Muṣḥafī's so vilely obscene that they are not fit to be in the memory," verses "at which

Refinement sometimes closed her eyes, and sometimes put her fingers in her ears" (303). Azad suggests—implicitly but strongly—that such verses should be put out of memory, and thus discreetly dropped from the canon.

Even worse than satire is the genre called *reḳhtī*, in which the poet assumes the persona of a woman—sometimes putting on a *dupaṭṭah* (a light veil-like shawl) and perhaps even adopting a falsetto voice—in order to recite suggestive verses in women's language. *Reḳhtī*, says Azad, was invented by Sa'ādat Yār Ḳhān "Rangīñ" with the aid of Inshā; it started as a "jest," for laughter and amusement among friends (221). But it plays the same role in creating entertainment that "filth" does in the growth of plants. "Leaving aside the question of style and dress," Azad says disapprovingly, *reḳhtī* has grave moral defects: "Its invention should be considered one cause of the effeminacy, lack of courage, and cowardice that grew up among the common people." Still, he manages to say a kind word for it: "The riddles and magic spells composed in this style show a fine taste" (259). Azad plainly considers that literary effectiveness can compensate, at least to some extent and in some cases, for moral turpitude.

· · ·

Moreover, Azad seemingly hesitates to condemn what was, from the Victorian point of view of his time, a particularly conspicuous form of immorality. For he considers "the love of boys instead of women" to have "special ties to Iran" (53), and he treats it as a part of Ṣūfism. In his account of the well-known Ṣūfī master Mirzā "Maẓhar" Jān-e Jānāñ (1699–1781), he presents Mirzā Maẓhar as an example of such tendencies. Yet Azad's account is far from straightforward, and his pretense of good faith as an objective "chronicler" (133) is not at all persuasive. His own real views remain finally obscure to us; perhaps his feelings were unresolved, and thus remained obscure even to him. The following account, therefore, is a case study not of Mirzā Maẓhar, but of Azad himself.

Mirzā Maẓhar was revered, Azad tells us, by great numbers of both Muslims and Hindus. "Many jests about him are well known, such that if such things were found in someone today, people now would not approve of his behavior. But that was a time when the aforementioned habits were considered aspects of excellence." As a second line of defense, Azad also maintains that small moral flaws can actually be thought of as beauty spots: "If on some clear, delicate, bright surface there is a scar, and it can be seen from a good angle, then it is not an ugly spot, but seems like embroidery; and the one who disapproves of it is not a person of good faith" (132).

This elaborately defensive preface introduces the life of Mirzā Maẕhar—who used to say of himself, according to Azad, "Love for beauty of Appearance (*ṣūrat*) and for the subtlety of Reality (*ma'nī*) was in my heart from the beginning" (132). Mirzā Maẕhar's father died when he was sixteen, and he at once entered into a lifelong commitment to Ṣūfism. Eventually he became not only a Persian poet and one of the early supporters of Urdu poetry, but also—and much more prominently—a well-known Ṣūfī religious figure (*pīr, murshid*) with many devoted followers (*murīd*). One of these followers was the aristocratic young poet Mīr 'Abd ul-Ḥayy "Tābāñ" (1715–1749), "whose great beauty was so universally famous that both high and low called him a second Joseph." Tābāñ was extremely aware of his charms: "With a fair complexion black clothes look very becoming, so he always dressed in black." Mirzā Maẕhar "looked on him with affection and kindness" (133).

The result, as Azad depicts it, was a kind of public flirtation: "Although Hazrat [Mirzā Maẕhar], in accordance with the etiquette of gatherings for instruction, did not openly show enthusiasm, it seemed that he looked at Tābāñ and inwardly overflowed with joy"; he "enjoyed conversing with his dearly loved one" and used to exchange witty and "spicy" (*namkīn, tez*) anecdotes with him in whispers. Without citing any authority, Azad offers a detailed, seemingly eyewitness account of such public intimacies—and contrives, in his uniquely vivid style, to make the relationship between Mirzā Maẕhar and Tābāñ appear vulgar and salacious. Azad even inserts a footnote in order to acknowledge, with an ostentatious show of reluctance, that Culture "casts a cold eye on these matters." Tābāñ's story ended sadly, for he died young. "When in the flower of his youth that second Joseph wounded all hearts [by dying], the whole city grieved for him." He thus became an even more poignant image of Azad's lost heaven: "Oh my Delhi, everything of yours is unique in the world!" (133–34).

Azad claims to be a bit at a loss to account for Mirzā Maẕhar's behavior. For Mirzā Maẕhar was a truly venerable religious figure, one who "fulfilled the commands of religious law with a sincere heart." We are not to take him lightly. "His manners and ways, his courtesy and refinement, were extremely sober and appropriate: whoever spent time in his company was careful to behave discreetly." He showed a great "delicacy of temperament" and an "inner equilibrium": he "could not tolerate improper and ill-regulated behavior" (134). At the same time, however, in his poetry "romantic images show a remarkable vividness, and this is no cause for surprise, because he had naturally the temperament of a lover." For other poets, "these *maẓmūn*s are merely imaginings"; but in his case, "they are his real state of mind" (135).

What are we to make of such an equivocal account? On the face of it, Azad seems to be asserting his own defiant, reactionary approval of now-discredited social norms. Still, he is a notably tricky writer, and one with strong personal prejudices. For example, without providing any source, he attributes to Mirzā Maẓhar a vulgarly insulting verse that contains a reference to pubic hair (92). And he mentions in a footnote, for the flimsiest of reasons and on no apparent evidence, that Mirzā Maẓhar "had installed a washerwoman in his house" (136). He also gives a deliberately distorted account of Mirzā Maẓhar's death.[2] Azad has been accused of systematically "making insinuations" about Mirzā Maẓhar, of "shaping events in such a way that they evoke not praise but blame"—and the accusation is entirely plausible.[3]

Mirzā Maẓhar, who was in any case a personage of far more religious than literary importance, seems to have been inserted somewhat arbitrarily into *Water of Life*,[4] and is the only figure about whom such markedly suggestive anecdotes are told. (Azad does describe Mīr Dard, another religious-cum-literary figure, as having courtesans among his followers; although their visits to him are innocent, his permitting such visits is made to appear reprehensible [178].)[5] By contrast, Azad gives Nāsiḳh, about whom pederastic anecdotes were well known,[6] an entirely respectable treatment, even praising him for keeping his work free from the "thorns of satire" (329–41). Azad, a determined Shīʿa, may in fact have inherited his father's well-documented taste for religious controversy. He has been suspected of indulging his partisan religious prejudices, both by presenting Ṣūfīs like Mirzā Maẓhar and Mīr Dard in a bad light and by giving favorable treatment to poets like Nāsiḳh, who was a convert to Shīʿism. Azad might thus have made an equivocal show of embracing and defending Mirzā Maẓhar—the better to slip a knife between his ribs.

But the knife he used was an unusual object: something like a genuine antique letter-opener, perhaps, with a newly sharpened edge. For Azad could claim to have based the general outlines of his portrayal at least loosely on extant source material. Farruḳhī, a fair-minded scholar in an excellent position to judge, identifies several sources from which most of Azad's anecdotes come, and does not seriously challenge any except the "washerwoman" one and the account of Mirzā Maẓhar's death.[7] One of Azad's primary sources describes Mirzā Maẓhar as "very fond of beautiful men" and says of Tābāñ that "Mirzā Maẓhar's heart was not the only one heated into a fiery oven by passion for him."[8]

Another tazkirah describes Mirzā Maẓhar as "suffering in his love for Mīr ʿAbd ul-Ḥayy Tābāñ" and as composing occasional verses in Urdu (rather than Persian) only out of regard for him.[9] Another describes him as having "by nature the temperament of a lover" and says that he was "wounded by the dagger of the coquetry of this beloved [Tābāñ]."[10] Another tazkirah describes Mirzā Maẓhar in more general terms: "He had an entire taste for the worship of beauty and the love of a beautiful form, and was involved with both divine and human love."[11] Another describes him as having "tasted the relish of love," so that he engaged in "the worship of beauty and the game of love."[12] The writers of all these tazkirahs speak of Mirzā Maẓhar in respectful and sometimes even reverent terms, with full regard for his religious eminence; all mention such tendencies simply as traits of his personality, without showing the slightest self-consciousness or unease.

But then, they all composed their works before 1857, and so could live more easily in the old world. Even today, some traces of that world occasionally come to the surface. In a recent (1988) and devoutly hagiographical biography, Mirzā Maẓhar is said to have "reached a high level and a supreme rank in loverhood (*ʿāshiqī*) and in the game of love (*ʿishq bāzī*)." But the author goes on to caution the reader most emphatically that for Ṣūfīs, human love "is not founded on lust" but in fact "acts as a staircase" to divine love. He illustrates this Platonic vision of love with a traditional anecdote. Once a venerable elder, while traveling, kissed "a moon-faced one" whom he passed on the road. His follower wondered, "Why are we forbidden to do these things?" When the elder became aware of his follower's doubt, he kissed "a red-hot iron rod." And he said to his follower, "When this much strength develops within you, then you too are entitled to kiss."[13]

By Azad's time, however, the old world had come under heavy Victorian attack—and the bombardment was to continue for decades. As the redoubtable Ram Babu Saksena put it in 1927, "vitiated and perverse" Persian poetry was the source of the problem: "The boy is regarded as a mistress and his curls, his tresses, the down on his cheeks, his budding moustache, the moles on his face are celebrated with gusto in a sensual manner revolting to the mind." This leads to unnatural, "pernicious and debased" poetry.[14] Certainly there was actual pederasty in the old culture, just as there was adultery, prostitution, drunkenness, gambling, and other behavior officially viewed as reprehensible. And certainly classical poetry did not legitimize the physical expression of pederastic desires, any more than it legitimized actual adulterous affairs with respectable ladies, or actual public drunkenness, or actual apostasy from Islam. But people of the old culture felt able to invoke attraction to beautiful boys as a powerful, multivalent poetic image, just as they invoked illicit heterosexual love, intoxication, apostasy, and other images of forbidden behavior.

Any attempt to move from poetic imagery to social reality, however, is destined to break down.[15] How negatively was pederastic behavior actually viewed in the society of the time? How widely was it practiced, and what forms did it take? The poetry itself, based as it is on well-established, universally accepted *maẓmūns*, provides no real evidence. The age of the beautiful boy, for example, is left quite unclear. He seems rarely to be envisioned as an innocent child. Quite the contrary, in fact: in general he is erotically aware, flirtatious, and ready to exploit his beauty to fulfill his own wishes and desires. He seems to be beardless, yet to reach his greatest beauty as his beard just begins to grow. When his beard has entirely grown, his charm is gone, and his lovers desert him. He seems never to be envisioned as a fully adult male, a peer of the lover himself. Yet the beautiful and universally admired Tābāñ, when he "wounded all hearts" by dying in "the flower of his youth," was thirty-four years old—and thus not exactly a "boy." The subject is such a touchy one that it is hard to find discussions that are not governed by obvious (and usually Victorian) emotional attitudes. The excellent work of C. M. Naim stands almost alone in considering poetic evidence in relation to social practice, with cross-cultural references to English poetry and society.[16]

In Azad's account of Mirzā Maẓhar, the strands of poetry, Ṣūfism, and love of masculine beauty seem impossible to separate; Azad both relishes and exploits their interconnections. Sometimes poetic personae are used as images of real personality. One tazkirah praises Tābāñ as "a beloved with the temperament of a lover."[17] Conversely, Azad praises Żauq's pride and sensitivity by calling him "a lover with the temperament of a beloved."[18] In Azad's more equivocal anecdotes he may indeed be playing both ends against the middle in some fashion; or he may even be confused between reality and poetry in his own feelings. For he elsewhere tells us that a certain minor poet died young: "He was himself beautiful, and loved to look at beautiful ones, and finally gave up his life in the grief of separation" (186). Did people really die of love in those days? Can ghazal conventions be said to operate as causes in the real world? Such tangles in the lines of thought are easy to see, but hard to unravel.

Azad's ultimate word on the subject of literary morality is, however, altogether clear: it is a tribute to the irresistible power of time. For he says of Inshā:

> People say that Sayyid Inshā's poetry is libertine, and that the obscenity in it is not by way of a spice, but has come forward to rank as the main dish. This is a correct statement. But the reason for it is that Time is a powerful lord, and the popular taste is his established law. At that time everyone, from the king and the nobles to

> the beggar and the poor man, delighted in just these things. . . . If Sayyid Inshā had not done this, then what would he have done? (271–72)

Whatever we may say about the past, however we may excuse or accuse it, Azad makes it clear that Time (working now through the agency of Queen Victoria) has decreed very different tastes for the future. People must now find fresher morsels of food to chew on—and must learn to use fewer, and milder, spices.

· · ·

Hali, in the conclusion of his *Life of Saʿdī* (1884–86), presents his own analysis of the problem of pederasty. He offers a remarkably sweeping generalization: "All the poets of Iran laid the foundation of 'ghazalness' (*taġhazzul*)—that is, romantic verses—only on the love of youths and beardless boys." But although on the face of it this seems "reprehensible and vile," Saʿdī and other Persian poets should not be accused of pederastic tendencies (*amrad parastī*) on these grounds alone. "In the Persian language, and under its influence in the Urdu language too, this style of poetry has come down from the beginning: that whether the poet be a man or a woman, a rake or a Ṣūfī, a lover of God or of [human] creatures, a lover of men or of women, or rather in the first place a lover or not a lover—he always writes ghazals in a manner that shows that the poet is in love with someone, and that he and his beloved are both men." By contrast, in "Hindi" (that is, Braj Bhasha) poetry, an equally powerful tradition causes the poet to write as a woman in love with a man; and in Arabic poetry, the poet writes as a man in love with a woman. Hali then offers, as proof of these indefensibly broad generalizations, the work of Amīr Ḳhusrau, who wrote poetry in Arabic, Persian, and Hindi, and did indeed, according to Hali, observe the poetic rules of each language.[19]

"Thus it is clear," Hali concludes, "that these are all imaginary and conventional forms of expression that have no relation to actual reality." As such, they do not please him: they show the "extreme unreality of Eastern poetry," the principles of which are based solely and entirely on "artifice and convention." Moreover, even as a literary convention the love of boys demands to be explained: to write as a man loving a woman (the Arabic mode) or a woman loving a man (the Hindi mode) is "according to nature," but "for a man to fall madly in love with a man, and seek union and enjoyment with him" is something "that human nature entirely rejects." How then did such a convention develop? Hali feels there is "hardly any doubt" that it was the genderless character of the Persian language that gave rise, over time, to misunderstandings. Another contributing factor might have been the extreme jealousy shown by Muslims toward their women, such that early ghazals depicting illicit love for women might have aroused suspicion and distrust in powerful patrons.[20] (Both these causes, however, imply gradual change over time, and thus conflict with the absoluteness of Hali's previous statements.)

But, Hali then adds, even if Shaiḳh Sa'dī and other venerable poets appear from some of their poetry to have been genuinely attracted to beardless boys, "I do not give this any bad meaning." For Ṣūfī sources make it clear that "human love, if it is pure and sinless, is a very major means to inner progress for the seeker, and in a number of venerable elders and mystics this quality has been seen, together with purity and chastity." Such Ṣūfī poets are even exempt from the accusations of artificiality and conventionality to which other poets are subject—for they recount, in the guise of human love, the real stages and events of their own spiritual progress.[21]

Hali does not, however, adduce any evidence for his extreme and sweeping claim of the primacy of the "beardless boy" as beloved in *all* Persian and Urdu ghazals. It is important to remember that in the overwhelming majority of verses, no clue at all is given about the gender of the beloved; most descriptions of beauty, cruelty, coquetry, and so on could apply either to a beautiful woman or to a beautiful boy—or, of course, to God, the ultimate Beloved. Grammar is no real help, for the beloved is by convention (almost) always grammatically masculine, even when "he" is described in terms appropriate only to a woman. Only in the occasional verse that mentions a gender-specific physical trait (beard, breasts), item of clothing (turban, blouse), or term ("boy"), can the gender of the beloved be known with certainty—for that one verse.

If the beloved indeed had a well-established gender, as Hali asserts, a gender that was tacitly assumed by all poets and audiences in the absence of specific countervailing evidence, no one has been able to prove it.[22] For the whole Perso-Arabic tradition of literary theory, which has so much to say about language and rhetoric in the ghazal, has virtually no interest in the question of the beloved's gender. The one real, crucial role of the beloved in the ghazal is to be *absent*—and a radically absent beloved becomes a fantasy being, endowed with a shifting set of traits that exist chiefly or only in the lover's imagination. In this respect the beloved resembles the *'anqā*, the bird defined by its elusiveness. All that can be said with real certainty is that the classical ghazal includes along with its great preponderance of sexually unspecific verses, some verses in which the beloved is clearly a beautiful woman,[23] and some verses in which the beloved is clearly a beautiful boy.[24]

· · ·

We have seen that in 1882 Hali planned "to set forth means for the *iṣlāḥ* of Urdu poetry, which has become extremely corrupt and injurious," and "to make clear how much benefit poetry, if it is founded on excellent principles, can bring to the community." This plan resulted in the *Introduction*, along with many other essays, books, and poems. Exactly a quarter of a century later (1907), in the last decade of his life, Hali felt that he had carried his plan through to fruition. For he wrote to a friend about his irritation when someone introduced him merely as "a poet in both Persian and Urdu" who had "no equal in India." This, in Hali's eyes, largely missed the point. For the speaker should have said that Hali had "made Asian poetry, which was only a useless thing, beneficial," and that "through him a great revolution has been brought about in the thinking of the Indian Muslims."[25]

Certainly if the *Introduction* has a central theme, it is the interdependence of poetry and society, and the need for poetry to change as society changes—or, if possible, even before society changes, so as to bring about desirable conditions in society and reverse undesirable ones. For poetry has a God-given power to excite the emotions, and can thus be used the way steam power can: to run a variety of machines (15–16). Civilized nations make good use of poetry (16). Bad poetry can corrupt, but good poetry can purify (29). At the worst, a vicious circle can develop: "In the beginning the corrupt taste of society ruins poetry; but once poetry is spoiled, its poisonous atmosphere inflicts extremely severe harm on society" (38). Poetry then tends to become full of wonders, fictions, and the supernatural—and hostile to history, geography, mathematics, and science (39). The poet must make careful, discerning use of his imaginative powers, for he alone can pick grains of silver out of sand (63). The poet is, for better or worse, "the tongue of the nation" (199).

Hali is concerned to improve all the principal genres of Urdu poetry. The ode, however, is almost a hopeless case: it is so out of accord with the times that poets will have no choice but to simply take their models from European poetry and start over (202). The *maśnavī* has good possibilities, but must be more refined in the future: some *maśnavīs*, like those of Nawab Mirzā "Shauq," are "immoral beyond all bounds and contrary to culture"; others are vague about their plots and explicit only about their "shamelessness," so that they pride themselves on "mentioning before all the world things that are not to be spoken of" (226). Mīr Ḥasan's, though, show "much respect for shame and modesty" (216); since Mīr Ḥasan was earlier than Shauq, it is not surprising that here and there, most commendably, he "painted visual pictures of natural situations" (218–19). The elegy, at its best, is the only Urdu genre worthy of being called "moral poetry." It can achieve a special "high level of morality" and religious pathos because it can make use of the events of Karbala (193)—a point that Hali chooses to emphasize, surprisingly, by telling the whole story of Karbala at considerable length (193–98).

But Hali recognizes that "*iṣlāḥ* of the ghazal" is the "most important and necessary" task, because the ghazal is so protean and widely popular; everyone, educated and illiterate, old and young, has at least some interest in it. Moreover, it needs quite a number of changes. Its formal structure must be made freer: the "bonds" of rhyme and refrain, which are "impossible to endure," must be loosened to some extent (127). And there must be changes in content as well, though these will of course be difficult, for speaking of "lust and desire" gives a pleasure that "not everyone can obtain from pure love" (128). Love is an indispensable foundation for the ghazal, but to have a real effect it must be sincere, not a literary pose or imitation. And why should it be limited to romantic love? The ghazal should find room for the love of "children for parents, parents for children, brother and sister for each other, the husband for the wife, the wife for the husband, the servant for the master, the populace for the king, friends for friends, a man for an animal, the house-dweller for the house, the homeland, the nation, the community, the family" (129–30).

In short, the ghazal should admit all the various kinds of love. Yet, most remarkably, Hali insists that a radical ambiguity is to be preserved: insofar as possible, no word is to be used that shows clearly whether the beloved is male or female! To hammer the point home, he actually provides a list of such forbidden gender-revealing words: names for items of clothing and physical traits, along with phrases like "son of," and so on (131). This would seem, however, to demolish his project of incorporating into the ghazal all the particular kinds of love he has just finished specifying; for how could they possibly be recognized and appreciated as such, if not even the gender of the beloved could be revealed? How to celebrate one's love for a son or daughter, a husband or wife, a brother or sister, a master—not to speak of an animal, a house, a country—without identifying them even so much as by gender? Hali seems not to realize that he has just called for a reform program with two parts that largely cancel each other out.

He then turns to the problem of the male beloved. Noting that he has already dealt with the question in detail in his conclusion to the *Life of*

Sa'dī, he briefly repeats his main points. The evocation of a man loving a man "is founded merely on a misunderstanding and a rashness in the thought of the community, not on realities and events." Nevertheless, it is such a "vile and unworthy custom" that it "creates a stain on the morality of the community." Thus "insofar as possible" it ought to be quickly abandoned, regardless of the fact that it has come down to us from "all the renowned poets" of Iran and India. "The claims of every age are different." If we imitate the "words of obscenity and shamelessness" found in the poetry of the great ancient poets of Iran and India, we will be "adjudged guilty according to the [British antiobscenity] law." Therefore just as we have abandoned many of our ancestors' follies out of fear of punishment by the courts, "we ought also to abandon one or two follies merely at the command of wisdom and morality" (131–32).

At this point Hali renews his insistence on evoking a beloved of indeterminate gender. If the beloved is depicted either as a respectable married or engaged woman, or as a prostitute (*bāzārī besvā*), it is shameful in either case to trumpet one's love in public (132). And a beloved left in a desirable state of "nonparticularity" (*iṭlāq*) requires grammatical masculinity, for in "the languages of the world" masculine forms are used for universal statements. Given this masculine grammatical form, if sexually specific words are used about the beloved, and if these words are sometimes male and sometimes female, "this will mean that the beloved is neither a man nor a woman, but a eunuch or a transsexual (*hījṛā*)." The best course is thus to continue the tradition of the numerous Persian and Urdu verses based on generalized or spiritual or divine love: the verse should give "absolutely no information" about whether the desired one is a man or a woman (133).

If poets observe this one great rule of gender ambiguity, they can say in the ghazal anything they want to say. They can write about "anything that arises with a true fervor" in their hearts: "happiness, or grief, or longing, or friendship, or gratitude, or complaint, or patience, or pleasure, or contentment, or trust, or desire, or hatred, or mercy, or justice, or anger, or surprise, or hope, or despair, or passion, or waiting, or love of country, or national (*qaumī*) sympathy, or turning to God, or supporting faith and religion, or the impermanence of the world and the thought of death, or any other human feeling." However much the ghazal takes as its true subject love alone, it can in fact say anything (138).

Hali recognizes that "moral *maẓmūns*" may prove less exciting than romantic ones; to make them effective is an "extremely difficult task." If the ghazal becomes too full of "advice and counsel," it may lose its charm. But a great revolution is now happening in the world. A lifetime is not long enough to describe it. New events constantly arouse strong emotions: surprise, regret, fear, despair. What better material could there be for the ghazal? If the scope of a two-line verse seems insufficient for the purpose, poets should remember the "continuous ghazal" used by many ustads, in which all the verses are part of a linear treatment of a single theme. "For example, the feelings aroused by every season, the scenes of morning and evening, the pleasure of a moonlit night, the verdancy of a forest or garden, the hustle and bustle of fairs and festivals, the desolation of a graveyard, the events of a journey, the heartfelt devotion to one's homeland, and many other things of this type" can be expressed very well in a "continuous ghazal" (140–41).

Despite—and also because of—the many self-contradictions in Hali's arguments, it is clear that poets of the future are being asked to destroy the classical ghazal in order to save it. In the space of a few pages Hali exhorts them: to loosen the ghazal's strict formal structure; to replace its vision of (illicit) erotic love with a variety of "virtuous" and almost entirely nonerotic loves; to be scrupulously careful never to reveal the gender of the beloved; to write not merely about love but about any emotion they genuinely feel; and to tie together the ghazal's autonomous two-line verses into a connected genre capable of natural description and even of narrative. We are back in the realm of Colonel Holroyd, whose chosen mushairah themes—"The Rainy Season," "Winter," "Hope," "Patriotism," "Peace," "Justice," "Compassion," "Contentment," "Civilization"—would fit excellently into Hali's lists of "moral *maẓmūns*." Except, of course, that all this naturalness is somehow required to coexist with a strikingly unnatural convention, emphasized by Hali as it never was in the classical ghazal: the absolute, rigorously maintained sexual indeterminacy of the beloved.

· · ·

Azad and Hali were thus doomed to twist and turn, vainly seeking to escape the horns of an impossible dilemma. Poetry must be natural—and poetry must also be moral. If the classical ghazal depicted real, actual loves, as natural poetry should, then it was thoroughly immoral: it spoke of a society obsessed with adultery, illicit seduction, prostitution, and pederasty. But if the ghazal in fact indirectly depicted (by exploiting its immense metaphorical resources) morally correct loves, then it had to be seen as so arcane, complex, and conventionalized that it could never be described as natural. Try as they might, Azad and Hali could never manage to make the ghazal both natural and moral at the same time. But they could never afford to abandon their grip on either adjective. For while the ghazal couldn't really be seen as having both virtues, it could all too easily be seen as having neither. And to be both unnatural and immoral was to be utterly decadent, to be without redeeming social importance, to be part of a page of history that had already been turned. "In a time of ascendant fortune, moods of love and desire were appropriate," Hali told his countrymen grimly. "Now that time has gone" (141).

EPILOGUE

Concluding his review of *Water of Life,* Hali said that the book offered to "people of judgment" a "detailed statement of the case, which contains sufficient testimony for a verdict about Urdu poetry."[1] He agreed with Azad about what that verdict should be, and he lived long enough to see the tide of opinion running strongly in his direction.

In retrospect, it can be argued that the year 1874 marked a kind of symbolic watershed for Urdu literature. That year saw both Azad's Anjuman-e Panjāb speech advocating a whole new English-based poetics, and the famous Anjuman mushairah series based on common topics rather than common formal patterns. Moreover, the year also saw the publication of the third novel in an extremely popular set written by Nażīr Aḥmad, Azad's fellow student at Delhi College, who had worked as an inspector of schools for the Department of Public Instruction before going on to a successful administrative career. This novel, *Taubat un-Naṣūḥ* (The repentance of Naṣūḥ), has been remarkably widely read and influential ever since. And it contains what has been called "one of the most horrifying scenes" in any Urdu novel.[2]

At a climactic point in the novel Naṣūḥ, whose recovery from an almost fatal illness has taught him new moral values, quarrels with his dandified son Kalīm, who has aristocratic tastes and a local reputation as a poet. Kalīm leaves home, and Naṣūḥ proceeds to investigate his son's rooms. The outer room, which Kalīm has named the "Palace of Delight," is elegantly and luxuriously furnished in the style of the old culture. Its ceiling forms a heaven of its own: "Without exaggeration, it was a replica of the sky, with the hanging fan in place of the Milky Way, the chandelier in place of the sun and moon, and the crystal light-trees exactly like stars." All the things Naṣūh sees in the room—carpets, huqqah, chandelier, playing cards, dice, music boxes, flower vases, perfume, and above all the "shameless" pictures (of artists and performers) and "irreligious" calligraphed verses on the walls—so offend him that he "picked up a carpet-weight and began to demolish them, and in an instant, tearing and smashing, he leveled them to the ground. And he put whatever was left in the courtyard and set fire to it."

When Naṣūḥ enters the inner room, the "Place of Retirement," he finds a wardrobe full of Kalīm's books, works of classical Persian and Urdu literature. He realizes that "the excellence of the binding, the pure lines of the calligraphy, the fineness of the paper, the elegance of the style, the correctness of the diction" all make the books a "priceless treasure." But "from the point of view of meaning and intention, every single volume was fit to be burnt and torn apart." Naṣūḥ is mesmerized by the books: he sits for hours, ignoring repeated calls to lunch, "looking at the books again and again, turning them over and over." But finally his resolve becomes firm: the whole wooden wardrobe full of books is carried out to the courtyard and turned into a flaming funeral pyre.[3]

Naṣūḥ's act creates turmoil—"an earthquake"—in his house. His wife Fahmīdah reproaches him for treating books with such flagrant disrespect. He responds that the books were full of "irreligion and idolatry and discourtesy and shamelessness and obscenity and slander and lies." He reminds Fahmīdah that even when he gave her the respectable *Gulistān* of Saʿdī to read, he had blacked out fully a quarter of the text—and for any other woman, he would have blacked out half. Because of the great power of poetry, he tells her, corrupting books are more dangerous than poisonous snakes: the errant Kalīm has been ruined by nothing other than his insidious books. Fahmīdah asks if there is any cure for this "poison." Naṣūḥ assures her that an antidote can easily be found—in better books, "books of faith and morality."[4]

The rejection of the old poetry (and prose) was thus enacted in a literal form as well: as a gesture of violent, deliberate physical destruction. And by no coincidence, the books were burned as part of a larger fire that included Kalīm's whole archetypally aristocratic world. At the end of the novel Kalīm, the son too old to reform, suffers and finally dies repentant; Naṣūḥ's two younger sons, much chastened, having voluntarily offered their own questionable books for burning, prepare to lead good Victorian lives.

Taubat un-Naṣūḥ earned the highest prize offered by the director of public instruction in the Northwestern Provinces for "meritorious treatises in the vernacular." The director himself, Colonel Holroyd's counterpart Matthew Kempson, liked the novel so much that he translated it (in abridged form) into English; it was published in London, with an approving preface by Sir William Muir. In Urdu, it has been read by countless adults and schoolchildren and has not been out of print since it first appeared.[5]

Naṣūḥ commits a powerful, drastic act of cultural destruction. There is no attempt at integration or synthesis. With one stroke of the new broom, the old debris is swept up into a funeral pyre—and Naṣūḥ nerves himself for the purifying conflagration. The old decadent books, full of "shamelessness" and "lies," are to be replaced by works of morality and faith—surely the same kind of works that Colonel Holroyd sought, ones "aiming at moral instruction, and presenting a natural picture of our feelings and thoughts."[6] The book-burning scene is only a bit more extreme and shocking than Azad's call for a whole new Anglicized, Victorian poetry and poetics.

As *Taubat un-Nuṣūḥ* went to press, there were other straws in the wind as well. During this same period, the members of a reformist committee on Muslim education set up by Sir Sayyid Aḥmad Ḳhān ended by denouncing their own traditional literary works, for these "teach men to veil their meaning, to embellish their speech with fine words, to describe things wrongly and in irrelevant terms, to flatter with false praise, . . . to speak with exaggeration, to leave the history of the past uncertain, and to relate facts like tales and stories."[7] In 1875, Sir Sayyid established the Muhammedan Anglo-Oriental College at Aligarh.

"The heresies of one age become the faith of another," as Sadiq duly noted, for Azad's views about poetry, which Sadiq described as "among the commonplaces of criticism today," were for the most part "anathema to Azad's contemporaries."[8] By now, however, Sadiq's "today" is itself long past. The faith in moral and "natural" poetry that may have been "among the commonplaces of criticism" in Sadiq's own time and place has come to seem—not so much heretical as irrelevant. Nowadays the "commonplaces of criticism" are hard-pressed to define themselves: they must find room for anti-novel novels, self-consuming artifacts, the cult of reflexivity and paradox, various kinds of "magical realism," authors who deliberately punch holes in their own narratives, and critics who deny the validity, or even the legitimacy, of the whole critical enterprise.

Moreover, the return of the repressed is in full swing. Even some of the more extraordinary performances of the classical literature are acquiring unexpected modern counterparts. The "Oulipo"—Ouvroir de littérature potentielle (Workshop of Potential Literature)—movement, founded in 1960, has been dedicated to the pursuit of literary structures that are "precisely definable and rigorous." The movement's goal has been called "constrictive form," since in its view "formal constraints spur the imagination."[9] As Raymond Queneau (1903–1976) put it, the Oulipo seeks to elaborate "a whole arsenal in which the poet may pick and choose, whenever he wishes to escape from what is called inspiration." The traditional Perso-Arabic poetic system produced tours de force like four-line verses that had the same meaning in whichever order the lines were read, verses divided into symmetrical phrases that could be read meaningfully in any order, and so on. But Queneau has given us *Cent Mille Milliards de poèmes* (One hundred thousand billion poems, 1961), a group of ten sonnets that is really "a combinatory ensemble: each line of each poem may replace (or be replaced by) its homologue in the nine other poems," so that something like 10^{14} potential readings exist.[10] And this has not exhausted Queneau's creativity. Urdu poets have composed, as we have seen, hundreds or even thousands of formally identical two-line verses about "sticks"—but Queneau has produced 195 stylistically distinct retellings of a single trivial moment on a bus.[11]

Such displays of technical virtuosity extended, in Perso-Arabic tradition, down to the level of particular letters of the alphabet. Azad tells us, for example, that Inshā "showed the power of his [poetic] temperament" by composing an ode, "adorned with many figures of speech," in which he confined himself to undotted letters (261). He was very proud of this feat—as well he might be, since he thus deprived himself of about half the alphabet. But another Oulipo member, Georges Perec (1936–1982), performed at least as impressive a feat: he wrote a whole novel without a single *e* in it—which is even harder to do in French than in English.[12] He also defended this achievement with (European) historical precedents and much theoretical verve.[13] Moreover, he composed poems with other remarkable alphabetical limitations, poems with restricted grammatical frameworks, bilingual poems, and—surely a supreme achievement of sorts—a palindrome five thousand letters long.[14]

The extravagance of such feats should not distract us from the larger implications of the method behind them. Such technically precise performances reawaken the vision of the "game of words" with its own cherished rules, and of the admirable and self-evident mastery of a real ustad. It is surely no accident that the members of the small, close-knit Oulipo movement worked for years in a mushairah-like atmosphere: they limited their numbers, learned from each other, and paid the closest attention to their emerging mutual body of work. Here once again was an intellectual lineage, a *silsilah* of sorts, in the process of formation. Here once again was a reinvention of the possibility of *iṣlāḥ*.

As we have seen, in the Urdu ghazal tradition *iṣlāḥ* had a precise technical meaning. The term was a valued part of the classical poetics, and had strongly positive connotations—which Azad and Hali were glad enough to exploit for their own anticlassical purposes. Azad put it very clearly: just as English arts and sciences continually improve "our clothing, houses, conditions, thoughts, and knowledge," in the same way "English literature too goes on giving *iṣlāḥ* to our literature." In the hands of Azad and Hali, the meaning of *iṣlāḥ* slides away from its clear poetic sense into a more general notion of "reform" or "improvement." As Hali ended his *Introduction,* he chose to insist above all on the need for this very abstract—and thus very slippery—*iṣlāḥ*: "Of the humble opinions about the *iṣlāḥ* of poetry that I have expressed in this essay, even if not a single one is accepted but still the thought becomes widespread in the country that truly our poetry is in need of *islāḥ,* then I will consider myself entirely successful. Because the first step toward progress is belief in one's decline" (233).

But Azad, despite all his attacks on the ghazal, ended *Water of Life* with a passionate plea to his elders for continuity and legitimation: "As time goes on, we keep lighting our lamps from yours. And however far we go forward, we move in your light alone" (528). Hali too recognized that later poets build on the work of earlier ones, as "one lamp is lit from another" (150). In our own generation, in defiance of all difficulties, the lamps continue to be lit. Despite the lack of a useful critical tradition, despite an almost universal ignorance of theory, despite the widespread, continuing, pervasive influence of Azad and Hali, the modern Urdu ghazal continues to be vigorously alive. What a supreme tribute to its powers! Somewhat narrower in scope it may be, but moribund it is not. Thus there can be great hope for the future. Modern poets still have open to them, in principle, all the literary possibilities so superbly deployed by Mīr and Ġhālib. We in our time can use the light of the great ustads' lamps not only for exploring the future, but also for recovering and reclaiming the past. Valī has said it beautifully:

> The road to fresh *maẓmūn*s is never closed—
> Till Doomsday the gate of poetry stands open.[15]

APPENDIX: A GHAZAL OBSERVED

In one passage of *Water of Life* Azad lovingly enumerates the parts of the ghazal: "That regularity of *qāfiyah,* or *radīf* and *qāfiyah* both. In the same way, first the *maṯlaʿ*, or a number of *maṯlaʿ*s, then some *shiʿrs*, finally a *maqṯaʿ*, and in it a *taḳhalluṣ*" (72). These parts can be seen in action in the following ghazal by Ġhālib (*Dīvān*, pp. 200–201), which has been translated in a way that preserves them. The cost, unfortunately, is clumsiness in English. This translation thus shows most of the formal structure—but alas, nothing of the *ravānī*, subtle wordplay, and beauty of the original.

To hell with all hindering walls and doors!
Love's eye sees as feather and wing, walls and doors. (1)

My flooded eyes blur the house
Doors and walls becoming walls and doors. (2)

There is no shelter: my love is on his way,
They've gone ahead in greeting, walls and doors. (3)

The wine of your splendor floods
your street, intoxicating walls and doors. (4)

If you're mad for waiting, come to me,
My house is a store of gazing, walls and doors. (5)

I never called down a flood of tears
for fear of my falling, pleading walls and doors. (6)

He came to live next door—
Doors and walls adoring walls and doors. (7)

A lively house stings my eyes
to tears, without you, seeing walls and doors. (8)

They greet the flood with rapture
From end to end all dancing, walls and doors. (9)

Don't tell love-secrets, Ġhālib
Except to those worthy of hearing: walls and doors. (10)

As can readily be seen, each of the ten two-line *shiʿrs*, or verses, ends in "walls and doors." This repeated refrain, called the *radīf*, is present in most ghazals, though it is not compulsory. And in each verse the word before the *radīf* ends in "-ing"; the rhyme in this position is called the *qāfiyah* and is compulsory. (It is much easier to sustain such rhyme in Urdu than in English.) The first verse sets the pattern, in a genre more often heard than read, by containing the rhyming elements twice—once at the end of each line—so that the hearer can immediately tell how much (if any) of the line is *radīf* and how much is *qāfiyah*. A verse of this special introductory form is called a *maṯlaʿ*, and most ghazals have one (although some may have more than one, and some may not have any). The last verse incorporates, by way of signature, the poet's pen name or *taḳhalluṣ* (which in this case is "Ġhālib") and thus earns for itself the special name of *maqṯaʿ*. The *maqṯaʿ* is optional; it is usually present in classical ghazals but is no longer so popular today. What has not been shown in English is the meter: every line of the ghazal is in the same rigorously defined Perso-Arabic quantitative meter.

The individual two-line verses reflect separate facets of the lover's experience. Azad described the contents of the ghazal as "romantic *maẓmūns*, intoxicated drinking of wine, creating imaginary colors and scents without the rose and the garden, lamenting the pain of separation, delighting in imaginary union, feeling alienated from the world, experiencing thus the hostility of the heavens" (77). He was not far wrong: this ghazal celebrates the flight of the lover's imagination as it soars above and beyond all barriers (verse 1); recognizes the overpowering force of pain (verses 2, 6, 9); exults in a vision of union (verses 3, 4, 7); wryly alludes to the experience of hope deferred (verse 5) and of loneliness in the midst of a cheerful crowd (verse 8); and concludes with a witty and cynical piece of advice addressed by the poet to himself (verse 10).

Individual verses not only do not follow from each other, but may flatly contradict each other. Verses 6 and 9 both rest on the same *maẓmūn*, that tears are a flood, and both envision the power of this flood to sweep away the walls and doors of the lover's house in its torrent. But verse 6 imagines the walls and doors as falling (under the impact of the flood) at the lover's feet and begging for mercy, so that the lover relents and spares them from being swept away, whereas verse 9 imagines the walls and doors as dancing with joy while they bob up and down in the flood waters, exulting (like the lover) in their own ruin. Such piquant double visions enhance, rather than diminish, the ghazal's appeal.

Equally characteristic is the ghazal's refusal to offer itself for any special mode of interpretation. There is not a simile in the whole poem, and the few explicit metaphors (in verse 4 splendor is wine, in verse 5 a house is a store) do not take us below the interpretive surface. The ghazal offers us only solidly developed, self-referential, interlocking *maẓmūns*. According to the ghazal itself, what it is "about" is doors, walls, tears, floods, and so forth; *we* may call this surface "metaphorical," but the ghazal does not. If we wish to look beyond the "metaphorical" surface and make allegorical or other interpretations, we must do so on our own responsibility. Is verse 4 addressed to God, and does it describe the way the natural universe is pervaded by divine glory? Does verse 3 express the attitude of a true revolutionary, sacrificing material possessions in the present for the sake of the imminent victory of the proletariat? Does verse 5 convey the poet's impatient longing for a pension to be provided by his dilatory patron? We may make or reject such interpretations at our pleasure, with no help from the poem itself. (And no help from the poet either, in most cases; even in the few cases where it can be adduced, such "help" is tricky, partial, and unreliable.) As Ġhālib reminds us, the poem always slips, like the imaginary *ʿanqā* bird, through even the finest nets of awareness.

GLOSSARY

Bayāẓ (notebook). A small personal notebook carried by poetry lovers; a *bayāẓ* normally contains a record of memorable verses its owner has heard or composed.

Bouquet. See *guldastah.*

Chronogram. See *tārīḳh.*

Closing verse. See *maqṭaʿ.*

Continuous ghazal. See *ġhazal-e musalsal.*

Dīvān (volume). A collection of poems by a single author. A *dīvān* is normally arranged in alphabetical order by the last letter of the *radīf* (refrain)—but not by the next-to-last, so that the poet is able to make his own arrangement.

Elegy. See *marṡiyah.*

Faqīr (faqir). A religious mendicant; ideally, one who lives an austere, simple life of wandering and meditation.

Ġhazal (ghazal). A genre of lyric poetry in Arabic, Persian, Turkish, Urdu, and other languages. See the appendix for a close look at a ghazal.

Ġhazal-e musalsal (continuous ghazal). A ghazal in which all the verses are linked into a sequence by a progressive development of meaning; it may even be used for narrative.

Ground. See *zamīn.*

Ground-sharing. See *ham zamīn.*

Guldastah (bouquet). An anthology of formally identical ghazals, often containing those recited at a particular mushairah.

Ḥajv (satire). A poem of (at least purportedly) humorous insult or abuse; some works in this genre are light and witty, others quite genuinely hostile; some are scatological or obscene.

Ham zamīn (ground-sharing). Having the same *zamīn* (ground), and thus formally identical.

Ḥaẓrat (Hazrat). "The Presence," a title given to honored personages.

Implication. See *kināyah*.

Inshā'iyah. A mode of discourse—exclamatory, interrogative, vocative, subjunctive, etc.—that does not purport to give factual information; opposed to *k̤habariyah*.

Intik̤hāb (selection). A sampler or selection of poetry (or prose), often in abridged form. An *intik̤hāb* may be based on a single poet, a single genre, or simply the taste of the compiler.

Iṣlāḥ (correction). In poetry, the process of pointing out technical errors in a line or verse, and/or suggesting specific improvements in word choice or arrangement.

Iẓāfat. A Persian and Urdu grammatical construction that connects two words—the first usually a noun, the second either a noun or an adjective—by means of a small linking vowel. See chapter 8.

Joining lines. See *miṣra' lagānā*.

Kaifiyat. "Mood." A term for the response evoked by a certain kind of verse: an ineffable, mysterious, melancholy, romantic mood in the reader or hearer. See chapter 8.

K̤habariyah. A declarative mode of discourse that does purport to give factual information; opposed to *inshā'iyah*.

K̤hiyāl bandī. A term used, either admiringly or disparagingly, for a tendency to carry *maẓmūn āfirīnī*, the creation of (complex) meaning, to extremes.

Kināyah (implication). The art of causing the (suitably knowledgeable) reader or hearer to draw inferences and perceive implications beyond what is specifically stated in the verse. This is one of the techniques of *ma'nī āfirīnī*.

Kulliyāt. The complete works of an author.

Line. See *miṣra'*.

Ma'nī. In both normal and poetic use, "meaning."

Ma'nī āfirīnī. "Meaning-creation." The multiplication and enrichment of poetic meaning; the art of creating a verse that will elicit two or more different interpretations, and/or will be surrounded by a penumbra of suggestion (*kināyah*). See chapter 8.

Maqṯa' (closing verse). Literally, "point of cutting off." In a ghazal, a verse that both includes the poet's pen name and occupies the last (or sometimes next-to-last) position.

Marṡiyah (elegy). A lament written to commemorate someone's death. Many—but not all—Urdu *marṡiyah*s are devoted to the death of Ḥaẓrat Ḥusain at Karbala.

Mashshāq (practiced). A term of respect for a poet who has, with time and experience, developed excellent technical skills.

Maṡnavī. A narrative or reflective poem, often longish but of no fixed length, often romantic but with no prescribed subject matter. Its two-line verses normally rhyme AA, BB, CC, etc.

Maṯla' (opening verse). Literally, "where the sun rises." In a ghazal, an introductory pattern-setting verse that has the rhyme (and refrain, if any) at the end of each of its two lines.

Maẓmūn. Roughly, a poetic theme or proposition. See chapter 7.

Maẓmūn āfirīnī. "Proposition-creation." The making of the (implicit or explicit) assertions of metaphoric identity from which the ghazal universe develops. See chapter 7.

Miṣra' (line). A single hemistich or line of poetry.

Miṣra' lagānā (joining lines). A technical exercise in which one line of a verse is provided and the poet is challenged to improvise another line that will complete the verse.

Miṣra'-e ṯaraḥ (pattern line). A line specified in advance, to which all the poems recited at a given mushairah are expected to conform in meter and rhyme and refrain. It is often part of a *maṯla'*, an opening verse.

Musaddas. A poem in stanzas of six lines, usually rhyming AAAABB.

Mushā'irah (mushairah). A gathering at which poets read their verses—which are usually, by prearrangement, formally identical ones—before an audience of ustads, shagirds, connoisseurs, and patrons. Mushairahs are discussed at length in chapter 5.

Nāzuk ḳhiyālī. A term used, either admiringly or disparagingly, for a tendency to carry *maẓmūn āfirīnī* to extremes.

Notebook. See *bayāẓ*.

Ode. See *qaṣīdah*.

Opening verse. See *maṭla*ʿ.

Pattern. See *ṭaraḥ*.

Pattern line. See *miṣra*ʿ*-e ṭaraḥ*.

Patterned. See *ṭaraḥī*.

Pen name. See *taḳhalluṣ*.

Practiced. See *mashshāq*.

Qāfiyah (rhyme). In a ghazal, the rhyming syllable at the end of the second line of each two-line verse. The *qāfiyah* is usually (though not in all ghazals) followed by a *radīf* (refrain).

Qaṣīdah (ode). A poem with a "purpose" (*maqṣad*). The term generally refers to poems in praise of something or someone—usually a patron. But a *ḥajv* too may be technically described as a *qaṣīdah*.

*Qiṭ*ʿ*ah* (verse-sequence). Literally, "cutting, section." Within a ghazal, a series of verses meant to be read as a connected sequence. The first verse of the *qiṭa*ʿ*h* is traditionally marked with the letter *qāf;* the last verse is not marked. Sometimes a *qiṭa*ʿ*h* outgrows the ghazal entirely and takes on an independent existence, as a unified poem in its own right; it is then usually given a title.

Quatrain. See *rubā*ʿ*ī*.

Rabṭ (connection). The quality of internal relationship and self-reflexivity within a single verse, especially between its two lines. See chapter 6.

Radīf (refrain). In a ghazal, the identically repeated word or words at the end of the second line of each two-line verse, after the *qāfiyah*. A *radīf* is extremely common but not compulsory.

Ravānī (flowingness). The quality of euphonious, harmonious sound that makes a verse effective when it is recited aloud. See chapter 6.

Refrain. See *radīf*.

Rhyme. See *qāfiyah*.

*Rubā*ʿ*ī* (quatrain). A four-line poem in one or more of a group of traditionally prescribed meters, and usually rhyming AABA.

Ṣāḥib (Sahib). A title of honor and respect.

Sanad (warrant). A verification of a usage: the word or *maẓmūn* in question is cited in the work of respected ustads, and thus legitimized.

Satire. See *ḥajv.*

Shāgird (shagird). An apprentice who has been accepted by an ustad for training in poetic composition.

Shiʿr. A distich or two-line verse, treated in the ghazal as an independent poetic unit; both lines must be in the same meter and must make a complete poetic effect of their own, without regard to the rest of the poem. The second line must end in the rhyming elements (*qāfiyah* definitely, and in most ghazals *radīf* as well).

Shorish. "Passion." Direct, powerful expression of the lover's experience of life; although charged with emotion, it is usually not narrowly personal. See chapter 8.

Silsilah (lineage). The chain of transmission from ustad to shagird, which over time becomes a line of descent that can reach far back into the past; a long and prestigious *silsilah* is a great source of authority and pride.

Taḳhalluṣ (pen name). A literary pseudonym adopted by a poet; it is often a meaningful word, and may or may not have some connection with the poet's real name. It is usually incorporated into the last verse of each poem.

Ṭaraḥ (pattern). A prescribed meter-rhyme combination, or *zamīn,* in which a ghazal is to be composed.

Ṭaraḥī (patterned). The classical kind of mushairah, in which all the verses recited are formally identical (i.e., *ham ṭaraḥ* or *ham zamīn*).

Tārīḳh (chronogram). A verse, line, or phrase composed in such a way that the numerical value of its letters according to the traditional Arabic *abjad* system adds up to the (A.H.) date of some event to be commemorated.

Tarkīb band. A stanzaic verse form that uses a single meter but varying rhyming elements. It has the following form: a *maṭlaʿ* (opening verse) and a certain number of *shiʿrs* (two-line verses) in rhyme-scheme A, followed by single *maṭlaʿ* in rhyme-scheme B, followed by a *maṭlaʿ* and the same number of *shiʿrs* in rhyme-scheme C, followed by a single *maṭlaʿ* in rhyme-scheme D, and so on.

Taẓkirah (tazkirah). A traditional genre of literary anthology in Persian and Urdu. A tazkirah consists of brief selections from the work of various poets, usually with some prefatory comments about each poet. The genre is discussed in detail in chapter 5.

Ustād (ustad). A recognized master-poet, one who has completed his apprenticeship and now accepts and trains his own shagirds. The term is discussed at length in chapter 4.

Vāsoḳht. A lyric genre, usually but not always in the six-line *musaddas* form, in which the lover expresses bitterness and quarrels with the beloved, after which they are reconciled.

Verse. The basic unit from which all longer poems were built up. A verse was always in one of the traditionally recognized meters. The most common unit of verse was the two-line *shiʿr,* but there was also the stanza (*band*), which might consist of three, four, five, or six lines.

Verse-sequence. See *qiṭaʿh.*

Volume. See *dīvān.*

Warrant. See *sanad.*

Zamīn (ground). The meter-rhyme pattern, or the formal specifications sufficient to define a particular ghazal: meter plus rhyme plus refrain (if any). Any two verses (*shiʿr*) in the same *zamīn* could be part of the same ghazal. Synonym: *ṭaraḥ.*

NOTES

Preface

1. Sadiq, *A History of Urdu Literature,* 14–19, 22, 24, 27, 29.

2. Ibid., 20.

3. Russell, "How Not to Write the History of Urdu Literature," 9. Russell notes one honorable exception: *Urdu Literature,* by D. J. Matthews et al. Russell's own work deserves pride of place on any such list; I would also add Ahmed Ali's general introduction to *The Golden Tradition* and Carla Petievich's more specialized study of the "two-school" theory.

4. Kalīmuddīn Aḥmad, *Urdū shā'irī par ek naẓar,* 69.

5. Mas'ūd Ḥasan Riẓvī "Adīb" claimed to have produced, in his immensely influential *Hamārī shā'irī* (1926–27), the first defense of the ghazal against such attacks. His method, however, was not to take issue with the criticism but to begin by accepting it, and then to "complete" the picture by adding "what had been left out"; where critics had presented "one side of the picture," he would supplement their work by showing "the other side," so that both sides taken together would enable people to form an accurate opinion about the poetry (15–16). On Adīb's approach, see Shamsur Raḥmān Fārūqī, "*Hamārī shā'irī* par ek naẓar-e s̤ānī," in *Tanqīdī afkār* (Allahabad: Urdu Writers Guild, 1984), 159–89.

6. See, for example, 'Alī Sardār Ja'frī, *Paiġhambarān-e suḳhan: Mīr, Ġhālib, Kabīr,* 2d ed. (Bombay: Adshot Publications, 1987 [1970]), which adopts the credo that "poetry is a part of prophecy." The author is very clear about his political intentions: "For modern political and revolutionary movements to become stronger, they must be joined in a relationship with medieval revolutionary thought"—which is to be derived from classical poetry (6).

7. Fārūqī, *Shi'r-e shor angez,* 3:42, 62. The point is discussed at length on pp. 61–62 and 75.

8. Because these two names constantly recur, they will be used in the text from now on without diacritics.

9. Āzād, *Āb-e ḥayāt* (Water of life), 14. Page references to this work will hereafter appear in the text.

1. The Lost World

1. Palam, now the site of the Indira Gandhi International Airport, is on the outskirts of Delhi.

2. Percival Spear, *The Oxford History of Modern India, 1740–1947* (Delhi: Oxford University Press, 1965), 37–43; Spear, *Twilight of the Mughuls*, 60.

3. Parvez, *Bahādur Shāh Ẓafar*, 272; see also 32, 344. Examples of Āftāb's Urdu ghazals appear on pp. 272 and 343.

4. Luṭf, *Gulshan-e hind*, 72.

5. Parvez, *Bahādur Shāh Ẓafar*, 38, 276.

6. Ibid., 38, 344.

7. Ibid., 234–37, 75–76, 60–74.

8. Na'im Aḥmad, ed., *Shahr āshob* (Delhi: Maktabah Jāmi'ah, 1968), 196. The word *firang*, used for Europeans, is a rendering of "Frank," and *qaid-e firang*, "Frankish captivity," was considered to be an especially harsh form of imprisonment. If given a mystical reading, the verse would refer to the wretched fate of everyone born into the world.

9. Spear, *Twilight of the Mughuls*, 72–73, 30.

10. Fisher, *A Clash of Cultures*, 146.

11. Spear, *Twilight of the Mughuls*, 78.

12. Andrews, *Zaka Ullah of Delhi*, 26–27.

13. Peter Hardy, "Ghalib and the British," in *Ghalib: The Poet and His Age*, ed. Ralph Russell, 55.

14. Āzād, ed., *Dīvān-e Żauq*, 145.

15. Gupta, *Delhi between Two Empires*, 5–8.

16. Spear, *Twilight of the Mughuls*, 194–200.

17. Andrews, *Zaka Ullah of Delhi*, 10. Sadiq (*Azad*, 2) also accepts the term *renaissance* for this period. Maulvī 'Abd ul-Ḥaq (quoted in Farruḳhī, *Āzād*, 1:43–44) presents a similar picture.

18. Spear, *Twilight of the Mughuls*, 82–83.

19. Gupta, *Delhi between Two Empires*, 5.

20. Russell and Islam, *Ghalib*, 23–27.

21. Ibid., 52–54, 49, 90–91.

22. Ibid., 219.

23. On the forms of this manipulation, see Bernard S. Cohn, "Cloth, Clothes, and Colonialism: India in the Nineteenth Century," in *Cloth and Human Experience*, ed. A. B. Weiner and J. Schneider (New York: Wenner-Gren Foundation for Anthropological Research, 1989), 303–53.

24. Russell and Islam, *Ghalib*, 63. This anecdote is first told by Azad (487–88),

and then repeated with minor changes by Hali in *Yādgār-e Ġhālib*, 28–29. Russell and Islam rely on Hali's version.

25. Like Ġhālib, Ḳhusrau listed a number of anecdotes about lavish royal generosity to poets, and emphasized the eternal fame that only poets can provide. See Mirza, *Life and Works of Amir Khusrau*, 108–12.

26. Ghalib, *Dastanbuy*, 48.

27. On the poet's role as *nadīm*, see Meisami, *Persian Court Poetry*, 6–11. Amīr Ḳhusrau (*Life and Works of Amir Khusrau*, 45, 78) used *nadīmī* to describe his own relationship with at least one patron.

28. Quoted in Russell and Islam, *Ghalib*, 73–74.

29. Parvez, *Bahādur Shāh Ẓafar*, 273, 278–85.

30. Russell and Islam, *Ghalib*, 71–75.

31. Ibid., 84.

32. Ġhālib, *Ḳhuṭūṭ*, 1:373–74.

33. It has been argued that the actual author of this tazkirah was the poet Imām Baḳhsh "Sahbā'ī." For my purposes, the identity of the author is not important.

34. ʿAbd ul-Ḥaq, *Marḥūm Dihlī Kālij*, 12–13.

35. Ṣābir, *Gulistān-e suḳhan*, 157–58, 166, 286, 337, 344–45, 390, 385. On "Farāso," see Husain, *Bahadur Shah II*, xli.

36. "Themes" is an umbrella term, a convenient starting point, but *maẓmūn* is difficult to translate with precision and will be discussed at length in chap. 7.

37. Ṣābir, *Gulistān-e suḳhan*, 345–46.

38. Imdād Ṣābrī, *Urdū ke aḳhbār navīs* (Delhi: Ṣābrī Academy, 1973), 1:146–48; Sadiq, *Azad*, 3–8. Until late 1843 the editor of record of the *Dihlī Urdū Aḳhbār* was in fact Maulvī Muḥammad Bāqir's father, Maulvī Muḥammad Akbar. The *Dihlī Urdū Aḳhbār* was probably the second Urdu newspaper in India: the first, a Persian-Urdu combination, had been started in Calcutta in 1822. But another was also started in 1837, and exact dates are hard to determine. For a detailed account of the available evidence, see Khan, *A History of Urdu Journalism*, 25–30, 65–73, 209–10.

39. Khan, *A History of Urdu Journalism*, 74–83. See also Ḳhvājah Aḥmad Fārūqī, ed., *Dihlī Urdū Aḳhbār* (Delhi: Shuʿbah-e Urdū, Delhi University, 1972), which reproduces selections from the paper for the year 1840.

40. ʿAbd ul-Ḥaq, *Marḥūm Dihlī Kālij*, 45–46.

41. Farruḳhī, *Āzād*, 1:80–82, 111; Khan, *A History of Urdu Journalism*, 71.

42. Farruḳhī, *Āzād*, 1:93.

43. Āzād, *Dīvān-e Żauq*, 2; Farruḳhī, *Āzād*, 1:88.

44. For a discussion and refutation of these claims, see "ʿĀbid" Peshāvarī, *Żauq*, 69–70. See also Farruḳhī, *Āzād*, 2:284–85.

45. Farruḳhī, *Āzād*, 1:94–98. The Urdu title of the poem was "Tārīḳh-e inqilāb-e ʿibrat afzā."

46. Some of Panipat's historical and religious associations are discussed in Steele, "Hali and his *Muqaddamah*," 2.

47. Leitner, *History of Indigenous Education*, part 2, 14.

48. Ḥālī, *Kulliyāt-e nas̤r*, 1:334.

49. Ibid.
50. Shujāʿat ʿAlī Sandīlvī, *Ḥālī,* 19.
51. Leitner, *History of Indigenous Education,* part 2, 2.
52. Ḥālī, *Kulliyāt-e naṡr,* 1:335.
53. Ibid., 1:335–36.
54. Spear, *Twilight of the Mughuls,* 83.
55. Andrews, *Zaka Ullah of Delhi,* 66.

2. *Beyond a Sea of Blood*

1. This is a de facto term of convenience; I do not mean to imply that sovereignty was legally vested in the British East India Company at the time.
2. Agha Mahdi Husain, in *Bahadur Shah II and the War of 1857,* makes this case strongly.
3. V. D. Savarkar, *The Indian War of Independence (National Rising of 1857),* 4th ed. (London: Mayuresh, n.d. [1909]), 101–2.
4. Kalb-e ʿAlī Ḳhān "Fāʾiq," in his introduction to Qurbān ʿAlī Beg "Sālik," *Kulliyāt-e Sālik* (Lahore: Majlis Taraqqī-e Adab, 1966), 11.
5. Spear, *Twilight of the Mughuls,* 224.
6. Ibid., 200–217.
7. Charles T. Metcalfe, trans., *Two Native Narratives of the Mutiny in Delhi* (Delhi: Seema Publications, 1974), 95, 123, 134, 181, 203.
8. K. C. Yadav, ed., *Delhi in 1857,* vol. 1, *The Trial of Bahadur Shah* (Gurgaon: The Academic Press, 1980), 52, 59, 333–35; Metcalfe, *Two Native Narratives,* 114, 122–23, 193.
9. Khan, *A History of Urdu Journalism,* 95–96.
10. Metcalfe, *Two Native Narratives,* 177.
11. Ġhālib, *Ḳhuṭūṭ,* 2:621.
12. Spear, *Twilight of the Mughuls,* 222–26.
13. Yadav, *Delhi in 1857,* 1:400, 345.
14. Parvez, *Bahādur Shāh Ẓafar,* 139–50.
15. Russell and Islam, *Ghalib,* 269.
16. For a look at the somewhat confusing evidence, see Gopi Chand Narang, "Ghalib and the Rebellion of 1857," in his *Urdu Language and Literature: Critical Perspectives* (New Delhi: Sterling Publishers, 1991), 10.
17. Russell and Islam, *Ghalib,* 137.
18. ʿAbd ul-Ḥaq, *Marḥūm Dihlī Kālij,* 72.
19. Spear, *Twilight of the Mughuls,* 218.
20. Russell and Islam, *Ghalib,* 142.
21. Ibid., 145, 149–50. According to yet a third account, he was released when a friend vouched for him; see Narang, "Ghalib and the Rebellion of 1857," 15.
22. Ghalib, *Dastanbuy,* 60.
23. Spear, *Twilight of the Mughuls,* 220–22.
24. Ġhālib, *Ḳhuṭūṭ,* 1:239.

25. Russell and Islam, *Ghalib*, 190–91.

26. *Gazetteer of the Delhi District, 1883–4* (Delhi: Punjab Government, 1884), 182, 184, 30. Lucknow too, after its recapture, was rebuilt with a view to preventing any future rebellions; for an account of the process, see Veena Talwar Oldenburg, *The Making of Colonial Lucknow, 1856–1877* (Princeton: Princeton University Press, 1984).

27. Sangat Singh, *Freedom Movement in Delhi, 1858–1919* (New Delhi: Associated Publishing House, 1972), 11–12.

28. Leitner, *History of Indigenous Education*, part 2, 2.

29. Ẓafar Ḥasan, *Sir Sayyid aur Ḥālī*, 41–42.

30. He used the evocative word *sannāṭā*: Ḥālī, *Yādgār-e Ġhālib*, 187.

31. Russell and Islam, *Ghalib*, 243.

32. Ibid., 153.

33. Ibid., 261, 224, 291.

34. Ġhālib, *Dīvān*, 333, verse 10.

35. Ġhālib, *Ḳhuṭūṭ*, 1:336; 2:556.

36. Russell and Islam, *Ghalib*, 162.

37. Ibid., 182.

38. Ibid., 233–34, 282–83, 347.

39. Khan, *A History of Urdu Journalism*, 86–87.

40. ʿAbd ul-Ḥaq, *Marḥūm Dihlī Kālij*, 71.

41. Khan, *A History of Urdu Journalism*, 92, 87–88.

42. Metcalfe, *Two Native Narratives*, 114.

43. Khan, *A History of Urdu Journalism*, 96; see also 95, 99–100.

44. Ibid., 101; see also 97–98, 102, 105, 109.

45. Sadiq, *Azad*, 14–16.

46. "Fingernails" had a well-established metaphorical role in loosening the "knots" of difficult problems.

47. Farruḳhī, *Āzād*, 1:98. The Arabic phrase in the last line yields the date of 1273 A.H. [1856–57].

48. Khan, *A History of Urdu Journalism*, 128–30.

49. Farruḳhī, *Āzād*, 1:104.

50. Ibid., 1:105–7.

51. Ibid., 1:76–77, 108–9.

52. Ibid., 1:113–24.

53. Ibid., 1:124–29.

54. Muḥammad Ḥusain Āzād, *Naṣīḥat kā karn phūl* (Delhi: Āzād Book Depot, 1945), 32. While this little book is indeed nostalgic at times (p. 22), it also shows a lively appreciation for the improved, secure roads (pp. 27, 31) and efficient trains (p. 37) provided by the English government.

55. Sadiq, *Azad*, 18.

56. Ḥālī, *Kulliyāt-e naṡr*, 1:336.

57. Metcalfe, *Two Native Narratives*, 113.

58. Ṣāliḥah ʿĀbid Ḥusain, *Yādgār-e Ḥālī*, 29.

59. Hali, *Hayat-i-javed*, 46.

60. Ṣāliḥah ʿĀbid Ḥusain, *Yādgār-e Ḥālī*, 30–31.

61. Shujāʿat ʿAlī Sandīlvī, *Ḥālī*, 30–34; Ḥālī, *Kulliyāt-e naṡr*, 1:337–39.

62. Ḥālī, *Dīvān-e Ḥālī*, 158; for the whole *marṡiyah*, see 156–63.

63. Shujāʿat ʿAlī Sandīlvī, *Ḥālī*, 34–35.

64. Thomas Metcalf, *The Aftermath of Revolt: India, 1857–1870* (Princeton: Princeton University Press, 1964), 289.

65. For a fuller account of this cultural devastation, see Syed, *Muslim Response to the West*, 18–20; and Narang, "Ghalib and the Rebellion of 1857," 2–3.

66. Husain, *Bahadur Shah*, 429–34.

67. Fisher, *A Clash of Cultures*, 156.

68. Ibid., 130–47. In 1857, however, the rebel troops insisted on taking orders directly from Delhi; the young Birjīs Qādir, whom they placed on the throne, became merely a *vazīr* in Bahādur Shāh's service. See Rudrangshu Mukherjee, *Awadh in Revolt, 1857–1858: A Study of Popular Resistance* (Delhi: Oxford University Press, 1984), 135–37.

69. Fisher, *A Clash of Cultures*, 180.

70. Tafaẓẓal Ḥusain Ḳhān "Kaukab," *Fuġhān-e dihlī* (Lahore: Akādamī-e Panjāb, 1954).

71. Metcalf, *The Aftermath of Revolt*, 295, 298.

72. Syed, *Muslim Response to the West*, 22, 40.

73. Hali, *Hayat-i-javed*, 56, 132.

74. Andrews, *Zaka Ullah of Delhi*, 67, 75.

75. Bashīr ud-Dīn Aḥmad, *Vāqiʿāt-e dār-ul ḥukūmat-e dihlī*, 3 vols. (Agra: Shamsī Mashīn Press, 1919), 1:702.

76. Sadiq, *Azad*, 11.

3. *Reconstruction*

1. For a study of this process, see Bernard S. Cohn, "Representing Authority in Victorian India," in *The Invention of Tradition*, ed. Eric Hobsbawm and Terence Ranger (Cambridge: Cambridge University Press, 1983), 165–209.

2. Ḥālī, *Yādgār-e Ġhālib*, 2.

3. Sadiq, *Azad*, 20–23; Farruḳhī, *Āzād*, 1:137–49.

4. J. F. Bruce, *A History of the University of the Panjab* (Lahore: Ishwar Das, 1933), 7.

5. Sadiq, *Azad*, 24. Actually, the full name of the organization was the Anjuman-e Maṭālib-e Mufīdah-e Panjāb, the "Society for Projects for the Welfare of the Punjab," but this name never became widely used: Farruḳhī, *Āzād*, 1:150.

6. Farruḳhī, *Āzād*, 1:154; see also 150–56.

7. Sadiq, *Azad*, 25–27; Farruḳhī, *Āzād*, 1:164–90.

8. Sadiq, *Azad*, 24–26.

9. Farruḳhī, *Āzād*, 1:193–94. The nature of this "trinket" (*ṭriñkaṭ*) is not clear.

10. Ibid., 1:193–98.

11. Sadiq, *Azad,* 27–28. Technically, what he wrote was part 2 of a three-part series.

12. Farrukhī, *Āzād,* 1:214–21.

13. Herbert L. O. Garrett and Abdul Hamid, *A History of Government College Lahore, 1864–1964* (Lahore: Government College, 1964), 29–31, 60–61. See also pp. 20–21 and 42 for further student reminiscences about Azad.

14. Ḥālī, *Kulliyāt-e naṡr,* 1:339.

15. Āzād, *Naẓm-e Āzād,* 46.

16. Ibid., 42–44.

17. Ibid., 47–48.

18. Ibid., 45. Azad's term *faṣāḥat,* which I have here translated as "eloquence," is almost impossible to convey properly in English; something like "appropriate speech" might be the best rendering.

19. Ibid., 50.

20. Sadiq, *Azad,* 32.

21. Ibid.

22. Farrukhī, *Āzād,* 1:241–43.

23. Ibid., 1:248–51.

24. Ṣāliḥah ʿĀbid Ḥusain, *Yādgār-e Ḥālī,* 35.

25. Ḥālī, *Kulliyāt-e naṡr,* 1:339–40.

26. Ḥālī, *Kulliyāt-e naẓm,* 1:51.

27. Ḥālī, *Makātīb,* 50.

28. Joseph Héliodore Garcin de Tassy, *La Langue et la littérature hindoustanies en 1874: Revue annuelle* (Paris: Maisonneuve, 1875), 26–28.

29. Farrukhī, *Āzād,* 1:257–78; Garcin de Tassy, *La Langue et la littérature hindoustanies en 1874,* 29–32.

30. Ḥālī, *Kulliyāt-e naẓm,* 2:415.

31. Sadiq, *Azad,* 33–39.

32. Farrukhī, *Āzād,* 1:255.

33. Ibid., 1:287–93.

34. Ibid., 1:280; see also 279–82. The *Avadh Panch* in fact lampooned Sir Sayyid as a *necharī yogī;* its caricature of him is reproduced in Lelyveld, *Aligarh's First Generation,* 140.

35. Garcin de Tassy, *La Langue et la littérature hindoustanies en 1875: Revue annuelle* (Paris: Maisonneuve, 1876), 20–22. In Aligarh, Sir Sayyid is said to have entirely banned the recitation of ghazals at college functions, seeking to replace them with poetry that "contained criticism of life and was purposeful and inspiring": see S. K. Bhatnagar, *History of the M. A. O. College Aligarh* (Bombay: Asia Publishing House, 1969), viii.

36. Sadiq, *Azad,* 39.

37. Leitner, *History of Indigenous Education,* part 1, 71.

38. Farrukhī, *Āzād,* 1:289–90.

39. Garcin de Tassy, *La Langue et la littérature hindoustanies en 1875*, 19–20.

40. Sadiq, *Azad*, 31.

41. Farrukhī, *Āzād*, 1:233–34.

42. This elegy, informally entitled "Nauḥah-e dihlī" (A lament for Delhi), is translated in Gupta, *Delhi*, pp. xviii–xix. It forms a verse-sequence within a ghazal; Hali published it in his first collection in 1893: Ḥālī, *Dīvān-e Ḥālī*, 87–89.

43. Farrukhī, *Āzād*, 2:618.

44. Ibid., 2:638; see also 606–7.

45. Azad implies that he might have done this work by writing from oral dictation of some sort: see Sadiq, *Azad*, 43–45 (a full list of the essays and their sources appears on p. 44). But Azad apparently had a reasonable reading and even writing knowledge of English: see Farrukhī, *Āzād*, 2:347–48.

46. Āzād, *Nairang-e khiyāl*, 11, 27.

47. Ḥālī, *Kulliyāt-e naṡr*, 2:182.

48. Ibid., 2:184–94.

49. Sadiq, *Azad*, 48.

50. Farrukhī, *Āzād*, 1:302–3. Dr. Leitner has been described as a self-willed, erratic, and "tendentious" administrator, whose own scholarly contributions have proved to be "more specious than was apparent to his contemporaries": see J. F. Bruce, *A History of the University of the Panjab*, 88–92.

51. Farrukhī, *Āzād*, 1:324–25; see also 314–15, 323.

52. Ibid., 1:326–54.

53. Ibid., 2:373; Muḥammad Ḥusain Āzād, *Sukhandān-e fārs* (Lucknow: Uttar Pradesh Urdu Academy, 1979).

54. Farrukhī, *Āzād*, 1:356–60, 362–63.

55. Ibid., 1:371–76.

56. Ḥālī, *Kulliyāt-e naṡr*, 1:340n.

57. Ibid., 1:340.

58. Garrett and Hamid, *A History of Government College*, 30.

59. Ṣāliḥah ʿĀbid Ḥusain, *Yādgār-e Ḥālī*, 41–43.

60. S. K. Bhatnagar, *History of the M. A. O. College Aligarh*, 47, 99–100, 147.

61. Ḥālī, *Dīvān-e Ḥālī*. On Sir Sayyid: 23, 26, 30–31; on the M. A. O. College: 170–71, and 178–82, 182–83; addresses to the Muhammadan Educational Conference: 183–90, 201–5; on poetic renewal: 28–29; on nationalism: 25, 27–28, 37.

62. Ṣāliḥah ʿĀbid Ḥusain, *Yādgār-e Ḥālī*, 44–45. An English version of *Yādgār-e Ġhālib*, prepared by K. H. Qadiri, has recently been published. However, many of Hali's words and Ġhālib's poems have been omitted from it—in favor of the translator's own literary comments and interpretations, which have been woven most confusingly into a text full of odd translations and typographical errors.

63. Both these works appear in Ḥālī, *Voices of Silence*, trans. Gail Minault.

64. A full bibliography is given in Shujāʿat ʿAlī Sandīlvī, *Ḥālī*, 77–92.

65. Ṣāliḥah ʿĀbid Ḥusain, *Yādgār-e Ḥālī*, 52–53.

66. Ḥālī, *Kulliyāt-e naẓm*, 1:349–57.

4. The Water of Life

1. ʿĀbid Peshāvarī, *Żauq,* 126.

2. The review is reprinted in Ḥālī, *Kulliyāt-e naṡr,* 2:184–94; the quotation is from pp. 190–91.

3. Ḥālī, *Makātīb,* 18; see also 15–19. See also Sadiq, *Azad,* 50; Farrukhī, *Āzād,* 2:11–12, 27.

4. Ḥālī, *Kulliyāt-e naṡr,* 2:186.

5. Sadiq, *Azad,* 47–53.

6. See Adīb, *Āb-e ḥayāt kā tanqīdī muṭāliʿah.*

7. For a thorough inventory of such errors, see Qāẓī ʿAbdul Vadūd, *Muḥammad Ḥusain Āzād bahaiṡiyat-e muḥaqqiq;* see also Shairānī, "Tanqīd bar *Āb-e ḥayāt,*" *Maqālāt,* 3:27–116.

8. ʿĀbid Peshāvarī, *Żauq,* 5.

9. Farrukhī, *Āzād,* 2:258.

10. For a flagrant example, see ibid., 2:276–78.

11. Azad further elaborates his allegations in *Dīvān-e Żauq,* 112. They are examined and refuted in Parvez, *Bahādur Shāh Ẓafar,* 313–33.

12. Ḥālī, *Yādgār-e Ġhālib,* 35. According to Hali's account, Ẓafar would sometimes write down "one or two lines" and then send the page to Ġhālib, who would complete the ghazal.

13. For this kind of modernization there do exist a few parallels: the editing of Muṣḥafī by "Amīr" Mīnāʾī and his ustad Muẓaffar ʿAlī "Asīr," and the editing of Nāsikh by ʿAlī Ausaṭ "Rashk."

14. For the most decisive evidence, see Shairānī, "Shams ul-ʿUlamā Maulānā Muḥammad Ḥusain Āzād aur *Dīvān-e Żauq,*" *Maqālāt,* 3:257–306; see also ʿĀbid Peshāvarī, *Żauq,* 130–322; and Farrukhī, *Āzād,* 2:514–50.

15. Farrukhī, *Āzād,* 2:533.

16. ʿĀbid Peshāvarī, *Żauq,* 110–27.

17. Farrukhī, *Āzād,* 2:87.

18. Shairānī, "Tanqīd bar *Āb-e ḥayāt,*" *Maqālāt,* 3:98–108; Farrukhī, *Āzād,* 2:129–41.

19. Fārūqī, *Shiʿr-e shor angez,* 3:89.

20. The pen names, since they had meaning, lent themselves elegantly to wordplay. The Indo-Persian poet Nūr ul-ʿAin "Vāqif" (died c. 1776) was once asked by a stranger, "Are you acquainted (*vāqif*) with Vāqif?" His reply: "I am *vāqif*" (Khatak, *Shaikh Muhammad Ali Hazin,* 114).

21. After a lifetime of practice, Amīr Khusrau claimed that he could often improvise faster than a scribe could write, and that even before kings he was usually "content to extemporise and to dispense with the services of the pen" (Mirza, *Amir Khusrau,* 167).

22. Ḥālī, *Yādgār-e Ġhālib,* 109; see also 108–13. This is still the commonly held view of Ġhālib's development, although a comparison of the ghazals he com-

posed in his early youth with those of his old age shows that his range was extremely wide—from radical simplicity to opaque complexity—throughout his poetic career.

23. Even more grandiose notions of royal gift giving were common in the tradition. One of Amīr Ḳhusrau's patrons boasted that since his father used to give "gold equal in weight to an elephant" to poets, he himself ought to give at least "an elephant-load of gold" (Mirza, *Amir Khusrau,* 125).

5. *Tazkirahs*

1. Ḥālī, *Kulliyāt-e naṡr,* 2:186.
2. Ibid.
3. Farruḳhī, *Āzād,* 2:651.
4. Compiling a volume was apparently a prolonged process. Mīr describes one poet as having completed a volume "up to the letter *mīm*" (Mīr, *Nikāt ush-shu'arā,* 77–78).
5. As Urdu newspapers began to be founded, they too were pressed into service: they often printed new ghazals and odes, or reprinted famous Persian poems. For examples, see Khan, *A History of Urdu Journalism,* 86, 147, 161–62, 168–69, 171, 195, 250–51, 292.
6. These numbers refer to the chronologically ordered list in "Farmān" Fatḥpūrī, *Urdū shu'arā ke tażkire,* 627–32.
7. Ibid., 147–48.
8. Ibid., 284.
9. On this notoriety, see Sayyid 'Abdullāh, *Shu'arā-e urdū ke tażkire,* 27–46.
10. Abu'l-Ḥasan, *Tażkirah-e masarrat afzā,* 23, 30, 172–73, 96, 85–93.
11. My translation of the title, while defensible, is slightly affected by loyalty to English. A more literal rendering might be "A fine and suitable [martial] contest."
12. For an interesting later effort in this direction, see Ḥasrat Mohānī, *Arbāb-e suḳhan* (Kanpur, 1929), reprinted in *Nigār* (Karachi) 67, no. 7 (July 1988): 4–47.
13. Nāṣir, *Ḳhush ma'rikah-e zebā,* 192, 229, 719, 722.
14. Ibid., 227, 508.
15. Ibid., 556, 122, 302–3, 485–87.
16. Ibid., 198–99, 272, 299.
17. Ibid., 374–76.
18. Ibid., 603. They might have slapped him, boxed his ears, or made rude gestures at him—anything to cause public humiliation.
19. He compared them to public polemical debates (*mubāḥiṡah*) between pandits, and said that both "attract numerous listeners from all creeds" (Leitner, *History of Indigenous Education,* part 1, 2).
20. Nāṣir, *Ḳhush ma'rikah-e zebā,* 309, 636.

21. Sayyid ʿAbdullāh, *Shuʿarā-e urdū ke taẓkire*, 67.

22. Khan, *A History of Urdu Journalism*, 250–53.

23. Mīr, *Nikāt ush-shuʿarā*, 61, 66, 81–82, 123, 132, 133, 142, 143.

24. Dargāh Qulī Ḳhān, *Muraqqaʿ-e-Dehli: The Mughal Capital in Muhammad Shah's Time*, trans. Chander Shekhar and Shama Mitra Chenoy (Delhi: Deputy Publications, 1989), 56.

25. Munibur Rahman, "The Mushaʿirah," *Annual of Urdu Studies* 3 (1983): 75–84; C. M. Naim, "Poet-Audience Interaction at Urdu Mushaʿiras," in *Urdu and Muslim South Asia*, ed. Christopher Shackle, 167–73.

26. Akhter Qamber, trans., *The Last Musha'irah of Dehli*, is the best such account. It is a translation of Farḥatullāh Beg's *Dihlī kī āḳhirī shamaʿ* (The last candle of Delhi). Farḥatullāh Beg, born in Delhi in 1883, claimed to have been inspired first by Azad's *The Wonder-World of Thought* and second by the tazkirah of Karīmuddīn.

27. Farmān Fatḥpūrī, *Urdū shuʿarā ke taẓkire*, 42–43.

28. Only two ghazals from this series—one of twenty-two verses and one of fourteen—survive in his collected works: see Shāh Naṣīr, *Kulliyāt-e Shāh Naṣīr*, ed. Tanvīr Aḥmad ʿAlvī (Lahore: Majlis Taraqqī-e Adab, 1971–77), 2:314–17.

29. Ṣābir, *Gulistān-e suḳhan*, 163.

30. Amīr Ḳhusrau said that a ghazal has merely "seven or nine verses," but the rule was more honored in the breach than in the observance, even by Ḳhusrau himself (Mirza, *Amir Khusrau*, 144). Ghazals did, however, usually have an odd rather than even number of verses.

31. Ṣābir, *Gulistān-e suḳhan*, 163. A different and much briefer account later appears in *Āb-e ḥayāt* (460) as well.

32. Āzād, *Dīvān-e Żauq*, 139–41. According to Azad, not all Żauq's ghazals in this *zamīn* survived the sack of Delhi: only two pages' worth came to hand—and parts of one page, including some verses of an ode, were illegible. Azad describes this mushairah series as so memorable that it had survived in oral tradition "for sixty years, to the present." For further discussion of the "*tīliyāñ*" affair, see Tanvīr Aḥmad ʿAlvī, *Żauq: savāniḥ aur intiqād* (Lahore: Majlis Taraqqī-e Urdū, 1963), 60–65.

33. Nāṣir, *Ḳhush maʿrikah-e zebā*, 278–80.

34. Ibid., 280. Azad too gives his own account of Inshā's and Muṣḥafī's "*-ūr kī garden*" ghazals (305–9), and of the retaliatory street processions by Muṣḥafī's shagirds (310–11).

35. Farmān Fatḥpūrī, *Urdū shuʿarā ke taẓkire*, 43. On the genre, see also Khan, *A History of Urdu Journalism*, 192, 197, 199–201.

36. Aḥsan Fārūqī, "Taẓkirah nigārī aur Muḥammad Ḥusain Āzād kī *Āb-e ḥayāt*" in *Āb-e ḥayāt*, ed. Sayyid Sajjād, 46–47; Kalīmuddīn Aḥmad, *Urdū tanqīd par ek naẓar*, 83. The question of who first composed the passage and who borrowed it without acknowledgment is not important for the present argument.

37. Farmān Fatḥpūrī offers a brief discussion in *Urdū shuʿarā ke taẓkire*, 78–85, as does Faiẓ in "Hamārī tanqīd kī iṣṭilāḥāt." The most serious and sustained

attempt, however, is that of ʿĀbid ʿAlī "ʿĀbid," in *Uṣūl-e intiqād-e adabiyāt,* 148–257. On the shortcomings of ʿĀbid's approach, see Fārūqī, *Shiʿr-e shor angez,* 3:96–97.

38. Mīr, *Nikāt ush-shuʿarā,* 163–64. The line quoted at the end is from Saʿdī.

6. Poems Two Lines Long

1. Farmān Fatḥpūrī, *Urdū shuʿarā ke tażkire,* 79.

2. Jerome W. Clinton, "Shams-i Qays on the Nature of Poetry," *Edebiyat* (n.s.) 1, no. 2 (1989): 101–27, on pp. 107, 115.

3. Ibn Ḳhaldūn, *The Muqaddimah,* trans. Franz Rosenthal, ed. N. J. Dawood (Princeton: Princeton University Press, 1967), 446, 445.

4. Muzaffar Iqbal, "A Conversation with Faiz Ahmed Faiz," *Pakistani Literature* 1, no. 1 (1992): 23–32; the quotations are from p. 30.

5. For example, Shāh "Ḥātim" (1699–1783) identified the great bulk of his ghazals as "*zamīn-e ṯaraḥī,*" and also borrowed *zamīns* from no fewer than twenty-three predecessors and contemporaries, chief among whom were Valī (eleven *zamīns*) and Saudā (twelve). See Ḥātim, *Dīvān zādah.*

6. Russell and Islam, *Ghalib,* 83–84.

7. Muzaffar Iqbal, "A Conversation with Faiz Ahmed Faiz," 32.

8. Russell and Islam, *Ghalib,* 343.

9. Ġhālib, *Ḳhuṯūṯ,* 1:114–15.

10. Browne, *A Literary History of Persia,* 3:293–99.

11. Hoshang was a legendary early Persian king who, according to the *Shāh nāmah,* flung one stone against another so that a spark leaped forth; thus fire came into the world. See Reuben Levy, trans., *The Epic of the Kings* (London: Routledge and Kegan Paul, 1967), 6–8.

12. For a thoroughgoing attack on the chronology, psychological plausibility, etc., of this anecdote, see ʿĀbid Peshāvarī, *Żauq,* 44–53.

13. Russell and Islam, *Ghalib,* 279.

14. Ṣafdar Mirzāpūrī, *Mashshāṯah-e suḳhan,* 2:8, from the "Tamhīd" by ʿAbd ul-Ḥaq.

15. Ibid., 2:14–15.

16. Ibid., 2:27. His expression is "*dast o garebāñ ho jāʾeñ.*"

17. Mīr, *Nikāt ush-shuʿarā,* 23, 114, 143. See also Fārūqī, *Shiʿr-e shor angez,* 1:275, 623, and, for more examples praising *rabṯ,* 3:113–14. Fārūqī's categories of *munāsibat* and *bandish kī chustī* (3:115–17) also, I would argue, fall within the domain of *rabṯ.*

18. Mirza, *Amir Khusrau,* 21.

19. Ṯabāṯabāʾī, *Maqālāt,* 127. Sayyid ʿAlī Ḥaidar "Naẕm" Ṯabāṯabāʾī (1852–1933) came from an old Lucknow family that had migrated to Matiya Burj with the deposed nawab of Avadh in 1856. He received a traditional education, and later had some exposure to English as well. His brief, aphoristic comments often leave the reader wishing for more.

20. A number of separate terms—*munāsibat-e alfāz̤* (suitability of words), *ri'āyat-e lafz̤ī* (wordplay), *ri'āyat-e ma'navī* (meaning-play), *īhām* (punning), etc.—may also be used for some of these different kinds of *rabt̤*.

21. The two basic structural genres in Urdu—those that provide formal frameworks for other, more topically defined genres—are ghazal and *maśnavī*. Of the two, the latter, with its AA BB CC rhyme scheme and habitual omission of the refrain, makes for much easier composition; on the *maśnavī*, see Fārūqī, *Dars-e balāġhat*, 131–32.

22. Ġhālib, *Dīvān-e Ġhālib*, 173. See, for example, the editor's defensive footnote in the *Dīvān-e Ġhālib*, ed. Ḥāmid 'Alī K̲h̲ān (Lahore: Panjab University, 1969), 16. The attack was first made by Ḥasrat Mohānī in 1918 in his *Sharḥ-e dīvān-e Ġhālib* (Delhi: S̤ā'iqah Book Depot, n.d.), 20, and has since evoked a number of responses. C. M. Naim, for example, points to the literal meaning of *qismat* as "division, separation"—the fate of a torn collar (personal communication, April 4, 1992).

23. See S. R. Faruqi and F. W. Pritchett, "Lyric Poetry in India: Ghazal and Nazm," *Journal of South Asian Literature* 19, no. 2 (1984): 111–27. See also Fārūqī, *Shi'r-e shor angez*, 3:105, 114–15.

24. Fārūqī, *Shi'r-e shor angez*, 1:216–19; 2:181–83.

25. Mīr, *Kulliyāt*, 709. As in this case, Mīr's favorite "Hindi" meter seems in general to lend itself especially well to *ravānī*.

26. Hali approvingly noted this practice, and the reason for it, in his review (*Kulliyāt-e naśr*, 2:189).

27. This argument is made at length in F. W. Pritchett, "Orient Pearls Unstrung: The Quest for Unity in the Ghazal."

7. The Art and Craft of Poetry

1. A good modern account of all these figures can be found in Fārūqī, *Dars-e balāġhat*, 9–85, on which I here rely. For an earlier account in English, see Pybus, *A Textbook of Urdu Prosody and Rhetoric*, especially "Part II—Rhetoric." Andrews, in *An Introduction to Ottoman Poetry*, gives a detailed analysis of the system as it developed in medieval Turkish poetry. The use of different theoretical sources, and of different vocabulary in translation, causes such accounts to differ in detail; but their basic agreement about the nature and use of verbal figures will be evident.

2. In many cases, it seems even to have been created orally. Hali says that Ġhālib often composed "eight or ten" verses in the course of a night, and tied a knot in his sash to remind him of each one. In the morning he would recall them and write them down (Russell and Islam, *Ghalib*, 36). Similar stories are told of other poets as well, including Dāġh and even Iqbāl.

3. Fārūqī, *Shi'r-e shor angez*, 3:89–90, 93–94.

4. Ibid., 3:74.

5. Ibid., 3:80, 84; see also 103–4. For examples of usage, and an account of the identity of *mazmūn* with metaphor, see 117–24.

6. Mark Turner, *Death is the Mother of Beauty: Mind, Metaphor, Criticism* (Chicago: University of Chicago Press, 1987), 18.

7. The pronoun might be "his," or the "His" of divinity, or "her"; ambiguity is the norm. Although the grammatical gender of the beloved is always masculine in classical Urdu poetry, the beloved sometimes has specifically boyish traits, and at other times specifically feminine ones. My use of "his" attempts to preserve an ambiguity that seems nevertheless weighted toward the abstractly masculine. This question will be discussed at length in chapter 12.

8. For Turkish examples, see *The Penguin Book of Turkish Verse*, ed. N. Menemencioglu and F. Iz (Harmondsworth: Penguin, 1978). An interesting Pashto anthology is Henry George Raverty, *Selections from the Poetry of the Afghans* (Calcutta: K. P. Bagchi and Company, 1981 [1862]).

9. Fārūqī, *Shiʿr-e shor angez*, 1:464–65; see also 37–39.

10. For his treatment of this *mazmūn*, see "*Rag-e sang se ṭapaktā*" (Ġhālib, *Dīvān*, 187).

11. In Urdu: *ġhalaṯīhā-e mazāmīñ mat pūchh / log nāle ko rasā bāñdhte haiñ* (Ġhālib, *Dīvān*, 222). The lover's laments are ineffective because it is a foregone conclusion that the beloved will be unmoved by them.

12. That is, if only they had finished me off and thus put me out of my misery. In Urdu: *ham pāyah hai do nālī bandūq se vuh bīnī / chharroñ kā kām rū-e qātil ke ḳhāl karte*. See Atāsh, *Kulliyāt-e Ātash* (Lucknow: Naval Kishor Press, A.H. 1280 [1863]), 247.

13. Ṭabāṭabā'ī, *Maqālāt*, 104.

14. For examples of the use of these terms, see Fārūqī, *Shiʿr-e shor angez*, 3:124–26.

15. This illustrative series of *shiʿrs* was in part developed by S. R. Faruqi for a talk at the University of Pennsylvania on May 6, 1988. I am much indebted to this talk and to the discussion that followed it.

16. Saʿdī, *Kulliyāt . . . Saʿdī Shīrāzī*, ed. ʿAbbās Iqbāl (Teheran: Shirkat, 1938), "Ṭībāt," 171.

17. Quoted in Ṭek Chand "Bahār," *Bahār-e ʿajam* (Delhi: Maṭbaʿ Sirājī, 1866 [compiled 1742]), 1:386.

18. Valī, *Dīvān-e Valī*, ed. Maḥmūd Ḳhān Ashraf and Ḥasrat Mohānī (Lahore: Maktabah Meri Library, 1965), 65.

19. Shākir Nājī, *Dīvān-e Shākir Nājī*, ed. Fazl ul-Ḥaq (Delhi: Idārah-e Ṣubḥ-e Adab, 1968), 12. In this edition, however, instead of *ek qadam adh* there appears *yak qad-e ādam*, which does not yield an intelligible meaning. My reading is that proposed by S. R. Faruqi.

20. Mīr, *Kulliyāt*, 557. See also Fārūqī, *Shiʿr-e shor angez*, 1:67–68.

21. Mīr, *Kulliyāt*, 657.

22. Shaiḳh Imām Baḳhsh Nāsiḳh, *Kulliyāt-e Nāsiḳh* (Lucknow: Maṭbaʿ Maulā'ī, A.H. 1262 [1846]), 229.

23. Nāsiḵh, *Kulliyāt*, 11.

24. Ḵhvājah Ḥaidar ʿAlī Ātash, *Kulliyāt-e Ātash,* ed. Ẓahīr Āhmad Ṣiddīqī (Allahabad: Rām Narāyan Lāl Benī Mādho, 1972), 23.

25. Ġhālib, *Dīvān*, 219.

26. Sulaimān Arīb, *Pās-e garebāñ* (Hyderabad: Anjuman Taraqqī-e Urdū, 1961), 33.

27. Fārūqī, *Dars-e balāġhat,* 40.

28. He also praised two of Maẓmūn's shagirds in the same terms (Mīr, *Nikāt ush-shuʿarā,* 34, 123, 125).

29. Ṭabāṭabāʾī, *Maqālāt,* 304.

30. Hiroaki Sato's *One Hundred Frogs: From Renga to Haiku to English* (New York: Weatherhill, 1983) is an excellent starting point for comparative study.

31. Ṭabāṭabāʾī, *Maqālāt,* 301.

32. Leitner, *History of Indigenous Education,* part 1, 98.

33. Ṣābir, *Gulistān-e suḵhan,* 346.

34. In Urdu: *asad uṭhnā qiyāmat qāmatoñ kā vaqt-e ārāʾish / libās-e naẓm meñ bālīdan-e maẓmūn-e ʿālī hai* (Ġhālib, *Dīvān,* 85). "Asad" was the pen name Ġhālib used at the very beginning of his career.

35. In Persian: *daftar babīñ kih maʿnaviyāñ chūñ navishtah and / alfāẓ rā figundah o maẓmūñ navishtah and.* See Ṭālib Āmulī, *Kulliyāt-e ashʿār-e malik ush-shuʿarā Ṭālib Āmulī,* ed. Ṭāhirī Shihāb (N.p.: Kitābḵhānah-e Sanāʾī, n.d.), 452.

36. Ṭabāṭabāʾī, *Maqālāt,* 295.

8. The Mind and Heart in Poetry

1. Fārūqī, *Shiʿr-e shor angez,* 1:46–47. The verse in Urdu: *agarchih shiʿr momin bhī nihāyat ḵhūb kahtā hai / kahāñ hai lek maʿnī band maẓmūñ yāb apnā sā* (Momin, *Dīvān-e Momin maʿ sharḥ,* ed. Ẓiyā Aḥmad "Ẓiyā" [Allahabad: Shāntī Press, 1970], 30).

2. Also sometimes called *maʿnī yābī, maʿnī parvarī,* or *maʿnī bandī.*

3. Ṭabāṭabāʾī, *Maqālāt,* 154.

4. Mīr, *Nikāt ush-shuʿarā,* 25, 48, 55, 60, 66, 130.

5. In Urdu: *ṭarfeñ rakhe hai ek suḵhan chār chār mīr / kyā kyā kahā kareñ haiñ zabān-e qalam se ham;* and again, *zulf sā pechdār hai har shiʿr / hai suḵhan mīr kā ʿajab ḍhab kā* (Mīr, *Kulliyāt,* 553, 615). For other examples of usage, see Fārūqī, *Shiʿr-e shor angez,* 3:129–31.

6. Ġhālib, *Ḵhuṭūṭ,* 1:114–15. The remark is also quoted by Hali in *Yādgār-e Ġhālib,* 139.

7. Ḥālī, *Yādgār-e Ġhālib,* 137.

8. Fārūqī, *Shiʿr-e shor angez,* 3:106; he develops the argument in some detail (106–9).

9. On *kināyah,* see also Fārūqī, *Shiʿr-e shor angez,* 2:136.

10. Mīr, *Kulliyāt,* 762.

11. The very first *iṣlāḥ* Mīr offered in his tazkirah involved simply a change

into the *inshā'iyah* mode: from *is qadar* ("to this extent") to *kis qadar* ("to what extent") (Mīr, *Nikāt ush-shu'arā*, 31).

12. On this topic, see Fārūqī, "Andāz-e guftugū kyā hai." This title itself can mean either (in the *inshā'iyah* mode) "What is the style of speech?" or (in the *k̲habariyah* mode) "What the style of speech is." The title is taken from a line of Ġhālib's (*Dīvān*, p. 321). See also John Hollander, *Melodious Guile: Fictive Patterns in Poetic Language* (New Haven: Yale University Press, 1988).

13. The English *of*, while similar, is less versatile: it must share its domain with the possessive *'s;* its nouns must generally be qualified by articles; and it must always be unambiguously present or absent.

14. Technically there might be as few as three, but then both *nishāṯ* and *dāġh* would be left as free-floating nouns, presumably vocatives, so that the interpretation would become impossibly clumsy and forced.

15. Ġhālib, *Dīvān*, 211.

16. Mīr, *Kulliyāt*, 192; see also Fārūqī, *Shi'r-e shor angez*, 2:366–69.

17. Ḥālī, *Ḥayāt-e Sa'dī*, 239.

18. Mīr, *Kulliyāt*, 111.

19. For a discussion of the universality of this metaphor, see George Lakoff and Mark Turner, *More than Cool Reason: A Field Guide to Poetic Metaphor* (Chicago: University of Chicago Press, 1989), 1–15.

20. Mīr, *Kulliyāt*, 161.

21. Fārūqī, *Shi'r-e shor angez*, 1:458; see also 455, 457.

22. Mīr, *Kulliyāt*, 550; see also Fārūqī, *Shi'r-e shor angez*, 2:376–80.

23. Ġhālib, *Ġhazaliyāt-e fārsī*, ed. Sayyid Vazīr ul-Ḥasan 'Ābidī (Lahore: Panjab University, 1969), 137.

24. Asġhar 'Alī K̲hān Nasīm, *Kulliyāt-e Nāsīm*, ed. Kalb-e 'Alī K̲hān Fā'iq (Lahore: Majlis Taraqqī-e Adab, 1966), 281.

25. Sayyid Muḥammad K̲hān Rind, *Guldastah-e 'ishq ma'rūf bah dīvān-e Rind* (Lucknow: Maṯba'-e Musṯafā'ī, A.H. 1267 [1850–51]), 66.

26. This *shi'r* (but not, alas, its location) was noted by S. R. Faruqi during his reading of the *Dāstān-e amīr Ḥamzah*, 46 vols. (Lucknow: Naval Kishor Press, c. 1883–1905).

27. Mīr, *Kulliyāt*, 138.

28. The correct Arabic spelling requires a *tashdīd* to double the *ye*, and that is how Mīr has spelled it in his verse, as the scansion makes clear. Normally, however, it is used in Urdu without the *tashdīd*.

29. For the former, see Ġhālib, *K̲huṯūṯ*, 1:277.

30. In Urdu: *har varaq har ṣafḥe meñ ik shi'r-e shor angez hai / 'arṣah-e maḥshar hai 'arṣah mere bhī dīvān kā*; and again, *jahāñ se dekhiye ik shi'r-e shor angez nikle hai / qiyāmat kā sā hangāmah hai har jā mere dīvāñ meñ* (Mīr, *Kulliyāt*, 692, 564). For other examples, see Fārūqī, *Shi'r-e shor angez*, 3:127–29.

31. Mīr, *Kulliyāt*, 109.

32. K̲hvājah Mīr Dard, *Dīvān-e Dard urdū*, ed. Ẕahīr Aḥmad Ṣiddīqī (Lahore: Nāmī Press, 1965), 103.

33. Ġhālib, *Dīvān-e Ġhālib*, 296.

34. Ibid., 250.

35. ʿAlī Sikandar "Jigar" Murādābādī, *Kulliyāt-e Jigar* (Lahore: Maktabah-e Urdū Adab, n.d. [c. 1979]), 154.

36. For examples of use of the term, see Fārūqī, *Shiʿr-e shor angez*, 3:126–27.

37. Ibid., 1:50.

38. Ṭabāṭabā'ī, *Maqālāt*, 285. I have been unable to trace this comment, which Ṭabāṭabā'ī attributes to Hali. S. R. Faruqi believes that it was actually based on an observation by Amīr Mīnā'ī in one of his letters and that Ṭabāṭabā'ī mistakenly attributes it to Hali.

39. T. S. Eliot, *On Poetry and Poets* (New York: Farrar, Straus, and Cudahy, 1957), 21–22. The poem in question was William Morris's "Blue Closet."

40. Ġhālib, *Ḳhuṭūṭ*, 1:277.

41. Mīr, *Kulliyāt-e Mīr*, 237.

42. Ibid., 196; the quotation is from Fārūqī, *Shiʿr-e shor angez*, 2:425.

43. Ḳhvājah Mīr Dard, *Dīvān-e Dard urdū*, ed. Ẓahīr Aḥmad Ṣiddīqī (Lahore: Nāmī Press, 1965), 146. I adopt Ṣafīr and Sheftah's version of the first *shiʿr*.

44. Shaiḳh Ġhulām Hamadānī Muṣḥafī, *Kulliyāt-e Muṣḥafī*, ed. Imtiyāz ʿAlī Tāj (Lahore: Majlis Taraqqī-e Adab, 1968), 1:83.

45. Faiẓ Aḥmad Faiẓ, *Nusḳhahhā-e vafā* (Delhi: Educational Publishing House, 1986), 360.

9. The Cycles of Time

1. An interesting exception was Shāh Ḥātim, who noted the year of composition for his ghazals in his *Dīvān zādah*.

2. This tendency goes back at least to Mīr, who made it clear that he did not consider any of the Deccani poets to be major figures (*Nikāt ush-shuʿarā*, 23, 90). Like so many other choices made in *Water of Life*, the use of Valī as a boundary marker has since become canonical.

3. Farruḳhī, *Āzād*, 2:110. In his extensive discussion starting on p. 108, Farruḳhī gives numerous examples of such internal contradictions.

4. Mīr agrees, describing punning (*īhām*) as a figure even more popular among the early (*qadīm*) poets than among his own generation—although, as he notes approvingly, "now it is done with greater sophistication" (*Nikāt ush-shuʿarā*, 163).

5. Aḥsan Fārūqī, "Tażkirah nigārī aur Muḥammad Ḥusain Āzād kī *Āb-e ḥayāt*," in *Āb-e ḥayāt*, ed. Sayyid Sajjād, 44–67. The *daur*s and their deficiencies are discussed on pp. 57–62.

6. William Wordsworth, *Lyrical Ballads: Wordsworth and Coleridge*, ed. R. L. Brett and A. R. Jones (London: Routledge, 1963), 314.

7. Ibn Ḳhaldūn, *The Muqaddimah: An Introduction to History*, trans. Franz Rosenthal, ed. N. J. Dawood (Princeton: Princeton University Press, 1967), 136–38.

8. Of these two writers, Karīmuddīn, in his tazkirah *Ṭabaqāt-e shuʿarā-e hind* (1847), set up a straightforward division into four *daurs*. Mirzā Qurbān ʿAlī Beg

"Sālik," in his essay in *Makhzan-ul favā'id* (1874–75), also created four *daurs* for the classical tradition—plus a current fifth *daur* that was "still incomplete," so that it would be "foolish" to record the names of its poets. See Farrukhī, *Āzād*, 2:101–7.

9. Āzād, *Nairang-e Khiyāl*, 11.

10. Farrukhī, *Āzād*, 1:107.

11. Ḥālī, *Muqaddamah*, ed. Vaḥīd Quraishī, 71.

12. Ḥālī, *Muqaddamah-e shi'r o shā'irī*, ed. Rashīd Ḥasan Khān, 32–33. Pages references to this work hereafter appear in the text.

13. Hali generally uses the English word "natural" (*necharal*); Azad, by contrast, prefers *qudratī*.

14. Ḥālī, *Kulliyāt-e nasr*, 2:188. Even in the last decade of his life, Hali was still basically dissatisfied with the state of Urdu poetry: he wrote to a friend in 1905 that the old style of poetry had "nothing new" to show him, while in the new style, "though the *maẓmūns* are quite new, the thing which must be called the life of poetry, and for which no other word than 'magic' can be used, is nowhere to be seen" (*Makātīb*, 21–22).

15. Hali normally uses *shā'istagī* for "civilization," but he explicitly identifies it with the English word "civilization" (*sivīlizeshan*) (25).

16. Again, Hali normally uses *takhayyul*, but he explicitly identifies it with the English word "imagination" (*imaijineshan*) (27).

17. Hali himself sometimes expressed strong support for this optimistic view. In his review of *Water of Life*, for example, he wrote: "The foundation for the real progress of poetry rests on the general civilization and education of the country" (*Kulliyāt-e nasr*, 2:192).

18. Ḥālī, *Muqaddamah*, ed. Vaḥīd Quraishī, 83. Vaḥīd Quraishī makes the case for Hali's inconsistency at length, with examples, on pp. 72–96.

19. Shamsur Rahman Faruqi, personal communication, October 1990.

20. Kalīmuddīn, *Urdū tanqīd*, 111, 113.

21. The second section is held to begin with the fiftieth chapter, entitled "What Excellences Ought to Exist in Poetry" (68); the third—much the longest—with the fifty-ninth chapter, entitled "Natural Poetry" (102).

22. Steele, "Hali and his *Muqaddamah*," 18–19.

23. Ḥālī, *Kulliyāt-e nasr*, 2:192.

24. Ibid.

10. From Persian to English

1. Yet quite inconsistently Azad also called attention, as we have seen, to the fondness for wordplay shown by both Sanskrit and "its offshoot Braj Bhasha"; in both languages, wordplay was actually "the foundation of verses" (75–76).

2. Āzād, *Nairang-e khiyāl*, 12.

3. The European's ungrammatical Urdu has been reproduced as exactly as possible.

4. As, for example, in his lively discussion of the simple style of Ātash versus

the complex style of Nāsikh (341–44, 375–77); behind a pretense of objectivity, he is really out to exalt the former at the expense of the latter.

5. Johnson in effect reverses the *daur* theory, since the classical discipline and technical control he admires in poetry are the fruit not of early natural simplicity, but of later and more mature development. As for Addison, he explicitly praises writing in which the poet "quite loses sight of nature" and presents persons (such as fairies, witches, magicians, demons) who have "no existence, but what he bestows on them." Poetry has, in his view, an admirably unbounded domain: it "has not only the whole circle of nature for its province, but makes new worlds of its own." See the discussion in Abrams, *The Mirror and the Lamp*, 274–75.

6. The one Westerner he names is Chaucer (83), whom he mentions as a founding poet parallel to Valī.

7. And they are a rather general lot, most of which appear only once: certificate, coat, committee, dictionary, double, fashion, government, lecture, member, nature, number, pension, photograph, review. Of them all, only "nature" appears repeatedly (though much less frequently than its Urdu counterpart, *qudrat*) as a part of Azad's literary discourse.

8. Ḥālī, *Kulliyāt-e nasr*, 2:187.

9. He does mention Rūdakī (chap. 11), 'Ūmar Khayyām (chap. 12), and Firdausī (chap. 14), but chiefly as individual examples of points he is making.

10. In his *Ḥayāt-e Sa'dī* he also refers to Carlyle (Syed, *Muslim Response to the West*, 100).

11. Macaulay wrote, "Poetry produces an illusion on the eye of the mind, as a magic lantern produces an illusion on the eye of the body. And, as the magic lantern acts best in a dark room, poetry effects its purpose most completely in a dark age. As the light of knowledge breaks in upon its exhibitions, as the outlines of certainty become more and more definite and the shades of probability more and more distinct, the hues and lineaments of the phantoms which the poet calls up grow fainter and fainter. We cannot unite the incompatible advantages of reality and deception, the clear discernment of truth and the exquisite enjoyment of fiction" (Thomas Babington Macaulay, "Milton," in *Critical and Historical Essays* [London: Longman, Green, 1865], 1:9).

12. Ibid., 1:5.

13. This attitude is discussed in Walter E. Houghton, *The Victorian Frame of Mind, 1830–1870* (New Haven: Yale University Press, 1957), 30–32.

14. Ḥālī, *Muqaddamah*, ed. Vaḥīd Quraishī, 69–70.

15. Quoted in Ḥālī, *Muqaddamah*, ed. Rafīq Ḥusain (Allahabad: Rā'e Ṣāḥib Lālah Rām Dayāl, 1964), 33.

16. Mumtāz Ḥusain, *Ḥālī ke shi'rī naẓariyāt*, 160.

17. For an inventory of various views of various possible influences, see 'Abd ul-Qayyūm, *Ḥālī kī urdū nasr nigārī*, 377–410.

18. Quoted in Viswanathan, *Masks of Conquest*, 160; Viswanathan discusses the debate over educating Indian students in such an alienating, English-literary way (159–62).

19. Joseph Héliodore Garcin de Tassy, *La Langue et la littérature hindoustanies en 1874: Revue annuelle* (Paris: Maisonneuve, 1875), 21.

20. John Milton, *The Prose of John Milton,* ed. J. Max Patrick (New York: New York University Press, 1968), 236.

21. The identification is made by Mumtāz Ḥusain in *Ḥālī ke shiʿrī naẓariyāt,* 52. A longer excerpt from Coleridge including this passage is reproduced in Ḥālī, *Muqaddamah,* ed. Vaḥīd Quraishī, 313–14; but the identification is not explicitly made.

22. Samuel Taylor Coleridge, "Shakespeare, with Introductory Matter on Poetry, the Drama, and the Stage," in *The Complete Works of Samuel Taylor Coleridge,* ed. Professor Shedd (New York: Harper and Brothers, 1853), 4:21.

23. On this question, see Fārūqī, "Sādagī, aṣliyat, aur josh."

24. Macaulay wrote, "We often hear of the magical influence of poetry. The expression in general means nothing: but, applied to the writings of Milton, it is most appropriate. His poetry acts like an incantation. Its merit lies less in its obvious meaning than in its occult power. There would seem, at first sight, to be no more in his words than in other words. But they are words of enchantment. No sooner are they pronounced than the past is present and the distant near. New forms of beauty start at once into existence, and all the burial-places of the memory give up their dead. Change the structure of the sentence; substitute one synonym for another, and the whole effect is destroyed. The spell loses its power; and he who should then hope to conjure with it would find himself as much mistaken as Cassim in the Arabian tale, when he stood crying, 'Open Wheat,' 'Open Barley,' to the door which obeyed no sound but 'Open Sesame'" ("Milton," in *Critical and Historical Essays,* 1:12).

25. The conclusion begins, "And thou, sweet Poetry, thou loveliest maid, / Still first to fly where sensual joys invade; / Unfit in these degenerate times of shame / To catch the heart, or strike for honest fame"; it continues for another twenty lines to the end of the poem. See *The Poems of Thomas Gray, William Collins, Oliver Goldsmith,* ed. Roger Lonsdale (London: Longman, 1969), 693–94. On the "luxury" passage (lines 295–98), see pp. 669 and 688.

26. Macaulay, "Moore's *Life of Lord Byron*", in *Critical and Historical Essays,* 1:165.

27. Graham, *Sir Syed Ahmed Khan,* 62.

28. Thomas Babington Macaulay, "Minute on Education," in *Sources of Indian Tradition,* ed. W. T. de Bary et al. (New York: Columbia University Press, 1969), 2:44–45.

29. Ibid., 2:49.

30. Graham, *Sir Syed Ahmed Khan,* 218; see also Lelyveld, *Aligarh's First Generation,* 207.

31. Viswanathan, *Masks of Conquest,* 149.

32. Their work, when read tendentiously and with retrospective partisanship, also provided a launching platform for what has been called the "two-school theory," a polarization of Urdu poetry into a simple, austere, chaste, dignified "Delhi

school" versus a convoluted, frivolous, sensual, decadent "Lucknow school." On this interesting case of literary schizophrenia, see Petievich, *Assembly of Rivals: Delhi, Lucknow, and the Urdu Ghazal.*

11. "Natural Poetry"

1. In Islamic tradition, the Water of Life (*āb-e ḥayāt*) enables one who drinks it to live till Judgment Day, which is as close to immortality as a human can come. It is thus a universal restorative and panacea.

2. But even then, the camera must be pointed only at the real world: as we have seen, in his famous Anjuman speech Azad implicitly criticized Urdu for reproducing a "photograph" of Persian literature.

3. Ḥālī, *Kulliyāt-e naṡr,* 2:190.

4. Ibid., 2:181–82.

5. Abrams, *The Mirror and the Lamp,* 33.

6. Samuel Taylor Coleridge, *The Collected Works of Samuel Taylor Coleridge* (Princeton: Princeton University Press, c. 1969–1978), vol. 7, ed. James Engell and W. J. Bate, part 2, 122.

7. Thomas Babington Macaulay, "Milton," in *Critical and Historical Essays* (London: Longman, Green, 1865), 1:6–7.

8. Saksena, *A History of Urdu Literature,* 23–25. The numbers are provided by Saksena himself. See also Russell, "How Not to Write the History of Urdu Literature," 1–2.

9. Sadiq, *A History of Urdu Literature,* 27–28.

10. Ḥālī, *Yādgār-e Ġhālib,* 138.

11. The five are Mīr Anīs, Mirzā Shauq, Żauq, Ẓafar, and Dāġh.

12. Ṣābir, *Gulistān-e suḳhan,* 346.

13. Elsewhere, however, as we have seen, Hali affirms the value of an ustad for reining in brilliant but wild young poets like the youthful Ġhālib.

14. Ṣābir, *Gulistān-e suḳhan,* 346.

15. Georg Brandes, *Naturalism in Nineteenth-Century English Literature* (New York: Russell and Russell, 1957), 71.

16. Matthew Arnold, "Wordsworth," in *Victorian Poetry and Poetics,* ed. Walter Stoughton and G. Robert Stange (Boston: Houghton Mifflin, 1968), 556.

17. Quoted in Abrams, *The Mirror and the Lamp,* 24.

18. Brandes, *Naturalism in Nineteenth-Century English Literature,* 7.

19. Fārūqī, *Shiʿr-e shor angez,* 2:38. Fārūqī notes that one favorite but particularly unfortunate emotion inherited from the Victorians was "pathos" (2:437).

20. For a chrestomathy of examples, see Fārūqī, *Shiʿr-e shor angez,* 1:11–14; 2:11–16.

21. There are, of course, honorable exceptions, such as the work of Muḥammad Ḥasan ʿAskarī, the later Salīm Aḥmad, and Shamsur Rahman Faruqi.

22. The situation is similar with regard to *dāstāns,* or traditional romances.

Of the few Urdu critics who study them, the majority are concerned, either offensively or defensively, with internally generated accusations that *dāstāns* are not realistic, relevant, sociologically descriptive, etc.—are not, in short, like nineteenth-century European novels. The *dāstān* tradition has been studied in F. W. Pritchett, *The Romance Tradition in Urdu: Adventures from the Dāstān of Amīr Ḥamzah* (New York: Columbia University Press, 1991).

23. For example, Shamsur Rahman Faruqi once spoke to a scholarly audience about Mīr's constant use of wordplay in his ghazals. During the discussion afterwards, he was indignantly reproached for insulting Mīr's memory. To "accuse" Mīr of enjoying wordplay was to question the spontaneity, simplicity, and pathos that were believed to constitute his greatness (S. R. Faruqi, personal communication, August 26, 1991).

12. *Poetry and Morality*

1. Mīr, *Nikāt ush-shuʿarā*, 46–48.
2. Maḥmūd Shairānī, "*Āb-e ḥayāt* aur *Majmūʿah-e naġhz*," p. *mīm dāl*; Qāẓī ʿAbdul Vadūd, *Muḥammad Ḥusain Āzād*, 2–3.
3. ʿAbd ul-Ḥayy, *Gul-e raʿnā* (Lahore: ʿIshrat Publishing House, 1964), 111.
4. Farrukhī, *Āzād*, 2:121.
5. When reproached for their presence, Mīr Dard replies, "To a faqir, they are all mothers and sisters." But he is then crushed into silence by the scornful retort, "Is it at all proper to bring out mothers and sisters and seat them in a public gathering?"
6. See, for example, Nāṣir, *Khush maʿrikah-e zebā*, 435, 530–33.
7. Farrukhī, *Āzād*, 2:124–27. Mirzā Maẓhar's death was in any case a confusing episode, about which the tazkirahs have different theories.
8. Karīmuddīn, *Ṭabaqāt*, 105, 166.
9. Nāṣir, *Khush maʿrikah-e zebā*, 83.
10. "Bāṭin," *Gulistān-e be-khizāñ*, 219, 51.
11. "Luṭf," *Gulshan-e hind*, 159.
12. Amrullāh, *Tażkirah-e masarrat afzā*, 202.
13. Tabārak ʿAlī Naqshbandī, *Mirzā Maẓhar Jān-e Jānāñ; un kā ʿahd aur urdū shāʿirī* (New Delhi: Author, 1988), 109, 121–22.
14. Saksena, *A History of Urdu Literature*, 25.
15. This case is argued in detail in F. W. Pritchett, "Convention in the Classical Urdu Ghazal."
16. C. M. Naim, "The Theme of Homosexual (Pederastic) Love in Pre-Modern Urdu Poetry," in *Studies in the Urdu Ġazal and Prose Fiction*, ed. Muhammad Umar Memon (Madison: South Asian Studies, University of Wisconsin, 1979), 120–42.
17. Ġhulām Ḥusain Shorish, *Tażkirah-e shorish*, ed. Maḥmūd Ilāhī (Lucknow: Uttar Pradesh Urdu Academy, 1984 [1777–80]), 125.
18. Āzād, *Dīvān-e Żauq*, 201.

19. Ḥālī, *Ḥayāt-e Saʿdī*, 237–38.

20. Ibid., 238–41.

21. Ibid., 243, 239.

22. Meisami shows that in Persian ghazal "the male gender of the beloved, often explicitly indicated, becomes a standard convention of the genre." But her argument is much more cautious and sophisticated than Hali's, and stops short of making universal claims. She also emphasizes the role of love in the Persian courtly ghazal as "an ideal and a fiction," so that it is not "the sex or even the 'real' status (human or transcendent) of the beloved that is of primary importance, but the qualities" (such as supremacy, nobility, and unattainability) that the beloved embodies. See her discussion in *Medieval Persian Court Poetry*, 245–55.

23. She may be envisioned as a respectable (*pardah nashīñ*) lady, or as a courtesan (*ṭavāʾif*); often she is too vague to be typed. There are no marriages, no wives, no children in the ghazal world. All the charges (hostility to "family values," etc.) made against courtly love poetry by Denis de Rougemont in his classic *Love in the Western World* apply equally to the ghazal. This is not surprising, after all, since courtly love poetry may well have been brought north over the Pyrenees from Moorish Spain with its Arabic ghazal tradition.

24. For a recent compilation of evidence on the subject, with a wide range of examples, notes, and references, see Tariq Rahman, "Boy-love in the Urdu Ghazal," *Annual of Urdu Studies* 7 (1990): 1–20.

25. Both passages are quoted in Ḥālī, *Muqaddamah*, ed. Vaḥīd Quraishī, 71, 372.

Epilogue

1. Ḥālī, *Kulliyāt-e naṡr*, 2:194.

2. C. M. Naim, "Prize-winning *Adab*: A Study of Five Urdu Books Written in Response to the Allahabad Government Gazette Notification," in *Moral Conduct and Authority: The Place of* adab *in South Asian Islam*, ed. Barbara Daly Metcalf (Berkeley: University of California Press, 1984), 311; see also 299–301.

3. The volumes of poetry singled out by name are *Kulliyāt-e Ātash, Dīvān-e Sharar, Vāsokht-e Amānat*, the "*Maṡnavī*" of Mīr Ḥasan, *Muntaḳhab ġhazaliyāt-e Chirkīn, Hazliyāt-e Jaʿfar Zaṭallī, Qaṣāʾid-e ḥajviyah-e Mirzā Rafīʿ Saudā, Dīvān-e Jān Ṣāḥib, Kulliyāt-e Rind*, and *Dīvān-e Naẓīr Akbarābādī*—a selection generally meant to suggest frivolousness, immorality, and obscenity.

4. Naẕīr Aḥmad, *Taubat un-Naṣūḥ* (Lahore: Majlis Taraqqī-e Adab, 1964), 251–55, 258–62.

5. Naim, "Prize-winning *Adab*," 301; Nazir Ahmad, *The Repentance of Nussooh*, trans. M. Kempson (London: W. H. Allen and Co., 1884), vii–viii.

6. Sadiq, *Azad*, 32.

7. Graham, *Sir Syed Ahmed Khan*, 159–62.

8. Sadiq, *Azad*, 33.

9. Harry Mathews, "That Ephemeral Thing," *New York Review of Books* 35, no. 10 (June 16, 1988): 35; see also 34, 36–37.

10. Warren F. Motte, Jr., trans. and ed., *Oulipo: A Primer of Potential Literature* (Lincoln: University of Nebraska Press, 1986), 11, 3. This book is an excellent basic source on the movement.

11. Raymond Queneau, *Exercises in Style*, trans. Barbara Wright (London: John Calder, 1979). The original French version was published in 1947.

12. Georges Perec, *La Disparition* (Paris: Denoël, 1969).

13. Georges Perec, "History of the Lipogram," in Motte, *Oulipo*, 97–108.

14. Mark Ford, "Pretzel," *London Review of Books* 11, no. 3 (February 2, 1989): 15–17.

15. In Urdu: *rāh-e maẓmūn-e tāzah band nahīñ / tā qiyāmat khulā hai bāb-e suḳhan* (Valī, *Dīvān-e Valī*, ed. Maḥmūd Ḳhān Ashraf and Ḥasrat Mohānī [Lahore: Maktabah Meri Library, 1965], 103).

BIBLIOGRAPHY

Works in English

Abrams, M. H. *The Mirror and the Lamp: Romantic Theory and the Critical Tradition*. New York: W. W. Norton, 1958.

Ali, Ahmed. *The Golden Tradition: An Anthology of Urdu Poetry*. New York: Columbia University Press, 1973.

Andrews, C. F. *Zaka Ullah of Delhi*. Lahore: Universal Books, 1976 [1929].

Andrews, Walter G. *An Introduction to Ottoman Poetry*. Minneapolis: Bibliotheca Islamica, 1976.

Bausani, Alessandro. "Alṭāf Ḥusain Ḥālī's Ideas on Ghazal." In *Charisteria Orientalia (in Honor of Jan Rypka)*, edited by Felix Tauer et al., 38–55. Prague: Ceskoslovenská Akademie Vèd, 1956.

Browne, Edward G. *A Literary History of Persia*. 4 vols. Cambridge: Cambridge University Press, 1964 [1902].

Faruqi, Shamsur Rahman. *The Secret Mirror*. Delhi: Academic Literature, 1981.

Fisher, Michael H. *A Clash of Cultures: Awadh, the British and the Mughals*. Riverdale, Md.: The Riverdale Company, 1987.

Ghalib, Mirza Asadullah Khan. *Dastanbuy: A Diary of the Indian Revolt of 1857*. Translated by Khwaja Ahmad Faruqi. Bombay: Asia Publishing House, 1970.

———. *Urdu Letters of Mirza Asadullah Khan Ghalib*. Edited and translated by Daud Rahbar. Albany: State University of New York Press, 1987.

Graham, G. F. I. *The Life and Work of Sir Syed Ahmed Khan*. Karachi: Oxford University Press, 1974 [1875].

Gupta, Narayani. *Delhi between Two Empires, 1803–1931: Society, Government and Urban Growth*. Delhi: Oxford University Press, 1981.

Hali, Altaf Husain. *Hayat-i-javed*. Translated by K. H. Qadiri and David Matthews. Delhi: Idarah-i Adabiyat-i Delli, 1979.

———. *Voices of Silence*. Translated by Gail Minault. Delhi: Chanakya Publications, 1986. [Translations of *Majālis un-nisā* and "Chup kī dād."]

———. *Yadgar-e-Ghalib*. Translated by K. H. Qadiri. Delhi: Idarah-i Adabiyat-i Delli, 1990. [The translator's own extensive comments are confusingly interwoven into an abridged text of the original.]

Husain, Agha Mahdi. *Bahadur Shah II and the War of 1857 in Delhi with Its Unforgettable Scenes*. Delhi: Atma Ram and Sons, 1958.

Khan, Nadir Ali. *A History of Urdu Journalism, 1822–1857*. Delhi: Idarah-i Adabiyat-i Delli, 1991.

Khatak, Sarfaraz Khan. *Shaikh Muhammad Ali Hazin: His Life, Times, and Works.* Lahore: Shaikh Muhammad Ashraf, 1944.

Leitner, G. W. *History of Indigenous Education in the Panjab since Annexation and in 1882*. Patiala: Punjab Government Languages Department, 1971 [1882].

Lelyveld, David. *Aligarh's First Generation: Muslim Solidarity in British India.* Princeton: Princeton University Press, 1978.

Malik Ram. *Hali*. New Delhi: Sahitya Akademi, 1982.

Matthews, D. J., C. Shackle, and Shahrukh Husain. *Urdu Literature*. London: Urdu Markaz, 1985.

Meisami, Julie Scott. *Persian Court Poetry*. Princeton: Princeton University Press, 1987.

Mirza, Mohammad Wahid. *The Life and Works of Amir Khusrau*. Delhi: Idarah-i Adabiyat-i Delli, 1974 [1935].

Naim, C. M. "Mughal and English Patronage of Urdu Poetry: A Comparison." In *The Powers of Art: Patronage in Indian Culture*, edited by Barbara S. Miller, 259–76. New Delhi: Oxford University Press, 1992.

Petievich, Carla R. *Assembly of Rivals: Delhi, Lucknow, and the Urdu Ghazal.* New Delhi: Manohar Publications, 1992.

Pritchett, Frances W. "Convention in the Classical Urdu Ghazal: The Case of Mīr." *Journal of South Asian and Middle Eastern Studies* 3, no. 1 (Fall 1979): 60–77.

Pritchett, Frances W. "Orient Pearls Unstrung: The Quest for Unity in the Ghazal." *Edebiyat* (n. s.) 4 (1993): 119–35.

Pritchett, Frances W., and Khaliq Ahmad Khaliq. *Urdu Meter: A Practical Handbook*. Madison: South Asian Studies, University of Wisconsin, 1987.

Pybus, G. D. *A Textbook of Urdu Prosody and Rhetoric*. Lahore: Rama Krishna and Sons, 1924.

Qadir, Abdul. *Famous Urdu Poets and Writers*. Lahore: New Book Society, 1947.

Qamber, Akhter, trans. *The Last Musha'irah of Dehli*. Delhi: Orient Longman, 1979. [A translation of Farḥatullāh Beg's *Dihlī kī āḳhirī sham'a*, c. 1935–36.]

Russell, Ralph, ed. *Ghalib: The Poet and His Age*. London: George Allen and Unwin, 1972.

———. "How Not to Write the History of Urdu Literature." *Annual of Urdu Studies* 6 (1987): 1–10.

———. *The Pursuit of Urdu Literature: A Select History.* London: Zed Books, 1992.

Russell, Ralph, and Khurshidul Islam, ed. and trans. *Ghalib: Life and Letters.* London: George Allen and Unwin, 1969.

Sadiq, Muhammad. *A History of Urdu Literature.* 2d ed. Delhi: Oxford University Press, 1984 [1964].

———. *Muhammad Husain Azad: His Life and Works.* Lahore: West-Pak Publishing Co., 1974.

Saksena, Ram Babu. *A History of Urdu Literature.* New Delhi: Asian Educational Services, 1990 [1927].

Shackle, Christopher, ed. *Urdu and Muslim South Asia: Studies in Honour of Ralph Russell.* London: School of Oriental and African Studies, 1989.

Spear, Percival. *Twilight of the Mughuls.* Karachi: Oxford University Press, 1980 [1951].

Steele, Laurel. "Hali and His *Muqaddamah*: The Creation of a Literary Attitude in Nineteenth-Century India." *Annual of Urdu Studies* 1 (1981): 1–45.

Syed, Muhammad Aslam. *Muslim Response to the West: Muslim Historiography in India, 1857–1914.* Islamabad: National Institute of Historical and Cultural Research, 1988.

Viswanathan, Gauri. *Masks of Conquest: Literary Study and British Rule in India.* New York: Columbia University Press, 1989.

Works in Urdu

ʿAbd ul-Ḥaq, Maulvī. *Marḥūm Dihlī Kālij* (Delhi College as it used to be). Delhi: Anjuman Taraqqī-e Urdū, 1989.

ʿAbd ul-Qayyūm. *Ḥālī kī urdū naṡr nigārī* (Ḥālī's Urdu prose). Lahore: Majlis Taraqqī-e Adab, 1964.

"ʿĀbid," ʿĀbid ʿAlī. *Uṣūl-e intiqād-e adabiyāt* (Principles of literary criticism). Lahore: Majlis Taraqqī-e Adab, 1966.

"ʿĀbid" Peshāvarī. *Żauq aur Muḥammad Ḥusain Āzād* (Żauq and Muḥammad Ḥusain Āzād). New Delhi: Idārah-e Fikr-e Jadīd, 1987.

Abuʾl-Ḥasan Amrullāh Illāhābādī, Amīruddīn Aḥmad. *Tażkirah-e masarrat afzā* (The enjoyment-enhancing tazkirah). Translated by Mujīb Quraishī. Delhi: ʿIlmī Majlis Kutubḳhānah, 1968 [1780].

"Adīb," Masʿūd Ḥasan Rizvī. *Āb-e ḥayāt kā tanqīdī muṭāliʿah* (A critical study of "Water of life"). Lucknow: Kitāb Nagar, 1953.

———. *Hamārī shāʿirī: miʿyār o masāʾil* (Our poetry: Standards and problems). Lucknow: Kitāb Nagar, 1987 [1926–27].

"Āzād," Muḥammad Ḥusain. *Āb-e ḥayāt* (Water of life). 2d ed. Lucknow: Uttar Pradesh Urdu Academy, 1982 (facsimile of 1907 ed., Lahore). The first edition was published in 1880; the second edition originally appeared in 1883.

———. *Nairang-e ḳhiyāl* (The wonder-world of thought). Edited by Malik Rām. New Delhi: Maktabah Jāmiʿah, 1987 [1880].

———. *Naẓm-e Āzād* (The poetry of Āzād). Edited by Tabassum Kashmīrī. Lahore: Maktabah ʿĀliyah, 1978 [1899].

———, ed. *Dīvān-e Żauq* (The poetry of Żauq). Delhi: ʿIlmī Printing Works, 1933 [1863].
"Bāṭin," Quṭbuddīn. *Gulistān-e be-ḳhizāñ* (The garden without autumn). Lucknow: Uttar Pradesh Urdu Academy, 1982 [1845].
"Faiẓ," Faiẓ Aḥmad. "Hamārī tanqīd kī iṣṭilāḥāt" (Our critical vocabulary). In *Mīzān* (Balance), 40–49. Calcutta: West Bengal Urdu Academy, 1982.
Farḥatullāh Beg. *Dihlī kī āḳhirī shamʿa* (The last candle of Delhi). Edited by Ṣalāḥuddīn. Delhi: Urdu Academy, 1986 [c. 1935–36?].
"Farmān" Fatḥpūrī. *Urdū shuʿarā ke tażkire aur tażkirah nigārī* (Tazkirahs and tazkirah writing about Urdu poets). Lahore: Majlis Taraqqī-e Adab, 1972.
Farruḳhī, Aslam. *Muḥammad Ḥusain Āzād*. 2 vols. Karachi: Anjuman Taraqqī-e Urdū, 1965.
Fārūqī, Shamsur Raḥmān. "Andāz-e guftagū kyā hai" (What is the style of speech?). *Ġhālib Nāmah* (New Delhi) 8, no. 2 (July 1987): 23–40.
———. "Sādagī, aṣliyat, aur josh" (Simplicity, truth, and fervor). *Aurāq* (Lahore) December 1990: 233–44.
———. *Shiʿr-e shor angez: ġhazaliyāt-e Mīr kā intiḳhāb aur mufassal muṭāliʿah* (Passionate poetry: A selection and detailed analysis of the ghazals of Mīr). 3 vols. New Delhi: Taraqqī Urdū Bureau, 1990–92 (vol. 4 forthcoming).
———, ed. *Dars-e balāġhat* (Lessons in rhetoric). New Delhi: Taraqqī Urdū Bureau, 1981.
"Ġhālib," Mirzā Asadullāh Ḳhān. *Dīvān-e Ġhālib* (The poetry of Ġhālib). Edited by Imtiyāz ʿAlī Ḳhān ʿArshī. 2d ed. New Delhi: Anjuman Taraqqī-e Urdū, 1982 [1958].
———. *Ḳhuṭūṭ-e Ġhālib* (Letters of Ghalib). Edited by Ġhulām Rasūl Mihr. 2 vols. Lahore: Panjab University, 1969.
"Ḥālī," Alṭāf Ḥusain. *Dīvān-e Ḥālī* (The poetry of Ḥālī). Delhi: Urdu Academy, 1991 [1893].
———. *Ḥayāt-e Saʿdī* (The life of Saʿdī). Edited by Shaiḳh Muḥammad Ismāʿīl Pānīpatī. Lahore: Majlis Taraqqī-e Adab, 1961 [1886].
———. *Kulliyāt-e naṡr-e Ḥālī* (The complete prose writings of Ḥālī). Edited by Shaiḳh Muḥammad Ismāʿīl Pānīpatī. 2 vols. Lahore: Majlis Taraqqī-e Adab, 1968.
———. *Kulliyāt-e naẓm-e Ḥālī* (The complete poetry of Ḥālī). Edited by Iftiḳhār Aḥmad Ṣiddīqī. 2 vols. Lahore: Majlis Taraqqī-e Adab, 1968 [1893].
———. *Kulliyāt-e naẓm-e Ḥālī* (The complete poetry of Ḥālī). Edited by Rafīq Ḥusain. Allahabad: Rāʾe Ṣāḥib Lālah Rām Dayāl, 1964 [1893].
———. *Makātīb-e Ḥālī* (Ḥālī's letters). Edited by Shaiḳh Muḥammad Ismāʿīl Pānīpatī. Lahore: Urdū Markaz, 1950.
———. *Muqaddamah-e shiʿr o shāʿirī* (Introduction to poetry and poetics). Edited by Rashīd Ḥasan Ḳhān. New Delhi: Maktabah Jamiʿah, 1969 [1893].
———. *Muqaddamah-e shiʿr o shāʿirī* (Introduction to poetry and poetics). Edited by Vaḥīd Quraishī. Lahore: Maktabah-e Jadīd, 1953. [See especially "Ḥālī kī tanqīd" (Ḥālī's criticism), pp. 49–96.]

———. *Yādgār-e Ġhālib* (A memoir of Ġhālib). New Delhi: Ġhālib Institute, 1986 [1897].
"Ḥātim," Shaikh Ẓahūr ud-Dīn Shāh. *Dīvān zādah* (Offspring of the *dīvān*). Edited by Ġhulām Ḥusain Żulfiqār. Lahore: Maktabah Khayābān-e Adab, 1975 [1781].
Kalīmuddīn Aḥmad. *Urdū shā'irī par ek naẓar* (A look at Urdu poetry). Patna: Book Emporium, 1985 [1941?].
———. *Urdū tanqīd par ek naẓar, ma' iẓāfah-e jadīd* (A look at Urdu criticism, with new additions). Patna: Dā'irah-e Adab, 1983 [1943?].
Karīmuddīn. *Ṭabaqāt-e shu'arā-e hind* (The categories of the poets of India). Lucknow: Uttar Pradesh Urdu Academy, 1983 [1847].
"Luṭf," Mirzā 'Alī. *Gulshan-e hind* (The garden of India). Lucknow: Uttar Pradesh Urdu Academy 1986 [1801].
"Mīr," Mīr Taqī. *Kulliyāt-e Mīr* (The complete works of Mīr). Vol. 1, edited by Ẓill-e 'Abbās 'Abbāsī. New Delhi: Taraqqī Urdū Bureau, 1983 [1968].
———. *Nikāt ush-shu'arā* (Fine points about the poets). Edited by Maḥmūd Ilāhī. In Persian. Lucknow: Uttar Pradesh Urdu Academy, 1984 [1752]. [An Urdu translation exists—*Tażkirah-e Mīr,* trans. M. K. Fāṭimī (Lucknow: Sājid Ṣiddīqī, 1962)—but since the text is so crucial, references in the present study are to the Persian original.]
Mumtāz Ḥusain. *Ḥālī ke shi'rī naẓariyāt: ek tanqīdī muṭāli'ah* (Ḥālī's poetic views: A critical study). Karachi: Sa'id Publications, 1988.
"Nāṣir," Sa'ādat Khān. *Khush ma'rikah-e zebā* (An elegant encounter). Edited by Shamīm Inhonvī. Lucknow: Nasīm Book Depot, 1971 [1846].
Parvez, Aslam. *Bahādur Shāh Ẓafar.* New Delhi: Anjuman Taraqqī-e Urdū, 1986.
Qāẓī 'Abdul Vadūd. *Muḥammad Ḥusain Āzād baḥaisiyat-e muḥaqqiq* (Muḥammad Ḥusain Āzād as a scholar). Patna: Idārah-e Taḥqīqāt-e Urdū, 1984 [1942–43].
"Ṣābir," Mirzā Qādir Bakhsh. *Gulistān-e sukhan* (The garden of poetry). Lucknow: Uttar Pradesh Urdu Academy, 1982 [1855].
Ṣādiq, Muḥammad. *Āb-e ḥayāt kī ḥimāyat meñ aur dūsre maẓāmīn* (In support of "Water of life" and other essays). Lahore: Majlis Taraqqī-e Adab, 1973.
"Ṣafdar" Mirzāpūrī. *Mashshāṭah-e sukhan* (The adorner of poetry). 2 vols. Lahore: Gīlānī Electric Press Book Depot, 1918, 1928.
Sāḥil Aḥmad, ed. *Muḥammad Ḥusain Āzād.* Allahabad: Literary Book Centre, 1985.
Ṣāliḥah 'Ābid Ḥusain. *Yādgār-e Ḥālī* (A memoir of Ḥālī). 5th ed. New Delhi: Anjuman Taraqqī-e Urdū, 1986 [1949].
Sayyid 'Abdullāh. *Shu'arā-e urdū ke tażkire aur tażkirah nigārī kā fan* (Tazkirahs of Urdu poets and the art of tazkirah writing). Delhi: Maktabah Shi'r o Adab, n.d.
Sayyid Āġhā Ḥaidar, ed. *Muṭāli'ah-e Āb-e ḥayāt* (A study of "Water of life"). Lahore: Sang-e Mīl Publications, 1969.
Sayyid Sajjād, ed. *Āb-e ḥayāt kā tanqīdī taḥqīqī muṭāli'ah* (A critical and scholarly study of "Water of life"). New Delhi: 'Ījāz Publishing House, 1985 [1966].

Shairānī, Maḥmūd. "*Āb-e ḥayāt* aur *Majmū'ah-e naġhz*" ("Water of life" and "Rare collection"). In Qudratullāh Qāsim, *Majmū'ah-e naġhz ya'nī tażkirah-e shu'arā-e urdū* ("Rare collection," a tazkirah of Urdu poets), edited by Maḥmūd Shairānī, pp. mīm jīm–mīm vā'o. Delhi: National Academy, 1973.

———. *Maqālāt-e Ḥāfiẓ Maḥmūd Shairānī* (Essays of Hāfiẓ Maḥmūd Shairānī). 3 vols. Lahore: Majlis Taraqqī-e Adab, 1969. [Vol. 3 contains "Tanqīd bar *Āb-e ḥayāt*," 27–116, and "Shams ul-'Ulamā Maulānā Muḥammad Ḥusain Āzād aur *Dīvān-e Żauq*," 117–306.]

Shujā'at 'Alī Sandīlvī. *Ḥālī bahaiṡiyat-e shā'ir* (Ḥālī as a poet). 2d ed. Lucknow: Idārah-e Furoġh-e Urdū, 1971 [1960].

Ṭabāṭabā'ī, Sayyid 'Alī Ḥaidar "Naẓm." *Maqālāt-e Ṭabāṭabā'ī* (Essays of Ṭabāṭabā'ī). Edited by Ashraf Rafī'. Hyderabad: Dā'irah Electric Press, 1984. [Essays originally written c. 1900–33.]

Ẓafar Ḥasan. *Sir Sayyid aur Ḥālī kā naẓariyah-e fiṭrat* (Sir Sayyid's and Ḥālī's view of nature). Lahore: Idārah-e Ṡaqāfat-e Islāmiyyah, 1990.

INDEX

'Abd ul-Ḥaq, Maulvī, 10, 37, 82
"'Ābid," 'Ābid 'Alī, 211n37
"'Ābid" Peshāvarī, 46, 48
"Adīb," Mas'ūd Ḥasan Riẓvī (1893–1975), 48, 201n5
"'Aish," Ḥakīm Āġhā Jān, 13
Akbar Shāh II "Shu'ā" (r. 1806–1837), 4
Amīr "Ḳhusrau" (1253–1325), 8, 85, 140, 177
Amrullāh Illāhābādī, Abu'l-Ḥasan, 67
Andrews, C. F., 6, 15
Anjumān-e Panjāb, 32–36
"Arīb,"Sulaimān (1922–1969), 103, 119
Arnold, Matthew, 167
Āṣif ud-Daulah, Nawab, 54
"Ātash," Ḳhvājah Ḥaidar 'Alī (1777–1847), 69–70, 83, 95, 101–2, 131
"Āzād"[Azad], Muḥammad Ḥusain (1830–1910): life, 11–13, 22–26, 31–33, 36–37, 40–42, 49–50; literary views, xv–xvii, 34–35, 39, 40, 50, 95, 132–34, 143–45; *The Court of Akbar (Darbār-e akbarī)*, 42; *Dīvān-e Żauq*, 49; *On Iranian Poets (Suḳhandān-e fārs)*, 41; *Stories of India (Qiṣaṣ ul-hind)*, 33, 40; *Water of Life (Āb-e ḥayāt)*, xv, 40, 46–48, 50–59, 63, 67, 88, 128–35, 141–43, 145, 155–58, 169–73, 189, 191; *The Wonder-World of Thought (Nairang-e ḳhiyāl)*, 40, 141, 144, 158

Bahādur Shāh "Ẓafar" (1775–1862): life, 4–7, 9–11, 16–18, 23, 28–29, 84; poetry, 5, 48–49, 66
"Baqā," Baqā Allāh Ḳhān, 53
Bashīr ud-Dīn Aḥmad (1861–1927), 30
"Bedil," 'Abd ul-Qādir (1644–1720), 120, 162
Beg, Farḥatullāh, 211n26
"Beqarār," Mīr Kāẓim Ḥusain, 9
Braj Bhasha, 4, 34, 132, 140, 145, 157, 177

Coleridge, Samuel Taylor, 149–51, 159

"Dabīr," Mirzā Salāmat ʿAlī (1803–1875), 57, 58
"Dard," Ḳhvājah Mīr (1721–1785), 58, 70, 117, 121, 174
Delhi Anglo-Arabic College, 42, 43
Delhi College, 6–8, 11–12, 14, 19–22, 69
Delhi Renaissance, 6, 11
Department of Public Instruction (Lahore), 26, 31, 38–39
Dihlī Urdū Aḳhbār, 12–13, 17, 22–23

Eliot, T. S., 112, 120
English language, 6, 34, 133, 141–43, 145

"Faiẓ," Faiẓ Aḥmad (1911–1984), 78, 121–22, 211n37
"Farmān" Fatḥpūrī, 211n37
Farruḳhī, Aslam, 12, 25, 32, 38–39, 41, 174
Fārūqī, Aḥsan, 75n
Fārūqī, Shamsur Raḥmān (1936–), 92–93, 106, 111, 167, 201n5, 211n37, 221n21

"Ġhālib," Mirzā Asadullāh Ḳhān (1797–1869): life, 7–10, 15, 18–22, 28, 158; views on poetry, 9, 78, 81, 106, 120; poetry, xiii, 20, 56, 86, 94, 102, 105, 108, 112–13, 117–18, 191–92
Goldsmith, Oliver, 151–52
Government College (Lahore), 31, 33, 41
Gupta, Narayani, 6

"Ḥālī" [Hali], Alṭāf Ḥusain (1837–1914): life, 11, 13–15, 26–28, 31, 33, 37–38, 42–44; literary views, xv–xvii, 36, 39–40, 49, 63, 185; *Conversations among Women (Majālis un-nisā)*, 44; *An Immortal Life (Ḥayāt-e javed)*, 44; *Introduction to Poetry and Poetics (Muqaddamah-e shiʿr o shāʿirī)*, xv, 43, 134–39, 146–52, 160–66, 179–82, 189; *The Life of Saʿdī (Ḥayāt-e Saʿdī)*, 43, 177–78; *Musaddas-e Ḥālī*, 42–43; *A Memoir of Ġhālib (Yādgār-e Ġhālib)*, 44, 203n24
Hardy, Peter, 6
"Ḥasrat"Mohānī, Faẓl ul-Ḥasan (1875–1951), 210n12, 213n22
Hollander, John, 108
Holroyd, Colonel W. R. M., 35–37, 39, 44, 144, 182, 187

Ibn al-Farāj Qudāmah, 77
Ibn Ḳhaldūn, 78, 133
Ibn Rashīq, 164
Iḥtishām Ḥusain, 147
"Inshā," Mīr Inshāʾallāh Ḳhān (1753–1817), 58, 70, 73–74, 81, 141, 171–72, 176–77, 188
"ʿIshq," ʿIzzatullāh, 9

Jaʿfrī, ʿAlī Sardār (1913–), 201n6
"Jigar"Murādābādī (1890–1961), 118–19
"Jurʾat," Shaiḳh Qalandar Baḳhsh (1748–1810), 68, 131, 171

"Kalīm," Abū Ṯālib, 103
Kalīmuddīn Aḥmad (1909–1983), 138
Karīmuddīn, 74, 211n26, 217n8

Leitner, Dr. G. W., 31–33, 38, 41, 69, 104

Macaulay, Thomas Babington, 146–48, 151, 153, 159

Madrasah of Ḥusain Bak̲h̲sh, 14, 20
"Makīn," Mirzā Fāk̲h̲ir, 51–55
Meisami, Julie, 223n22
Metcalf, Thomas, 28
Mill, John Stuart, 169
Milton, John, 148–51
"Mīr," Mīr Taqī (c. 1722–1810): general, 48, 50, 58, 66, 70, 75–76, 84, 103, 119, 130, 141, 170; poetry, 7, 87, 99–100, 105–7, 109–12, 115–16, 120–21, 131, 158
Mīr Ḥasan (1727–1786), 180
Mirzā "Maẕhar" Jān-e Jānāñ (1699–1781), 57, 172–75
Muhammedan Anglo-Oriental College (Aligarh), 43, 153, 187
"Momin," Momin K̲h̲ān (1800–1852), 27, 48, 58, 106, 131
Muḥammad Bāqir, Maulvī (c. 1810–1857), 11–12, 22–25
Mumtāz Ḥusain, 147
"Muṣḥafī," Shaik̲h̲ G̣hulām Hamadānī (1750–1824), 58, 66, 68, 73–74, 121, 171, 209n13

Naim, C. M., 176
Nashe, Thomas, 119–20
"Nāsik̲h̲," Shaik̲h̲ Imām Bak̲h̲sh (1776–1838), 51, 57–58, 68–70, 81, 100–101, 131, 171, 174, 209n13
"Nasīm" Dihlavī (1794–1864), 113–14
"Nāṣir," Sa'ādat K̲h̲ān, 67–69
"Naṣīr," Shāh. *See* Shāh Naṣīr ud-Dīn "Naṣīr"
Naẕīr Aḥmad (1836–1912), 6, 14, 30, 185–87; *Taubat un-Naṣūḥ*, 185–87

Oriental College (Lahore), 32
Oulipo, 187–88

Perec, Georges, 188
Persian language, 4, 34, 135, 140–41, 145, 157, 162
Petievich, Carla, 201n3, 220n32

"Qatīl," Mirzā Muḥammad Ḥasan, 171
Queen Victoria, 8, 19, 44, 169
Queneau, Raymond, 188
Quraishī, Vaḥīd, 147

"Rangīñ," Sa'ādat Yār K̲h̲ān, 172
Rebellion of 1857, xv, 16–30, 32, 47, 175
Red Fort, 3–4, 6, 9, 18, 20, 22, 69
"Rind," Sayyid Muḥammad K̲h̲ān (1797–1857), 114
Russell, Ralph, xiv

"Ṣābir," Mirzā Qādir Bak̲h̲sh, 10–11, 66, 72–73, 104, 163–64
"Sa'dī" Shīrāzī (c. 1200–1290), 96
Sadiq, Muhammad (d. 1984), xiii–xvi, 30, 38–39, 41, 48, 161, 187
"Ṣafdar" Mirzāpūrī, 82–84
Saksena, Ram Babu, 159, 175
Ṣāliḥah 'Ābid Ḥusain, 27, 39
"Saudā," Mirzā Muḥammad Rafī' (1713–1780), 51–55, 58, 66, 68, 79–80, 115, 170–71
Sayyid Aḥmad K̲h̲ān, Sir (1817–1898), 7, 28, 30, 38, 42–43, 144–45, 153, 187
Scott, Sir Walter, 152
Shāh 'Ālam II "Āftāb" (r. 1759–1806), 3–4, 58
Shāh "Ḥātim" (1699–1783), 130, 212n5, 217n1
Shāh Naṣīr ud-Dīn "Naṣīr" (d. 1838), 9, 56–57, 69–70, 79–80, 131
"Shākir" Nājī (1690?–1774?), 98
Shams-e Qais, 77
"Shauq," Nawab Mirzā, 179–80

"Sheftah," Nawab Musṯafā Ḳhān (1806–1869), 27–28, 69
"Siṯvat" Lakhnavī, 114–15
Spear, Percival, 5, 17
Steele, Laurel, 138
Sulaimān Shikoh, Mirzā, 69, 73, 171

"Tābāñ," Mīr 'Abd ul-Ḥayy (1715–1749), 173–75
Ṯabāṯabā'ī, Sayyid 'Alī Ḥaidar "Naẕm" (1852–1933), 85, 95, 106, 120, 212n19, 217n38
Tahżīb ul-Aḳhlāq (Sayyid Aḥmad Ḳhān, editor), 38, 42, 145
"Ṯālib" Āmulī, 105
"Tāṡīr," Muḥsin, 80, 96
Turner, Mark, 93

Urdu, 4, 10, 29, 34–35, 107–8, 133, 139–42, 145, 155, 169

"Valī" Dakanī, Shamsuddīn Valī Muḥammad (1667–1720/25), 97, 130, 189

Wordsworth, William, 132, 147–48, 166–67

Yeats, William Butler, 115

"Ẕafar." *See* Bahādur Shāh
Żakā'ullāh, Maulvī (1836–1907?), 14, 30
"Zaṭallī, Mīr Ja'far (c. 1659–1713), 170
"Żauq," Shaiḳh Ibrāhīm (c. 1788–1854): general, 9–10, 12–13, 48, 51, 55, 120, 131, 141–42; poetry, 25, 49, 56, 73, 78–80, 84–85, 130, 162

Compositor: Graphic Composition, Inc.
Text: 10/13 Aldus
Display: Zapf Chancery Light
Printer: Braun-Brumfield, Inc.
Binder: Braun-Brumfield, Inc.